W9-AZW-968

A MILLION IS NOT ENOUGH

HOW to RETIRE with the MONEY YOU'LL NEED

MICHAEL K. FARR

WITH GARY BROZEK

NEW YORK BOSTON

This publication is designed to provide competent and reliable information regarding the subject matter covered. However, it is sold with the understanding that the author and publisher are not engaged in rendering legal, financial, or other professional advice. Laws and practices often vary from state to state and if legal or other expert assistance is required, the services of a professional should be sought. The author and publisher specifically disclaim any liability that is incurred from the use or application of the contents of this book.

Springboard Press
Hachette Book Group USA
237 Park Avenue, New York, NY 10017
Visit our Web site at www.HachetteBookGroupUSA.com.

Springboard Press is an imprint of Grand Central Publishing.
The Springboard Press name and logo is a trademark of Hachette Book Group USA, Inc.

First Edition: March 2008

Library of Congress Cataloging-in-Publication Data:

Farr, Michael K.
A million is not enough : how to retire with the money you'll need / Michael K. Farr with Gary Brozek; foreword by P. J. O'Rourke.
p. cm.
ISBN-13: 978-0-446-58223-0
ISBN-10: 0-446-58223-9
1. Retirement income—Planning. 2. Saving and investment. 3. Investments. I. Brozek, Gary. II. Title.
HG179.F36 2008
332.024'014—dc22 2007019274

10 9 8 7 6 5 4 3 2 1

Book design by Giorgetta Bell McRee

Printed in the United States of America

For Laurie, Robert, and Maggie,
I love you up to the sky!

Acknowledgments

I am very grateful to so many friends and colleagues who helped with this book. Scott Sobel suggested I write it. Gary and Don Brozek were wonderful collaborators. Keith B. Davis, CFA, is due enormous thanks and credit. Keith helped me write, rewrite, and research large portions of this text. His clear, thoughtful approach is evident throughout. He should really have his name on the cover, too. P. J. O'Rourke guided me through my first book and coached me at every step. His humor and support are beyond measure. My great friends David Lyons and Kenneth Parkinson proofread early, awkward versions for me. Ted Rorer and Jack Whitcomb introduced me to this wonderful business twenty years ago, and each preached ethics, ethics, ethics! Thank you to Natalie Kaire and everyone at Springboard Press. My agent Jane Dystel has been outstanding. Finally many thanks to Susan Cantus, Sunny Miller, John Washington, Taylor McGowan, Caroline Savage, Keith Davis, Chris Meeker, Michael Fox, Joe Lott, Freeman Jelks, Sheldon Cohen, Joe Coreth, Tom Meisse, Scott Quinlan, and Ashley Staten.

Contents

Foreword

Do you hear a horrible noise on the demographic horizon? That would be us Baby Boomers and our infantile thundering as we throw a huge tantrum about getting old. It's one of the two things we promised ourselves that we'd never do. We'd never get old, and we'd never care about money. And here I am turning sixty and, not only that, but when I go to the ATM machine it acts like my father did when I asked for the car keys in 1963.

I am the ideal person to be writing this preface, alas. That is, I did some financial calculations and discovered that I had about two and a half hours to achieve my investment goals if I wanted to retire in comfort at the time of my choosing. The time of my choosing was in about two and a half hours, when I finished writing this preface. And that was assuming that Michael Farr was going to pay me a million dollars to write it. Then I actually read his book. Now I realize that even if Michael *does* pay me a million (something that, my agent informs me, would require a really serious error in decimal point placement by the accounting department of Michael's publishing house), I'll still be working until I'm 103. Don't let this happen to you.

In fact I'm not even going to let it happen to me. I've gone further than just reading Michael's book. I'm actually doing what his book tells me to do. Or most of what it tells me to do. I'm finding it difficult to make the same kind of arrangements for my "sunset years" that most people my age do. For instance, being a freelance writer, I cannot take the usual approach to retirement. "Retirement from *what*?" as my wife puts it.

Nonetheless, using insights and information gained from Michael Farr, I have been able to escape the snares of typical Baby Boom financial planning strategy. Either that or, as a result of early-onset Alzheimer's, I've been able to forget them.

Typical Baby Boom Financial Planning Strategy

1947–1969	Mooch off parents.
1970–1974	Invest in bong futures.
1975	Briefly diversify into powdered Peruvian commodities before coming to senses and/or going to rehab.
1976	Get a job.
1977–1978	Save loose change in coffee cans.
1979	Spend all weekend putting contents of coffee cans into coin wrappers; buy two Kruggerands, and bury them in a safe place.
1980	Utilize liquid assets and debt instruments to rent tux for wedding.
1981–1990	Mortgage self to eyeballs.
1991	Reallocate equity positions and income flow. (House goes to ex-wife, salary goes to child support.)
1992	Try to remember where Kruggerands are buried.
1993–1999	Pad resume, get new job, receive unmerited promotion, and be over-compensated.
2000	Put everything into cousin's kid's roommate's dot-com start-up.
2001	Get original job back.
2002–2006	Use sub-prime lending to buy residential real estate for investment purposes.
2007–?	Worry self to death.

Personally my own financial planning strategy was even worse than that. I had an entire decade when I, um, "forgot" to pay my income taxes. The following is a true story (unless the statute of limitations hasn't run out on this sort of thing, in which case I'm kidding here). In the middle 1970s it finally dawned on me that the federal government might not find my IRS amnesia quite as amusing as my beatnik pals did, so I went to a tax accountant. The tax accountant gave me the same look that you gave yourself in the mirror after you put everything into your cousin's kid's college roommate's dot-com start-up. The accountant made me spend the next two months getting in touch with various hippies, stoners, lay-abouts, bums, head cases (or, as they were called in those days, novelists, poets, and musicians). From this crew of reprobates I had to extract affidavits to the effect that for the past ten years I had been living an utterly unproductive and virtually unremunerated existence, in which I had been paid nothing and was worth it. The paperwork I collected (crumpled, soiled, scrawled on the back of overdue rent notices, and in one case, I think, block printed in body paint) was presented to the IRS auditor. The IRS auditor beheld the testimonials. He beheld me. And—this is the sad part—he let me off scot-free.

I'm a reformed character now, of course, a solid member of the bourgeoisie, provident, frugal, and thrifty. I know that if I take care of the pennies the dollars will...run off to Paris with some hunky Euro they met at the Federal Reserve, or something. Those dollars sure aren't where I left them, in that emerging market commodities fund where they were supposed to be buying Chinese wheat gluten futures.

That's why I'm reading Michael's book and doing what it tells me to do. In Chapter Five Michael asks me to rate my Risk Tolerance. He provides a brief questionnaire to help me gauge the degree of risk that I'm willing to take to build my retirement portfolio. And I'm filling out that questionnaire this very moment. Although, to tell the truth; I'm not filling it out exactly the way Michael asks because, economically, I'm an idiot. Michael's book is addressed to a variety of readers ranging from the financially highly astute to the budgetarily mildly feckless. It is not addressed to morons like me. I've had to take a few liberties with Michael's Risk Tolerance quiz. The italicized portions of the following are answers I made up because Michael's questions are too hard. Choose one answer for each question:

RISK TOLERANCE

1. Which statement best matches your attitude toward investment risk?
   a. I am very comfortable with and willing to take more risk to pursue maximum growth.
   b. I have a moderate appetite for risk as long as I feel I am being compensated over time.
   c. I am uncomfortable with risk, and short-term volatility in my investments makes me nervous.
   d. *Can I freshen that up for you? A bird can't fly on one wing! I'm thinking that going long on the Zimbabwean dollar looks like a good bet.*

2. At what level of loss in a single year would you start to feel very uncomfortable about your investment decisions and start to question your willingness to continue investing?
   a. More than 20 percent.
   b. 6 to 20 percent.
   c. 5 percent or less.
   d. *When I notice that the Mrs. is serving Hamburger Helper for dinner and there's no hamburger in it.*

3. How did you react when an investment suddenly dropped by 20 percent?
   a. Nothing, as long as I still believed my investment had good long-term potential.
   b. Worry a little, reassess the situation, but take no action.
   c. Bail out and go to cash.
   d. *My only recent investment was a gerbil for the kids at Christmas. It took at least a 20 percent drop when the cat knocked the Have-A-Trail off the ping-pong table. We buried it in an old cuff-link box.*

4. Which alternative would you prefer?
   a. A 50 percent chance of winning $2,000 but a 50 percent chance of losing $500.
   b. A 75 percent chance to gain $1,000 but a 25 percent chance of breaking even.
   c. A sure gain of $750.
   d. *Or a chance to go back to high school and take Practical Math again so that I would know what the hell Michael Farr is talking about.*

5. Which of these alternatives would you prefer?
   a. A 50 percent chance of losing $2,000 but a 50 percent chance of gaining $500.
   b. A 75 percent chance of losing $1,000 but a 25 percent chance of breaking even.
   c. A sure loss of $750.
   d. *A new gerbil and a nice family to adopt the cat.*

Give yourself 2 points for each a answer, 1 point for every b answer, and 0 points for every c answer *and –1 point and a leftover, half-empty bag of gerbil food that may end up as a Hamburger Helper side dish for every d answer.*

If you scored 7–10, your risk tolerance is *high.* You want high returns, and you're willing to take risks to get them.

If you scored 4–6, your risk tolerance is *moderate.* You prefer to strike a balance between risk and reward. You don't want to risk it all, but you do want high performance.

If you scored 0–3, your risk tolerance is *low.* You don't like risk; you believe slow and steady wins the race.

If you scored –5 to –1, *P. J., you'd better pray that the Social Security system remains solvent.*

All right, I'm still a moron. But the wonderful thing about this book is that it has turned me into an attentive moron. At long last I'm listening to some sound financial advice. I'm paying particular attention to Chapter Eight, which contains "Farr's Financial Rules," each of which Michael explains in depth—something that

I'm sure the reader will be grateful to me for not trying to do myself. But here are a few in capsule form:

Make decisions with your head and not your gut and your heart

And don't make decisions with other people's guts or hearts either—or with their arms and legs for that matter. It's always tempting to skip the annual college fund contribution. But I've watched my daughters play sports. They've got physical coordination like their dad has business acumen. I don't care how hard it is for schools to meet Title IX obligations; my daughters aren't getting athletic scholarships until Barbie Clothes Changers have a varsity team.

Do what feels bad

This one's so simple, but nobody does it. Every investment nitwit, myself included, knows to "buy low and sell high." Well, wake up!, says Michael. When the price of a stock is high and it's time to sell it, is the price high because people are feeling *bad* about owning that stock? And when the price of a stock is low and it's time to buy it, is the price low because people are feeling *good* about owning that stock? It's like what the nuns taught us at school—you've got basic animal urges, now do the opposite.

Don't try to find fresh grass where the herd has already trampled and gathered

This not only explains my portfolio, it explains my lawn.

Don't underestimate how long trends will last

So maybe my Beanie Baby collection was a good idea after all.

Don't become a trend investor

Or not.

Michael Farr's advice is as powerful as the optical prescriptions that we're all starting to need, as reliable as our nightly trip to the bathroom at 3AM, as solid as…No, middle age is sad enough without Levitra jokes. Instead let me tell you a reason to listen to Michael Farr's advice that you won't find in this book. I was talking to Michael a few years ago, back when Ken Lay, Jeffrey Skilling, et al., were getting indicted. And I asked Michael, "Did you get burned on Enron stock?"

Michael said, "No, but I tried."

I said, "You tried?"

Michael said, "Sure. Enron is going up like a rocket. So I call in a couple of our financial analysts and say, 'Take a look at this Enron thing and bring me a buy strategy.' Two weeks later I haven't heard anything from them so I call them in again and say, 'What about Enron?' And they say they're working on it. Two more weeks go by and I still haven't heard anything, and I call them in a third time and I say, 'Come on, come on. Everybody's making a fortune on Enron. We need to get in on this.' And they say, 'Boss, when we got hired, do you remember the advice you gave us?'"

"Did you?" I asked Michael.

"Nope," he said, "but they did."

"Well," I said, "What advice did you give them?"

"I advised them to never buy a company that's making money if they can't figure out how the money's being made."

And that was what the financial analysts advised Michael. They said, "We've looked and we've looked and we can't figure out how the hell Enron is making its money."

It's a rule of life: You can tell how good advice is by how hard the advice is to take. (And if you think I'm even slightly wrong about that I ask you to recall any and all of the advice your mother gave you.) Anyway, that's why I am (a bit belatedly) listening to Michael. Michael Farr's advice is so damn good that it almost wasn't taken by Michael Farr.

—P. J. O'Rourke

A MILLION IS NOT ENOUGH

Introduction

A Million Dollars Isn't What It Used to Be!

The Union of Soviet Socialist Republics ended on December 25, 1991. I was there in June 1991, helping to lay the groundwork for that fall.

George H. W. Bush and Mikhail Gorbachev were playing nicely. The heated Cold War rhetoric had cooled. Gorbachev had endorsed the idea of a stock exchange, and Bush offered to help. I'm not sure how the call to the CEO of Alex. Brown & Sons, the oldest investment banking firm in the United States, ultimately reached my desk, but it did. There I was, a thirty-year-old former high school teacher and now vice president of the old, revered banking firm, teaching communists how to be capitalists. In many ways I myself had just made that transition: from altruistic schoolteacher to Wall Street financier.

My Pan Am flight arrived in Moscow before heading on to Leningrad. We taxied to a lifeless-looking brown brick terminal, an enormous red flag emblazoned with yellow hammer and sickle billowing ominously overhead. As the plane stopped, a dozen young men in Soviet uniforms with machine guns ran toward us from all angles. They stopped in unison, stared at the windows with their angry, peach-fuzzed baby faces, and turned on their heels with their backs to us, keeping guard. The Cold War was still alive and well, and I was wondering if I had been sent because I was young and dispensable.

I lectured to three hundred people from the various Soviet states and Eastern Bloc countries for ten days. Their questions and desire for knowledge and information seemed insatiable. The tough part was teaching culture and not content. Intellectually, they understood me, but culturally, they did not. There were shortages of most staples in the USSR at the time, so I used a local example. I suggested, "If you are at the front of a long line to buy butter and are able to buy the last two pounds for two rubles per pound, you might declare yourself a butter broker and sell one of your pounds of butter for five rubles to the remaining crowd." The reaction of these nascent brokers was remarkable: They were outraged. "You would not do such a thing to a comrade." "In difficult times, all comrades should help one another." "A good Russian would share his butter with the rest of the crowd." Do you see the hurdle presented? For the rest of my examples, I suggested profiting from trade with other countries and profiting from investments from which your comrade would also profit.

The Soviets got it. The Moscow and St. Petersburg Stock Exchanges now boast some of the most sophisticated and successful traders in the world. If communists could overcome seventy years of opposite thinking, we can certainly take hold of our finances and become masters of our retirements.

What about *your* culture? Did you grow up in a home that saved or spent? Your attitudes toward money will make investing easier or harder. This book will help. It's very hard to take responsibility for something that you don't understand. *A Million Is Not Enough* will empower you to understand the task of managing your assets, do the right thing, and enjoy the retirement you deserve.

The Million Mystique

For most of us who came of age in the years after World War II, the term *millionaire* has held a special place in our imaginations. We grew up revering "one million dollars" as a kind of mythic amount conferring on those who've attained it a sort of elevated status. Our parents thought of captains of industry when they pictured a millionaire; people like the Vanderbilts and the Rockefellers embodied this concept for them. But we Baby Boomers were more likely to think of a millionaire as someone like Thurston Howell III and his wife, Lovey, from *Gilligan's Island*—the old-money, East Coast, pampered, privileged few who were more likely to be found on the society pages than the financial pages. However, our concept of who a millionaire is (and what constitutes wealth in the twenty-first century) has probably matured as we've aged. Entertainers, athletes, and CEOs have raised the bar of what it means to be rich in America, and we now realize that joining the ranks of the million-dollar club doesn't automatically entitle us to a life of luxury, champagne, and caviar—nor does it even earn us a place on the honorable mention list of *Forbes* magazine's wealthiest individuals. Put simply, a million dollars isn't what it used to be!

Still, the million-dollar mark is not without its privileges. Bloated corporate salaries aside, for most of us a million dollars retains a mythic appeal and is a goal worth aiming for. For most Americans facing retirement, saving that amount means abundant security and being able to maintain the kind of life in our post-work days that we've always envisioned. Too bad too many of us waited a bit too long before getting serious about attaining this goal. This is particularly true of Baby Boomers.

No generation in American history has experienced such widespread abundance and enjoyed it *less* than Baby Boomers. This relentlessly restless and striving group has been responsible for creating unparalleled economic growth and prosperity for ourselves and future generations. Perhaps best characterized by an *everything to excess* approach to life, Boomers remain unfulfilled—and largely unprepared for the next several decades of our lives. We live in times of unparalleled economic growth and prosperity, and yet only 22 percent of Boomers in a recent survey stated that they were satisfied with their future financial picture. So why can't we truly enjoy the fruits of our labors? Why are only 22 percent of us happy about our financial futures?

Three reasons for Boomers' economic instability emerge:

- First, many of us were slow to start planning for our financial futures. Let's face it, figuring out how to save and invest for the next twenty to forty years of financial needs is a daunting and complex proposition. As a result, many of us have put off looking at our finances carefully because we are afraid of what we might find.
- Second, we Boomers are an active and busy bunch. We think it takes a lot of time and hard work to save for retirement... and that's time many of us just don't have. Sometimes we manage to fit so much into our waking hours that we leave no time in the day for ourselves. Anyway, we think we're going to live forever—and given our healthy, active lifestyle, new medications for nearly every ailment, and a dash of Botox, we look and feel as though we just might make it. We show no signs of slowing down soon!
- Third, we Boomers suffer from what I call Abundance Guilt.

What Is Abundance Guilt?

We are among the most fortunate generations in American history. Since World War II—the time period that covers our lives—America has enjoyed unparalleled economic growth. We escaped the hard times that our Depression-era parents experienced. Even memories of the economic fallout of September 11, 2001, and the bursting of the dot-com bubble have receded in our collective rearview mirrors as the Dow Jones Industrial Average continues to climb to record heights. McMansions sprout up behind gated entrances the way that tract homes and cookie-cutter subdivisions did in the 1950s. Yet within each Boomer echoes the siren song of the '60s, when the bulk of us came of age politically and spiritually. That era and its protests against what we viewed as a repressive regime typified by the Vietnam War, hippies dropping out, the initial call to save the planet from ecological disaster, and all the other humanitarian and idealistic visions we had compete with our acquisitive nature. We want more and more material goods, higher salaries, better benefits—everything that constitutes the good life—but we also seek a kind of spiritual enlightenment that will make us feel better about a lifestyle that teeters on the brink of excessive. We're torn in two by these twin desires. We'll learn more in this book about Abundance Guilt and how it affects our finances.

How do I presume to know all this about Boomers? I am a Boomer. Also, as president and majority owner of Farr, Miller & Washington, a Washington, DC-based investment firm that manages more than half a billion dollars in individual and institutional assets, I know what it takes to plan for a sound financial future. The majority of my clients—ranging from celebrities and famous entrepreneurs to smart investors—are members of the Baby Boomer generation, and I know their needs, their strengths, and their weaknesses well.

In *A Million Is Not Enough: How to Retire with the Money You'll Need,* I want to help us take the guilt out of abundance. As a necessary first step toward completion of this mission, we have to understand that Abundance Guilt doesn't only deny us the pleasure of our financial success—it is the root cause of our worries about our financial future. When we acknowledge the conflicts inherent in our successes and the childhood lessons of austerity our Depression-scarred parents taught, our strengths and weaknesses as intense strivers, we can harness them and use them to our advantage.

Is $1 Million Enough?

A Million Is Not Enough is a book about achieving financial security in our retirement years. I believe that we should view one million dollars as the minimum requirement for any married couple wishing to achieve self-sufficiency while still being able to leave an inheritance to children or a charity. You may ask, *Why one million dollars?* Well, $1 million will generate $50,000 per year for twenty-five or thirty years while adjusting for inflation. If you consider retiring at sixty-five and living until you are eighty-five or ninety, $1 million, invested prudently, should be sufficient to meet a $50,000 annual need. If your spending is in excess of $50,000 per year, you will need to either cut your spending or increase your savings. And yes, those who want (or need) to spend $250,000 per year in retirement will need $5 million in today's dollars. This means that our goals, standard of living, and risk tolerance may indeed require much more than a million dollars in savings by retirement. My job in writing this book is to help you identify your goals and how to go about achieving them.

Because we Boomers will live longer and consequently will have a longer retirement period than any previous generation, we will need a bigger and better nest egg. Additionally, we aren't about to settle into a gentle good night of retirement. We will remain highly active. Most of us aren't planning the kind of full-stop retirement our parents might have enjoyed—we don't see ourselves moving into a Florida condominium to await the end of our days. Many of us will continue to work in some capacity, or volunteer, or start a new business or career. We want to travel, take classes, and live our lives to the fullest. In order to meet our needs over the estimated twenty years of retirement (again, assuming $50,000 a year for housing, travel, entertainment, and general living expenses), $1 million is the minimum needed to maintain our present lifestyle.

This book is divided into three sections: The Million-Dollar Mind-Set, The Million-Dollar Groundwork, and The Million-Dollar Maneuvers.

As it would be in any campaign, understanding the rationale for the actions you are being asked to take is important, and that's what I'll cover in the first section. Once you have an understanding of what's being asked of you and why, then you enter the second, more active phase: preparing. Like anything worth doing, choosing to save at least a million dollars for retirement requires you to do some evaluating and planning of your current situation and resources. Rushing headlong into anything is unwise, and especially so when it comes to your financial future. The heart of the book, of course, is the third phase of your Million-Dollar Mission—engaging in the Million-Dollar Maneuvers that will help you reach your stated goal.

Step One: Evaluate It. Calculate your net worth and determine your monthly budget. Using the worksheets provided, you can create a picture of where you stand today.

Step Two: Save It. Find ways to allocate more money for investments. I provide you with twenty-five suggestions for cutting costs and increasing your investment budget.

Step Three: Understand It. How risk tolerance and returns needs shape portfolio choices. The goal is at least a million dollars before retirement, but depending upon your age, circumstances, and risk tolerance, your necessary return on investment will vary.

Step Four: Build It. Construct an individualized portfolio. Based on all the factors above, investment suggestions are provided to help you reach your stated goal.

Step Five: Manage It. Monitor and protect your investments. Once your plan is firmly in place, you can adjust it according to your evolving needs. By adhering to Farr's Rules, you can rest secure in the knowledge that your long-term planning will help you realize the vision you created years before.

Step Six: Pass It On. Create a financial legacy for your family. One of life's inevitabilities is that you can't take it with you. I offer some advice on how to make sure the government doesn't take too much of it from you after you're gone.

The age at which you begin investing plays a significant role in determining the approach you take, so I've included strategies for three age groups:

- **Investment plans for thirty-five.** A "Just in Time" plan for those entering the peak earning years with an emphasis on a long-term vision and investment strategy.
- **Investment plans for forty-five.** An "It's Not Too Late" plan for those who've delayed planning, with an emphasis on a controlled but aggressive approach to maximizing their power-earning years.
- **Investment plans for fifty-five.** A "Catch-Up" plan for those who've either delayed their planning or experienced some other financial setbacks that have them feeling as if they are

trailing the rest of the field. This plan focuses on strategies you can employ to make up for lost time while still feeling secure.

Along with Farr's Rules, I have provided specific recommendations and rationales for why certain stocks should be a part of nearly every portfolio. By focusing on a new task—the creation of one million dollars in assets by age sixty-five—we Boomers can accomplish what seem to be two conflicting goals: saving for the future and enjoying our present life. Using real-world examples of clients who've chosen this baseline figure as their goal, I'll show you how a little thoughtful refocusing of purpose, a little saving, and some wise investment choices can lead to a prosperous retirement and beyond.

We have a lot of ground to cover, so let's get started by looking at the unique challenges facing Boomers as we move toward the next stage in our lives.

PART ONE

The Million-Dollar Mind-Set

Understanding the Mission

CHAPTER ONE

This Is Not Our Parents' Retirement

Why Boomers Are Reinventing How We Will Fund Our Golden Years

Jason Lee thought he had his life and his future figured out. He worked as a research assistant at the Library of Congress. He loved his work, pursued a passionate interest in World War I aviation history, spent his off days at the Air and Space Museum, and planned vacations to visit various collections of vintage aircraft, private and public, around the world. He had a lot of friends who shared his interest, but at age forty-five considered himself a confirmed bachelor. He didn't spend lavishly, but he indulged his hobby without restraint. *Why not?* he figured: He was going to support himself for the rest of his life. Love intervened. On a visit to the Old Rhinebeck Aerodrome in upstate New York, he met a woman whose father was a collector and piloted one of the vintage aircraft that flew in the show. Six months later, they were married.

Jason gave up his job at the Library of Congress, moved to Rhinebeck, and secured a job as a librarian at the local high school. His wife, Alicia, was a widow who had received a $100,000 insurance settlement on her first husband's passing five years earlier. She'd invested wisely but, since receiving the money, had only worked part time at the aerodrome's museum in the summer and doing freelance aircraft restoration consulting the rest of the time. Exclusive of returns on her investments, she'd earned an average of a little more than $24,000 per year for the previous five years.

She was fairly frugal, traveled to and from her home on a bicycle most days, and kept a 1992 Toyota Corolla around for emergencies and winter days when she couldn't ride. Her husband had been a non-union carpenter, but had been good about putting a modest amount in his IRA plan for each of the fifteen years he was married to Alicia. In total, he'd put away $45,000. Alicia still owed $97,000 on the remaining eighteen years of the thirty-year fixed mortgage they'd taken. Of that original $100,000 nest egg, she had $48,000 in her investment portfolio and $16,000 in savings.

Since Jason had always figured that he'd only be supporting himself for his entire life, he hadn't been very good about contributing toward his retirement. He'd designated a modest 5 percent of his income to his 401(k) plan at the LOC, and when he left, he rolled over just shy of $30,000 into an IRA plan. He had no other savings, had rented an apartment in the Georgetown area, used mass transit exclusively, and, other than his extensive library and home computers, had few other assets. His starting salary at the high school was $32,000, and based on the terms of the current contract between the certified staff and the school district, the most he could hope to earn with his master's degree was $48,000.

Jason's father, Adam, was one of my clients, and once his son got married, he made sure that Jason and Alicia came to see me. I knew that Adam Lee had told all his kids that when they turned sixty, they would each receive an incremental gift (to avoid tax penalties) from each of their parents equal to the amount of money that they had in their various retirement accounts. The remainder of his parents' money would go toward various charitable organizations. Adam wanted his kids to learn some valuable lessons about saving, and though his plan may on some levels sound harsh, if his kids saved, they'd be amply rewarded. Jason had no problem with the arrangement his father had made; he simply had chosen not to take full advantage of it.

When I first met the newlyweds, I asked them what their financial and personal lifestyle goals were. They told me that they wanted to begin a family as soon as possible. Jason had attended the University of Virginia, paying out-of-state tuition, so he knew the high costs of a college education. They frankly admitted they were scared about the future and their retirement. Jason had never thought much about it because he figured he'd be okay living solo; Alicia and her first husband had only begun to think about it when he was diagnosed with cancer and their financial priorities radically shifted.

Alicia's parents were struggling with their own retirement issues and weren't likely to be able to leave much for their two children. Because of the arrangement the elder Lee had created, Jason and Alicia knew that they wouldn't starve, but Jason was determined to provide his kids with the kind of educational opportunities that his father had—along with ensuring that they would be debt-free upon graduation.

Fortunately, given the combination of Jason's father's future gift, their own modest savings, and a history of frugality, we were able to put together a plan that would make certain that the Lees' future children would have their educations paid for and the couple would be able to fund a secure retirement—even though they would be enrolling their children in college at an age when most of their Tail End Boomer peers were either within a few years of retirement or would have already retired. While the Lees' situation may differ in its particulars, it shares many similarities with those of others of their age group. And the lesson is clear: If you don't plan early, you can still plan smartly. I'll talk more about the particulars of their plan in later chapters.

The Boomer Generation, Defined

Today the largest generation to ever move toward retirement takes another step in that direction. In the time required to read this sentence, another Boomer turns fifty. That's right: Every seven seconds of every day, another Boomer reaches that milestone. Because our rate of progression into this age group is unprecedented, and because we Boomers possess unique personality traits and a conflicted relationship with our money, we face unique challenges and opportunities as we plan for our financial future. We're going to examine some of these complicating personal factors in the pages that follow. Before we do that, I need to make clear some points about how I use the term *Baby Boomers.*

Throughout this book, I'm going to use three ages to represent the broad spectrum of Boomers.

- The first group I will use are those age fifty-five. Born in 1951, they represent the heart of that generation, and thus I call them **Core Boomers.**
- The second group, those age forty-five, are what I call **Tail End Boomers.** Born in 1961, they are representatives of the last of the "official" Boomer generation.
- Thirty-five-year-olds are what I will refer to as **Neo-Boomers.** Because they were born in 1971, they don't fit into the traditional definition of Baby Boomers—those born between the years 1944 and 1964. I include them because they are now at a transitional point in their lives when they have outgrown the *Generation X* label often placed on them and are in their prime earning years. Like it or not, they share many of the same traits as their Boomer parents—thus the name *Neo-Boomers.*

While all of these groups share common traits, the major difference in their retirement-planning scenarios is time. Though it is obvious, it needs to be stated: The more time you have before you retire, and the sooner you begin to put money away for that eventuality, the better off you are. Also note that the advice and recommendations covered in this book are applicable to the generations that follow the Boomers as well.

My, How Things Have Changed

Just to give you a better sense of time and where we were in the years that our representative Core Boomers, Tail End Boomers, and Neo-Boomers were born, here's a thumbnail sketch of what the economy looked like in those three years. Consider these bits of economic and historical trivia:

1951 This year represents the beginning of the Baby Boomer era. Along with that first vintage of Boomers, Americans also saw these events:

- The first power-producing nuclear fission reactor goes online.
- The Univac computer is introduced.
- US pay phone rates rise from 5 to 10 cents.
- Jackie Gleason makes $11 million for a two-year contract for *The Honeymooners*.
- The US gross domestic product rises to $339.7 billion.
- The median household income reaches $3,709.
- The unemployment rate is 5.3 percent.
- Per capita expenditures for housing reach $157.49.

1961 The last of the true Boomers are born. That same year:

- Drs. Crick and Watson break the DNA genetic code.
- IBM introduces the Selectric typewriter.
- First National Bank of New York is the first financial institution to offer fixed-term certificates of deposit.
- The US gross domestic product reaches $544.8 billion.
- Median household income rises to $5,735.
- The unemployment rate grows to 5.5 percent.
- Per capita expenditures for housing reach $278.73.

1971 Twenty years after the first Boomers are born, some of that generation have already begun to reproduce and are now parents of the first group of Neo-Boomers.

- President Nixon orders a ninety-day freeze on wages and prices.
- First-class postal rates rise to 8 cents per ounce.
- The US gross domestic product climbs to $1,125.4 billion.
- Median household income increases to $9,028.
- The unemployment rate is 4.9 percent.
- Per capita expenditures for housing reach $494.56.

As you can see, the US economy was booming for much of this period, though many of us can remember the stagflation of the mid- to late 1970s. We all know that period was tough for many, but most Core Boomers and Tail End Boomers came out of it in fine fashion. For Neo-Boomers, that period isn't even really a deposit in their economic memory bank. Things have been so good for so long, most of us can't even begin to imagine what our lives would be like if we couldn't count on a continuing upward trend. I have to admit that the creeping sensation that this incredible run could end one day—whether due to economic factors outside our control or our own failure to save for our retirement—has more than a few of us tossing and turning at night.

The Costs and Benefits of Living

We live in a consumer culture, so in order to round out the picture of where we were and how much things have changed over time, a few select costs and salaries are shown in tables 1.1 through 1.7 to give you a sense of how the economy has evolved in the years since our Core Boomers were born. The culture has changed over the last fifty years, and our spending power has along with it. Even adjusted for inflation, many fixed costs such as housing, college tuition, a car—even admission to a baseball game—have increased at a faster rate than our salaries. In tables 1.1 through 1.7, the first figure is the actual dollar amount, and the second is its 2006 equivalent, adjusted for inflation.

Table 1.1
PUBLIC SCHOOL TEACHER SALARY

Year	Salary	2006 Equivalent
1951	$2,998	$23,394
1961	$4,991	$33,797
1971	$8,813	$44,188
2001	$43,740	$51,538
2006	$47,203	$47,203

Table 1.2
AVERAGE NEW HOME PRICE

Year	Price	2006 Equivalent
1951	$9,422	$82,871
1961	$15,200	$108,051
1971	$23,400	$127,839
2002	$177,300	$208,909
2006	$238,400	$238,400

Table 1.3
ANNUAL TUITION AT THE UNIVERSITY OF SOUTH CAROLINA

Year	Price	2006 Equivalent
1950	$80	$673
1960	$80	$510
1970	$150	$787
2000	$3,768	$4,440
2006	$7,808	$7,808

Table 1.4
FORD'S LEAST EXPENSIVE CAR

Year	Price	2006 Equivalent
1955	$1,606	$12,129
1965	$2,313	$18,892
1975	$2,769	$10,457
1998	$11,280	$14,034
2006	$13,995	$13,995

Table 1.5
TICKET TO A CHICAGO CUBS BASEBALL GAME

Year	Price	2006 Equivalent
1950	$1.44	$12.67
1960	$1.83	$13.10
1970	$2.08	$11.36
2000	$14.30	$17.60
2006	$30.00	$30.00

Table 1.6
AVERAGE MAJOR LEAGUE BASEBALL PLAYER SALARY

Year	Salary	2006 Equivalent
1951	$13,300	$103,782
1967	$19,000	$115,398
1975	$44,676	$168,720
1999	$1,377,196	$1,678,099
2006	$2,866,544	$2,866,544

Table 1.7
HERSHEY BAR

Year	Price	2006 Equivalent
1951	$.05	$.45
1961	$.05	$.35
1971	$.05	$.30
2000	$.50	$.59
2006	$.75	$.75

Besides invoking a bit of nostalgic longing for the good old days, what does all this mean? We can see clearly that salaries have gone up, as well as prices. But are we really better off? On the average, yes, but by and large by only a slim margin. Unfortunately, the differential between the haves and the have-nots in American society is greater than at any time since before World War I. As we Boomers have come of age, so has our economy. And these changes in the financial landscape have altered the ways in which we need to save and invest to assure a safe retirement. In other words, our parents' retirement strategies (mostly born of a Depression-era save-it all mentality) aren't enough to get us Boomers to the finish line with the money we need for the retirement we want. We have to do more.

Defining Our Mission

A million dollars is an ambitious goal, but the truth is that all of us have our own particular needs. I tell my clients to use the million-dollar benchmark as a guideline, but they'll need to refine that goal depending on a number of factors, including their lifestyle and the number of years they have left until retirement. One million dollars certainly sounds like a lot of money, but it clearly isn't what it used to be. As we've seen, price increases are constantly eating away at our buying power. In fact, inflation, as measured by the Consumer Price Index, has averaged 4.4 percent per year since 1975. We would have needed only $263,200 in 1975 to buy the same basket of goods that would cost us $1 million today. *Therefore, our minimum goal of one million dollars by retirement is constantly increasing.* If you expect to retire in thirty years, your goal will be much higher than if you're retiring in five years. The following formula gives an estimate of the goal in achieving the Million-Dollar Mission:

$$\text{retirement goal} = \$1{,}000{,}000 \times (1 + \text{expected inflation rate})^{\text{number of years until retirement}}$$

Using this formula, we can derive rough estimates of what it will take to achieve the Million-Dollar Mission for different age groups and inflation rates. Notice that the goal increases as both years to retirement and the inflation rate increase. This is because inflation is eating away at more and more of our purchasing power. If inflation were to continue at the historical average of 4.4 percent since 1975, we would need nearly $3 million to retire in twenty-five years!

In the chapter 7 case studies, I assume that the inflation rate will average 3 percent in the future. I believe that the Federal Reserve Board has become much more effective in staving off inflation in recent years. Hyperinflation such as that experienced in the late 1970s and early '80s should be a thing of the past. I encourage you to use this assumption as well. Table 1.8 illustrates the effect of these two forces and gives a rough guideline of what might be needed to maintain a $50,000-per-year retirement (by today's standards) as we move into the future.

Don't let this table scare you! If you'll be retiring in twenty-five years, you have plenty of time to get your financial house in order. If you are older and are retiring in just five years, you may not need to save nearly that much. The point is that time is on our side if we map out our goals and are willing to make some sacrifices. This has always been true, but recent developments in the economy have made it clear that the old retirement strategies Americans once employed are no longer going to work for this generation. With retirement visible on the horizon, Boomers are looking at a very different financial landscape.

What Is the New Economy?

Our parents spent the vast majority of their working lives in the prime post–World War II industrial era. For many, that meant working in the same field, possibly with the same company, throughout their careers, with employers contributing to their retirement through a traditional pension plan.

The Greatest Generation worked hard and built their fortune on global expansion and the national boom created by our

Table 1.8
SAVINGS REQUIRED TO ACHIEVE $50,000 IN ANNUAL RETIREMENT INCOME

Years to Retirement	Inflation Rate								
	1.0%	**1.5%**	**2.0%**	**2.5%**	**3.0%**	**3.5%**	**4.0%**	**4.5%**	**5.0%**
5	$1,051,010	$1,077,284	$1,104,081	$1,1[illegible]1,408	**$1,159,274**	1,187,686	$1,216,653	$1,246,182	$1,276,282
10	$1,104,622	$1,160,541	$1,218,994	$1,280,085	**$1,343,916**	$1,410,599	$1,480,244	$1,552,969	$1,628,895
15	$1,160,969	$1,250,232	$1,345,868	$1,443,298	**$1,557,967**	$1,675,349	$1,800,944	$1,935,282	$2,078,928
20	$1,220,190	$1,346,855	$1,435,947	$1,63[illegible],616	**$1,806,111**	$1,989,789	$2,191,123	$2,411,714	$2,653,298
25	$1,282,432	$1,450,945	$1,640,306	$1,85[illegible],944	**$2,093,778**	$2,363,245	$2,665,836	$3,005,434	$3,386,355
30	$1,347,849	$1,563,080	$1,811,362	$2,097,568	**$2,427,262**	$2,806,794	$3,243,398	$3,745,318	$4,321,942
35	$1,416,603	$1,683,881	$1,999,890	$2,373,205	**$2,813,862**	$3,333,590	$3,946,089	$4,667,348	$5,516,015

existence—the Boomers. They started the Electronic, Atomic, and Space Ages—we took them to new heights. They benefited from the strength of our economy and the peak of the union movement to amass pension plans that most of us will never see. I don't mean to begrudge them their largesse—they worked extremely hard to build a world that made it possible for us Boomers to accomplish all we have. I am proud and grateful to stand on the shoulders of such a strong and accomplished group of people. Theirs was not a world of computer screens, gigabytes, and ergonomic workstations but of hammers and bulldozers and torrid steel mills. Many Boomers may have begun our careers in the waning years of that same era, but since the late 1990s the American economy has undergone a transition. Many economists call today's financial landscape the New Economy. Though not every financial expert agrees with this assessment, everyone *can* agree that retirement's different today than it was for our parents. Today's economic landscape is characterized by a few specific traits:

- **The absence or minimization of business cycles or inflations.** Consistent growth without deep recessions reduces, but doesn't eliminate, the risks of investing. Individual stocks carry risk, of course, because of their strategies and markets, but overall market risk is reduced by a steady hand at the national and global economic wheel. Predictable and favorable tax and fiscal policies lead to more investment and a stronger economy.
- **The rise of new industry sectors, such as e-commerce, that produce computers and related goods and services.** We have experienced a revolution in information technology. Not only do these industries employ vast armies of people, but think of how ubiquitous technology has become. Nearly every aspect of our lives has been transformed. Even a restaurant server needs to know how to use a computer to get orders into the kitchen. Kitchen appliances have chips that monitor performance and warn of impending service. They can even link to the factory for diagnostics and ordering of replacement parts.
- **An accelerated rate of productivity growth.** Yes, we work longer hours than nearly any other First World country, but it

goes beyond that. Technology and modern business practices have boosted productivity. There is a downside—workers are sometimes discarded as easily as a piece of equipment—but a vital economy and an ability to learn new fields make the workforce more fluid than ever.

- **The globalization of business as capitalism spreads around the world.** More easily than ever, money flows around the world to fund the best ideas and businesses. Markets are freer than ever before, and US companies have benefited immensely by selling their goods in foreign markets.

What's in This for Me?

So if this were a book about macroeconomics, you might find this talk about the New Economy pertinent at first glance. But what does this really mean for us and our retirement? To me, it means that the days of relying on wages and the ability of a corporate "parent" to sustain us through our retirement are things of the past. We need to be more involved in our own retirement planning, and we need to become investors if we hope to share in the unprecedented wealth creation our economy produces.

Why can't we rely on wages? After all, a penny saved is a penny earned. Critics of the New Economy say that increases in productivity that have driven the stock market—as well as the resulting corporate profits—are all really powered by labor. Basically, their argument is that the wealth that investors have amassed over the last thirty years has been wealth created by or taken from labor—meaning us—through lower real wages, lost jobs, huge productivity gains, and reduced pensions. Stock prices and corporate profits have been rising at double-digit rates, but only twice in the past three decades have wages risen more than 2 percent above the inflation rate.

Real wages have been essentially stagnant for years, and at best they are barely outpacing inflation. What about all that restructuring? Talk to folks who have been downsized, right-sized, or simply laid off, and you'll find that they aren't feeling all that efficient as they struggle to find new jobs. Most important for us to consider is how corporations care for their employees once they are no longer active in the workforce. The so-called liquid workforce—one that is easily accessible and easily disposed of—has been the subject of a great deal of debate and analysis. Much of the focus has been on the dearth of middle-class, midlevel, living-wage jobs. It seems that the economy continues to eliminate midlevel jobs while creating many low-wage retail positions and some high-level professional positions, with a vast chasm in between.

Pensive About Pensions

Previous generations did not have to plan for their retirement in quite the same way that Boomers and Neo-Boomers now have to. For most Americans who were a part of the so-called Greatest Generation, the two most significant sources of their retirement income were the pension plan set up for them by their employers and Social Security. If you are a working person in your midthirties to your fifties, you are certainly aware of the sea change that has taken place in this regard. Consider May 2005, when a federal bankruptcy judge ruled that United Airlines could default on its pension programs to tens of thousands of current and future retirees. By so ruling, the judge allowed United to turn over control of its pension fund obligations to a federal agency already swamped with similar corporate pension defaults. United's $9.8 billion plan default is the largest in US corporate history.

So what did that mean to the employees of United? The Pension Benefit Guaranty Corporation (PBGC)—the federal agency that took over the plan—has to pay United's pensions, but it doesn't have to pay the full amount United originally promised its workers. Federal guidelines limit the amount of pension payments to any individual to $45,000 per year if you retire at sixty-five, and $20,526 if you retire at fifty-five. That doesn't sound like too bad a deal, but consider this: The highest-paid United employees faced pension cuts of 50 percent, while lower-paid workers faced cuts of 20 percent under these new guidelines. A lot of workers getting paid far less than they planned on for their retirement doesn't sound very good, now, does it?

It gets worse. Unfortunately for United's workers, that's the best-case scenario. The actual amount the PBGC will likely pay out is sure to be far less than that $45,000 maximum. Experts predict that the PBGC's funds will likely run out given the number of other corporate pension funds that have defaulted in the last five to ten years. It had, as of May 2005, a $23 billion deficit. Add to that the difference between what United owed its workers ($9.8 billion) and what the PBGC assumed as an obligation—$6.6 billion. That $3.2 billion gap simply won't be paid out to any of the airline's employees. Those are staggering responsibilities that the airline was able to walk away from.

Let's put this shortfall in perspective. That $3.2 billion that won't be paid works out to a little over $250,000 per employee. Fortunately for the company's CEO, his annual $4.5 million pension was guaranteed.

The airline industry has struggled, and the auto industry is not far behind. Reports have recently surfaced regarding GM, its pension plan, and questionable accounting practices regarding pension assets and liabilities that help show better corporate earnings. In 2003, GM faced the largest pension fund deficit in history—$25 billion. At present, the company provides health and income benefits to 161,500 retirees and surviving spouses—that's three times as many people who are actively in its workforce.

Those two industries are not alone in their pension woes. The latest statistics available are from 2004, when the PBGC reported that the number of underfunded pension plans rose from 166 in 1999 to 1,050 in 2003. The total cash shortfall from the underfunded pension plans in 2003 was $279 billion, with an estimated $400 billion shortfall for 2004. The Cato Institute—a policy research group—states that by 2014, the PBGC's shortfall may top $50 billion.

On the Brighter Side

So pensions may not be what they were cracked up to be, and they were never really guaranteed for every employee anyway. What's the big deal? Well, the other element that our parents relied on—and that's also in jeopardy—is Social Security. I won't belabor the point, but we all know that Social Security reform has been hotly debated at the national level for years. One plan would put much of the responsibility for managing your Social Security account on your own shoulders. That is also what many corporations and businesses have done in establishing 401(k) programs for their employees. Depending upon your perspective, these reforms (real and proposed) are either a blessing or a curse. If you are the kind of person who likes to be in control of your own financial life, the move to privatize Social Security has some advantages. At the very least, it's a harbinger of what's to come. We will all need to take a surer, more active hand in our own retirement planning.

I prefer to look at the situation with this perspective: From those to whom much has been given, much is expected. In other words, I do believe that the American economy is stronger than ever. I do believe that productivity will continue to increase; that the massive stock market correction that everyone predicted would spiral us all into poverty is speculative fiction; and that the predicted bursting of the housing bubble and the overextension of credit and a tidal wave of defaults on mortgages are real concerns, but have all been seen before. All historical economic hurdles have been endured and surmounted. I also firmly believe that the move from pension plans to IRAs and 401(k) plans and other iterations of individual retirement planning is a boon and not a potential bust. Of course, my heart goes out to those who have lost so much due to corporate mismanagement and outright malfeasance. But I most certainly believe we have to take more responsibility for making decisions and choices to manage our financial future.

I don't know about you, but I want to be in control of the financial decisions that so directly correlate what I do now with how I will be able to live later. I've never been one to shirk responsibility. I also know that some people shy away from what they consider to be risky ventures. I can't tell you that no risk exists in investing. I *can* tell you that much of what we view as risk is all about our perception of control. I view flying in an airplane as riskier than driving my car, even though the statistics tell us that thousands more people die in automobile accidents than airplane crashes. Why do I feel this way? It's all about control. When I fly on a commercial airliner, I'm not able to go out and kick the tires, check the fluids, make sure the wings are properly de-iced; I'm not the one who sits at the controls, executes the commands to get airborne or land, or makes the decision about how much turbulence is too much. In my car, though, I'm king. I'm responsible for its purchase, maintenance, and speed; its direction and route; when I leave; even what food I serve on board. If I get in an accident, I won't hesitate to accept my part of the responsibility, and I like the feeling of knowing that if I arrive safely, I'm the one who can take the credit for it.

I hope that you feel the same way about your financial future. Yes, we live in a new economy, and there are large forces at work determining the shape of this country's and the world's financial future. But in my financial life, I concentrate on working with the elements I can control. Focusing on the task at hand and not the unpredictable lurking in the dark has always served me well, and it is the philosophy I employ in working with my clients. That's also the philosophy that underpins this book. Control is good. That you've decided to take hold of your financial future and assume the responsibility of undertaking the Million-Dollar Mission is the first step toward taking control of your financial future.

What Makes Us Unique

For a host of reasons, retirement is a tricky concept for Baby Boomers especially. Here's what we Boomers had to say about retirement in a 2004 AARP "Boomers at Midlife" survey:

- Boomers feel they need to make the most progress in their lives in the area they feel most behind in—personal finance. Every year of the survey, that has remained their number one concern. In 2006, 36 percent said that improved personal finances was their main focus over the next five years.
- About 23 percent of Boomers said their personal finances are the worst thing in their lives right now.
- Only 22 percent reported being satisfied with their personal financial situation.

But here's the good news:

- By and large, Boomers feel they can shape their futures by working hard to take steps to accomplish their goals.

These concerns have informed the approach I've taken in crafting this book. These concerns, real or imagined, need to be addressed. The message in most retirement books is that planning for your financial future results in a kind of zero-sum game. These volumes offer advice on how you can get through the last years of life safely to ensure that you cross the finish line financially solvent. Well, for most of us, finishing isn't enough. For us it's always about winning, about staying at the top of our game. Based on my years of experience in dealing with fellow Boomers, I know that what troubles us is not whether we will survive, but whether we will continue to thrive. I don't know many of today's working Baby Boomers who will be content to simply sit idly by and watch as our money supply dwindles. Yet we're also pulled in another direction.

An Abundance of Guilt

Baby Boomers are perhaps history's most studied and talked-about generation. We've read about our restless adolescence and campus unrest, our intense self-interest (the Me Generation), and our lavish lifestyles. With labels from *Yuppies* to *DINKs,* the media have seldom been kind. Is it any wonder then that many of us suffer from Abundance Guilt?

What is Abundance Guilt? As I touched on in the introduction, this complex of beliefs, values, and behaviors plays a significant role in shaping Boomers' financial outlook, spending and saving patterns, and thoughts about retirement, as well as our worldview. Having had the intense frugality of our Depression-era parents and grandparents drummed into our heads in our formative years, having rebelled against what many saw as another facet of a repressive and joyless authority, most Boomers are deeply conflicted about material wealth. Not only are we members of a generation that has enjoyed unparalleled financial success, but we also spend more, save less, and claim to value "experiences" or "the journey" over goals and destinations—while simultaneously possessing deeply held values about nurturing the environment, aiding the poor, and ridding the world of disease.

The desire to drop out of corporate culture still beats strong in the hearts of many Boomers, yet that impulse lives side by side with our overreaching ambition to be at the head of the class. We are textbook studies in internal conflict. We shop in specialty grocery stores, drive gas-guzzling and expensive SUVs festooned with WORLD WILDLIFE FUND bumper stickers, turn yoga into a competitive sport, yearn for the simpler life in a remote wilderness (just so long as all the amenities are within a five-mile drive), adopt Buddhist serenity practices, and quaff double-caffeinated lattes to unwind.

The workaholic Boomer is the master of multitasking and victim of the pathological next. You know the pathological next: It's what we whisper to ourselves whenever we are surprised by a free moment or the end of a current task. Boomers are right on to the next thing. "What will I do *next*?" We seem to value time over money, paying a premium for conveniences, splurging and not researching, all because our time is so precious. Overwhelmed with the fullness of our days, we Boomers have created a new economic dynamic that I call egonomics: buying not only those things we need but also those we feel we deserve. In addition, we harried Boomers will spend an extra dollar for fresh pasta, an upgrade to the rental car or hotel room, or designer shampoo in the hope of adding a little luxury and serenity to our horrid, hectic days. Those purchases made, the desires indulged, we still don't find the satisfaction we'd hoped for. What's next for us? How do we cross this divide?

The key first step is to recognize how Abundance Guilt has shaped our choices. Unless we act now, we will carry that same conflict through to our retirement planning and eventually into our postwork years. I want you to enjoy the fruits of your labor when you can truly have the time to enjoy them. I don't want you to be fretting away those moments. I know many of my clients have the added responsibility of caring for their parents and assisting them financially. They constantly remind me that they don't want to be in their parents' position themselves.

An Abundance of Drive

What critics of our generation don't often recognize is the positive side of Baby Boomer traits: Our dogged determination, fierce competitiveness, relentless searching, and tireless work ethic have helped us succeed at almost everything we've attempted. These traits, which define us as a generation, are the same ones that will allow us to catch up on saving for our retirement—and create a financial plan that allows us to not only survive, but also continue to thrive and prosper. It's not about being able to meet all our expenses; it's about exceeding those needs and continuing to fund our desires—without the guilt and conflict. I subscribe to the philosophy of wealth that Malcolm Forbes espoused. When asked, "How much money does it take to be really rich?" he responded, "Enough to live the lifestyle of your choice to the fullest aspect and a little more." Whether that lifestyle choice means remaining able to travel extensively, maintain multiple residences, fund charitable works, or ensure that our children and their children's children are well educated, we Baby Boomers are not about to simply settle down to a quiet contemplative life. Nor should we feel any of the Abundance Guilt that takes the joy out of our prosperity. After all, what is the point of working hard, earning a good income, if we can't enjoy it?

My message: We need to get over the guilt and take control of our spending so we can truly *enjoy* what we've earned.

We are the first generation for whom an extended postwork period has become a reality. In many ways, we have been and continue to be trailblazers. And we are not about to settle for anything less than excellence. After all, a generation that produced the likes of Bill Gates, Larry Ellison, Sir Richard Branson, and Michael Dell, among countless others, doesn't seem likely to be content with the break-even approach of most retirement books.

The fundamental flaw in the thinking of most retirement planners and financial gurus currently on the bookshelves is that they don't recognize that Baby Boomers don't have the same on-off switch as previous generations. Just because we are approaching retirement doesn't mean we're about to undergo a fundamental change in our high-achieving, goal-oriented personalities. Does it really make sense to think that we are going to let Abundance Guilt drag us down—to stop being competitive and accept a middle-of-the-pack finish?

For evidence of this relentlessly striving nature, we only have to look at a few areas of our lives. We are perhaps the most athletic generation, and as we age, we continue to seek out new challenges. In last year's New York City Marathon, half of the thirty-six thousand finishers were between the ages of forty and seventy. In that most physically demanding of challenges, we Boomers demonstrated the dedication, willingness to sacrifice, and commitment to a goal that are the hallmarks of our generation. While not every one of us tackles the challenge of running a marathon, the principle is undeniable—those of us born between 1944 and 1964 will enjoy a more athletic lifestyle, and enjoy it longer, than any previous generation. But that active lifestyle costs money. This book will show you how you can continue to lead your active lifestyle without breaking the bank.

Are You Ready?

This book, then, is for our generation of strivers. And for this trailblazing generation working toward retirement in the New Economy, nothing but a new approach is necessary. The million-dollar question is: Are we ready to do what it takes to attain a safe and secure retirement? Are we ready to undertake the Million-Dollar Mission?

For many of us Boomers, the answer to the million-dollar question will be simple. *Yes, I have decided that the goal of putting away a minimum of a million dollars for retirement by age sixty-five is worthwhile. Beyond that, I am willing to commit to continued growth past sixty-five so that I don't just stagger to the finish line, but break the tape and look for further challenges to enrich my life. Regardless of the New Economy, my old habits, my inherent contradictory feelings about wealth, and the negative side of the legacy I've inherited from my Depression-era parents, I'm ready to do what I've always done: Go to work.*

In the next chapter, we will take a closer look at this quest and how it impacts our financial future.

CHAPTER TWO

What Do You Want Out of Retirement?

Imagining Your Future

On a fishing pier in Florida a few years ago, I met a man named Bill who lived in a mobile home park. He told me he went there to fish almost every day. Bill would also drive once a month to visit his daughter and grandchildren in North Carolina. He said he wanted for nothing. Receiving a retirement income of around $30,000 per year, Bill told me that he was rich; he couldn't ever spend all the money that kept "rolling in."

This man was content to slow down and enjoy a relaxed flow of life, along with the warmth of his relationships with his fishing buddies, his daughter, and his granddaughter. That's all he wanted. I don't know how he got to that point in his life. He may have been a hard-charging entrepreneur who decided he had given up too much human contact in order to succeed in the business world and now wanted to focus on relationships. He may have been a guy who lived a workaday existence and simply loved to fish. The point is, he was doing exactly what he wanted to do. Bill's vision for his retirement may not be your idea of ecstasy, but he was happy.

In this book, I hope to assure you that while the numbers may be large by present standards, you can create a nest egg that will allow you to partake in the possibilities those numbers represent. For now, though, let's forget about the numbers and take the first and most important step in the planning process—creating a vision of what your retirement life will be so that you can be as happy as Captain Bill.

A New Stage in Life

In chapter 1, I hinted at the vast opportunities your later years offer. No longer yearning for a time to slow down and hope our health holds up, we Boomers will bend retirement to our will. Living longer and healthier and with greater resources to allow for untraditional choices, we will carry our endless striving forward and create a wholly different lifestyle to replace "retirement." Sure, some of us will by circumstance or choice end up in the traditional retirement mode. Others will completely redefine ourselves and what can be accomplished in our later years. The term *Golden Years* with its associated images of relaxation and winding down doesn't fit this new life stage; we Boomers plan to make some of our most valuable contributions during this period. As a result, I like to call this time *pretirement*. Eventually, we may reach a point when traditional retirement catches up to us—when illness or age or finances will prevail—but pretirement is the time between full-blown career life and that traditional version of retirement that we'll be dragged into kicking and screaming. That's where we have another chance to explore a whole new set of dreams and goals.

Retirement is the classic period of porch sitting and walking with a cane. Pretirement is exemplified by the seventysomething who books a round-trip world cruise that includes bike expeditions and rafting. Pretirement is the longed-for multiyear vacation at the rainbow's end when you can enjoy the fruits of your years of twelve-hour workdays. That is the Million-Dollar Mind-Set—wanting to continue to enjoy the kind of life we led while working with the added bonus of having even more time to enjoy what we love.

What are some of the options for pretirement? They're as vast as your imagination.

- Adventure travel for people over fifty-five is a booming industry. More of us are combining the pent-up quest to travel with our desire to remain in good physical shape by scaling mountains, kayaking rapids, and experiencing hands-on the cultures and wild areas of our world.
- New careers are possible, from supporting favorite causes

to starting new businesses. Mentoring or lending our hard-won expertise to fledgling enterprises can be rewarding and profitable.
- Hobbies can become passions that we eventually transform into businesses.
- We can move to a new location and start a different existence, or we can dig in and become even more deeply entrenched in our current home.
- We can be as close or as far away from civilization as we like:
  - Make connections. Social networking sites help reconnect classmates, co-workers, and others, as well as bringing together people who've never met but have similar interests.
  - Drop out. We can move to the country and raise llamas or grow organic spices.
- We can learn, or teach:
  - Lifelong learning can mean developing proficiency in a new language, learning to play a musical instrument, or studying the ancient philosophers. We can even learn a new career. I know of one corporate executive who retired and became a chiropractor.
  - Those already expert can teach the many people out there who are interested in the same subject.

These are just a few of the possibilities. Whether we enrich or enhance what we've previously experienced, or explore new avenues of possibility, our pretirement will be marked by activity. For us, retirement isn't like a river drying up or slowing to a trickle; instead, it's a river diverted to power new enterprises—personal, social, emotional, and financial.

Seeing Your Future

Goal setting and investing for the future need to be thought about in two steps: where you want to go and how you plan to get there. The first step is to establish the goals you would like to achieve. At this stage, you should not be concerned with monetary targets, but rather the dreams you have always envisioned for retirement.

I'm giving you a blank sheet and allowing you to put your personal vision to paper.

It is also important to note that everyone's goals are different. According to the *Certified Financial Planner Licensee Manual*, "Personal values and attitudes shape a client's goals and objectives and the priority placed on them. Accordingly, these goals and objectives must be consistent with the client's values and attitudes in order for the client to make the commitment necessary to accomplish them." I believe this is a key point. Not only will identifying and prioritizing specific objectives help you in your quest to achieve those objectives, but it will also give you the incentive you need to make the necessary sacrifices. The *CFP Manual* goes on to state, "Goals and objectives provide focus, purpose, vision and direction for the financial planning process." Therefore, to simply establish a monetary goal of one million dollars by retirement is not enough. *The only reason to have money is to enhance the quality of life!*

Unless you have a vivid picture of how you want to utilize your pretirement years, all the money you could possibly amass won't help you feel fulfilled and happy. The emotional and psychological aspects of retirement can be tough unless you're prepared. The sudden amputation of something that has been a part of your entire adult life can be devastating even when you know it's coming. Without a plan for something meaningful to fill the void, you could feel lost and unvalued. More and more books are beginning to deal with these softer but extremely important retirement issues, and I highly recommend reading them.

If you're thirty-five, you might not have as clear a vision of how you want to spend your retirement as someone closer to retirement age. It's a faraway concept you know you need to save for (you bought this book, so you're at least that far along in the process!), but you haven't spent a lot of time imagining the reality of it. Don't fret. What you come up with today will not go on your permanent record. It can be changed, and likely will be no matter when you craft it. The objective is to get a sense of your goals and ensure that your retirement planning is consistent with those goals as they stand today. Periodic ponderings of your life and retirement goals will continue to be a good idea. At the same time, review your savings progress and make sure that the two are in harmony.

One thirty-five-year-old couple, Lisa and Henry, fit the prior description. In the throes of raising two infants and getting their lives established, thoughts of saving and retirement are rarely possible. They've been married five years and live in the good-size home they were able to purchase just after their wedding. Henry, an accountant for a large conglomerate, makes $85,000 per year. Lisa was a dental hygienist until the boys were born, but looks forward to getting her $40,000 salary again. They are house-rich but pretty cash-flow-poor. They had once talked about retiring to Florida because their parents have enjoyed their lives down there, and both of them have had fond memories of childhood trips and vacations together while dating. Their thoughts have never progressed much past that phase.

Just as I recommended to Lisa and Henry, the first step to take is to spend some time gathering ideas. Write down some of the thoughts you've had over the years about what you would like to accomplish in your life. Notice I didn't say *during your retirement*. Remember, we're viewing retirement as just another phase of life to be used to accomplish things that have meaning for us. These could be random ideas that come while jogging or musings during a stressful day at work. Maybe neighbors or co-workers have crafted retirement into something that appeals to you. Unfulfilled goals or hobbies possibly dating back to childhood might still be important. Traveling the world, playing golf, doting on grandchildren, moving to the beach, or rediscovering your love for painting watercolors can all be satisfying and meaningful objectives. Maybe you'd like to devote more time to a favorite cause or finish writing a novel begun in college. Whatever those aspirations are, take a few weeks or months to let the ideas percolate into your thoughts and list them.

After you have a list, try to rate each of them. I'm a list maker, so I use the old *pros on one side of the sheet, cons on the other* system. Again, don't list financial issues at this point. Focus on all the other items that go along with each possibility. For instance, moving to a lake home might require giving up the social and cultural benefits of your current location. You might not be as close to your grandchildren as you'd like. On the other hand, you might be better able to relive your love of sailing or walks on the beach at sunset.

Do some research. Find books, people, or Web sites devoted to your goals and understand the implications. It's nice to dream about all the wonderful parts of the goal, but ideas need to be grounded with some thought to the day-to-day reality. Athletes and performers seem to have a charmed life of endless resources and free time to completely indulge themselves. But that's not the day-to-day reality. All-night shoots, living away from home for ten months of the year. Not being able to go anywhere like a normal person without being bombarded with attention. Living under a microscope. These folks have to be sure that's the kind of life they want and can handle. The same goes for whatever you choose to do with your retirement years.

Of course, you cannot go through this process without including the people who will be directly impacted by your decisions. Your significant other absolutely needs to be part of the process, and to some degree children, parents, and your close social network. Unless they are all on board or at least understand your thinking, you may run into problems later on. Your own peace of mind and commitment to your decision likely will be impacted by the support you get from the people who mean the most to you, so get their buy-in as soon as you can.

Once you have narrowed the possibilities, you can put some numbers to them—the job of a later chapter. Don't discard the remaining ideas, though. Keep your list handy and update it when new ideas pop up. I'm sure you'll be revisiting this issue often, and your choices may change.

Pretirement Realities

Okay, we've indulged our whimsical side. It's time to think about some of the realities of pretirement that will directly impact our ability to be whimsical.

The most significant issue facing us Boomers is the fact that we are all living longer. That's good news and bad news. With life expectancies rising, many Boomers fear that they will run out of money before they die. Being relatively healthy actually becomes a catch-22. We live longer and are able to enjoy life more, yet we might reach the day when we run out of money and can't afford to live any longer.

How long will we live? The actuarial statistics (table 2.1), used by the Social Security Administration, flesh out this idea:

Table 2.1
PERIOD LIFE TABLE, 2001

	MALE		FEMALE	
Current Age	***Remaining Life***	***Total Life Expectancy***	***Remaining Life***	***Total Life Expectancy***
0	74.14	74.14	79.45	79.45
21	54.27	75.27	59.28	80.28
35	41.23	76.23	45.71	80.71
40	36.64	76.64	40.97	80.97
45	32.16	77.16	36.31	81.31
50	27.85	77.85	31.75	81.75
55	23.68	78.68	27.31	82.31
60	19.72	79.72	23.06	83.06
65	16.05	81.05	19.06	84.06
70	12.75	82.75	15.35	85.35
75	9.83	84.03	11.97	86.97
80	7.31	87.31	8.95	88.95
85	5.24	90.24	6.42	91.42
90	3.70	93.70	4.47	94.47
95	2.64	97.64	3.13	98.13
100	2.00	102.00	2.29	102.29

Source: Social Security Administration; updated April 6, 2006

When increasing life expectancies are cited, they usually refer to the rising life expectancy of a newborn. A newborn in 2006 will certainly live much longer on average than a baby born in 1906.

And a thirty-five-year-old alive in 2006 (thus born in 1971) can expect to live longer than a thirty-five-year-old in 1906 (born in 1871). What is fascinating is the fact that the older you already are, the longer you can expect your total life expectancy to be. How can that be? We have to look at the statistics cited and how they reflect the reality we all experience.

The infant and adolescent mortality rates in America are quite high. We rank thirty-sixth in the world with 6.63 deaths per 1,000 live births; annually, 700 out of 100,000 children who survive childbirth die before they reach age one. For children ages one through four and five through fourteen, that rate drops substantially, then rises again to 66 deaths per 100,000 among fifteen- through nineteen-year-olds. So once we get past the blips of the still very high infant and adolescent rates, our chances of living long increase greatly.

From birth to the age of twenty-one, the average total life span increases less than one year because of those mortality rates. In other words, if you make it to age three, your chances of reaching age four are less than those of a twenty-one to thirty-five-year-old man making it to his next birthday. And if you make it through the cancer and heart disease risks of middle age, your chances of celebrating a centennial birthday skyrocket. From ages seventy through seventy-five, a male will pick up an additional two years of life expectancy. Put simply, the older we get, the greater the chance we have to reach that full life-expectancy figure. Infant mortality, accidents, and other sudden deaths skew the numbers.

Of course, these tables cannot possibly take into account medical breakthroughs to come. The tables merely represent actuarial estimates given today's realities. Tomorrow might bring a stem-cell breakthrough or cancer eradicator that prolongs life for every age group. Just because you are now thirty-five doesn't mean you should plan on a shorter life span than a fifty-five-year-old. By the time you reach that age, life-span estimates could increase substantially beyond the average 82.31 years today's 55-year-old woman is expected to live.

If you are now thirty-five, you are projected to live on average to seventy-six if you are a man and eighty-one if a women. That means you will have, on average, eleven and sixteen years of retirement, respectively, if you choose to retire at age sixty-five. If you're presently age fifty-five, you will have an even longer retirement period to fund—fourteen years for a man, and seventeen years for a woman. If you've worked a traditional career span from age twenty-two to sixty-five, you'll now have to live one-third to one-half of that forty-three-year span using what you earned from that period.

Another way to think of this is that you need to save enough each year of your career to fund four to six months of retirement—when you'll need to stretch one year's income to cover up to eighteen months of living expenses. I hope that convinces you that making a maximum contribution to your 401(k) plan and maximizing your employer's contribution is a wise choice!

Obviously, in addition to representing the number of years of retirement living expenses you'll need to fund, retirement life span also represents the number of years that you'll continue to be taxed by inflation rates. You may be on somewhat of a fixed income, but you'll continue to be subject to inflation and its erosion of purchasing power.

A second major factor is Boomer consumerism. We spend more than any previous generation, and unless we're going to become Taoist monks late in life, we're going to continue to spend even after we stop working full time. Factor in inflation and that initial living-expense estimate of $50,000 per year during pretirement balloons as we go out ten, twenty, or, for some of us who may retire early or enjoy greater longevity, fifty years. We'll also be spending more on health care—elective or otherwise. And many of us will be part of the Sandwich Generation, accepting some responsibility for our parents and our children while navigating our own middle and later lives.

In addition, as we discussed in chapter 1, the future of Social Security is anything but secure; no one should rely upon it as the foundation of a retirement plan. We also know that, along with Social Security worries, most of us Boomers face a different retirement funding source than our parents did. Many of them had a pension plan firmly in place that offered a secure, if fixed, income. Today's employers offer us more flexible programs, but with that flexibility comes responsibility. If you were fortunate to be in the market or making maximum contributions to your 401(k) through the boom years of the 1990s, you were smart and lucky. Count your blessings, but recount how much you currently have in that account. In light of the downturn in the market since that incredible run, do you have any sense of how much of those gains have subsequently diminished?

To further complicate matters, unlike our parents, we Boomers aren't savers. Mom and Dad saved roughly 25 percent of their yearly income. We save 12 percent. That's less than half as much, and I'd venture a guess that we own twice as much as our parents do and are deeper in debt than they've ever been. Certainly, most of us earn more than our parents were able to, but prices have risen, inflation has eaten away at our earning power, and we want more and more. How have many of us gotten that "more"? Through credit in many instances. Figures vary, but the typical American household carries anywhere from $7,000 to $12,000 in credit card debt alone. I won't frighten you by providing the figures for total indebtedness including mortgages, car payments, and all the rest. Later on, in chapter 3, you'll calculate your net worth and look at how you spend your money each month, including how much of it goes to savings.

What Will Retirement Look Like?

Chances are, our overspending habits will not change when we retire. We know ourselves, we know our habits, we know the current economic picture, and as a result more than 50 percent of Americans ages forty to fifty indicated in a recent survey that they don't expect their living expenses to decrease when they retire. That's a far cry from our parents, who settled into a quiet postwork life. As you sit there reading this today, can you honestly picture yourself going to an afternoon matinee at the Cineplex and heading for the early-bird buffet at the local diner? I can hear your screams of protest now. They don't call us Boomers for nothing—we are not about to go quietly into that good night of retirement.

As I said previously, for us life isn't merely about numbers but about experiences, and making the decision to pursue this million-dollar goal will lead us on an extraordinary journey. Fortunately for us, our parents instilled in us a fundamental sense of values that will serve as a starting point—and a point of departure from the previous Depression-scarred generation.

There are other real-world considerations that you need to at least think about before getting to the numbers. Consider all the following and more when undertaking this exercise:

- At what age would you like to retire, if at all?
- What other careers or activities do you want to pursue after your retirement from your current career?
- Will you be living in the same house?
- Do you plan to buy a second home?
- Will you be helping to pay for your grandchildren's education?
- Will you be providing financial assistance to your children? In particular, a special-needs child can greatly complicate retirement planning.
- Will you be responsible financially for any part of your parents' health care or end-of-life expenses?
- Is leaving an inheritance to your children important, or are your heirs self-sufficient?
- What other special income needs will you have (traveling, for example)?
- Is it important for you to leave money to a charitable organization?
- Do you have adequate resources to fall back on in the event of a major health problem that causes disability or assisted-living requirements?

These considerations all must be prioritized before you can even think about putting our money to work. While optimism is a positive virtue, you must recognize that you may not be able to achieve all your goals for retirement and postretirement. Starting early is a huge first step toward the realization of your goals, but a limited time horizon may force some difficult choices.

Envisioning Your Retirement

Goal setting is tough. Goals are personal and change over time. Financial and lifestyle goals range between necessities and luxuries. The crowd mentality does not work here. What you may want and need financially is not dependent on society's standards and norms. A comfortable and appropriate amount of risk for you may be very different from your brother-in-law's. So investing isn't about beating the S&P 500 Index or your bragging golf partner or bridge group; investing is about getting what you want.

Here's a worksheet that I've devised and used successfully with some of my clients who are in need of help focusing on and fine-tuning their future.

RETIREMENT WISH LIST

1. At what age do you want to retire?

____ 55 ____ 65
____ 60 ____ other

2. What percentage of your retirement time do you envision spending on:

Hobbies and interests	________%
Education	________%
Travel	________%
Spending time with family or friends	________%
Working	________%
Volunteering	________%
Other	________%
Total	________%

3. I envision being able to:

Participate in my hobby/interest ______ hours per week.
Enroll in ______ classes per year.

Travel ______ weeks per year.
Spend ______ hours per week with family or friends.
Work ______ hours per week.
Volunteer ______ hours per week.

4. Where will you choose to live during your retirement? Check one:

____ Present location(s)
____ Somewhere else

5. I envision:

____ Living in one location
____ Living in two or more locations
____ Traveling all the time

6. If you selected "somewhere else" in question 4, which of the following will you base your location selection on? Rank them in order from 1 to 12:

____ Proximity to family and/or friends
____ Proximity to/availability of favorite leisure activities
____ Climate
____ Aesthetics/beauty of the area
____ Proximity to airport
____ Proximity to health care facilities
____ Convenience/proximity to people and services
____ Privacy/distance from others
____ Cost-of-living issues (rank order these factors from A through D)
 ____ cost of residence
 ____ property taxes
 ____ services
 ____ availability of public transportation
____ Availability of work opportunities
____ Safety
____ Educational opportunities

7. I haven't been involved in this yet, but I would love to try:

   1. ______________________________
   2. ______________________________
   3. ______________________________
   4. ______________________________
   5. ______________________________

8. I've always dreamed of owning:

   1. ______________________________
   2. ______________________________
   3. ______________________________
   4. ______________________________

9. Even if I had to give up doing everything else, I would still want to remain able to:

   ______________________________.

   I would still want to own:

   ______________________________.

10. What I'm most afraid of when I think of retiring is:

    ____ Not having enough money
    ____ Illness/death
    ____ Illness/death of spouse and/or friends
    ____ Boredom
    ____ Losing my independence
    ____ Other: ____________________

11. What I'm most looking forward to when I think of retiring is:

    ____ Flexibility of my time
    ____ Reaping financial rewards
    ____ Contributing more to the greater good
    ____ Spending time with family/friends
    ____ Pursuing new interests
    ____ Pursuing present interests
    ____ Learning more

Keep in mind that at this stage, with the exception of geographic and cost-of-living issues, you aren't concerned with your financial picture yet. We'll turn to all those issues in the next chapters. For now, you want to create an idealized version of your retirement. After all, the point of this book is to help realize your personal vision for the future.

Retirement as a Second Career

Most of us work too hard already. We slog through ten- to twelve-hour days, traveling to places that take us away from family and friends. Why would we want a second career on top of our already too busy lives? Well, here's the deal. I'm about to propose a job that uses the same skill set you presently employ. In other words, you're going to have to do some analysis and problem solving. You're going to have to make some tough choices and battle the risk-reward demons. You may have to stretch yourself a bit and do some weekly reading, but you could cut down on that by watching television or listening to the radio. What I'm proposing is a job that has the potential—if you're successful and sharp (and we already know you're both those things, since you bought this book)—to allow you to earn as much in a retirement year as you do presently. And as an added bonus: You only have to devote about two hours a week to it. Think about it. Two hours a week. What is that? Less than the time it takes to work your way around the front nine; about the time it takes to watch a DVD at home or catch a movie at the local Cineplex. (Just FYI: Purchasing and watching a DVD from the comfort of your own home as opposed to going to the movie theater once a week will save more than $1,000 a year for a family of four—more on that in chapter 4.) Two hours a week, and you'll get the holidays off, so that means about a hundred hours a year.

And what is this job? Working on your retirement plan. If you can set aside a total of two hours a week—preferably two consecutive hours, but that's not completely necessary—you can achieve the loftiest financial goals. Now, I'm a busy guy myself, and I know that if it's important to me, I'll find a way to get those two hours in. Guaranteed. Even if that means listening to NPR's *Marketplace* for half an hour on the way home from work or TiVoing *Nightly Business Report* and watching it before bedtime.

You can do it; I promise. Don't let fear win out. While financial planning can appear complex, when you break it down into simple steps, it is no longer daunting. Investing and financial planning require nothing more than a series of simple, commonsense action plans. Let's take the first step together. Having trouble? Shoot me an e-mail at invest@farrmiller.com, and I will help.

There's very little mystery involved in developing a solid financial plan. It's been demonstrated time and again that quick, easy-money systems don't work; that if you follow the advice of writers who encourage you to run with the bulls, you're as likely to slip in the mud as you are to grab the horns. Essentially, what this book will show you is how to be your own investment firm. Sure, you don't have access to all the personnel resources that I do, but every bit of the same information I have is available to you. As an added bonus, instead of four hundred clients, you have only one account that matters to you—your own. That trade-off results in you coming out ahead every time. Throughout this book, I will show you how.

It's Never Too Late to Get Started

Ideally, you've been thinking about your retirement since you started working. Many corporations make this possible through matching contributions to 401(k) and other plans. The reality is that most twenty- and thirtysomethings aren't as focused on retirement as they are on other crucial life experiences—getting married, buying their first home, and raising children. All those things cost money, of course, and when it comes to deciding among your many expenses, setting aside additional funds for retirement can often slip down the list of priorities.

Fortunately, even as late as age sixty-five, you can still catch up. While many of my clients start their retirement and investment management much earlier, Robert and Erica Fleming came to me shortly after Robert lost his job as a CIO at a prominent midlevel

Beltway financial institution. Erica had been through minor heart surgery and stopped working as a fund-raiser for a local charitable organization five years earlier. When Robert came to see me, he was scared. The job loss was a tough blow, and he and Erica had had some bad luck with previous investments. Though they owned their own condo, they only had $400,000 in total savings, primarily from his pension. How were they going to make it?

Robert was a smart man, and he knew that he faced a make-or-break decision. I told him several times about the high level of risk involved, and he was willing to entrust me with his future. Despite his age, we had to be aggressive, so we created a portfolio that was allocated 60 percent in stocks and the rest in bonds. We had to grow his money or the two of them weren't going to have enough to last—especially considering that Erica's mother was ninety-one years old and in good health.

Nine years later, they have supplemented their Social Security income with account withdrawals, and their portfolio has a value of $700,000. Of that total, $100,000 came from Erica inheriting money at her mother's passing, but it is still an impressive rate of return in a relatively short period of time. Robert and Erica can sleep well at night, and so can I knowing that we took some real chances early on. We've since backed away from that aggressive position into more fixed income holdings.

While I don't recommend that you wait until the age of sixty-five like Bob and Erica did, it's helpful to know that you can expect a successful income even at that late stage with smart money management and wise investment decisions. Later on in the book, I'll look in more detail at the kinds of plans those of us who have fallen behind can implement to avoid such risky times.

Now that you have a vision for what your retirement should look like, and a target goal in mind—a million dollars—it's time to devise a strategy for getting there. In chapter 3, we'll take a look at the initial assessment and planning stages necessary to implement your mission.

PART TWO

The Million-Dollar Groundwork

Prepare to Invest Wisely and Well

CHAPTER THREE

Evaluate It

Knowing Where You Stand Today

In the last couple of years, I've run into a number of people I haven't seen since college or even earlier. I don't know if it's that time in our lives when our kids are growing up and we start really focusing on ourselves again, but many of us seem to be training for a marathon or some other form of extreme physical challenge. Triathlons, bicycling, mountain climbing, river running, and other extreme endeavors are on many of our agendas. A few of my friends have jumped right into training and seem to be well on their way to their goal. But most of them who leap in have stories to tell of injuries and setbacks that have put the accomplishment of their goals on hold—or even in total jeopardy.

On the other hand, several of my peers were careful and visited their doctors for a workup before they even embarked on their training program. They had a general physical along with a stress test and other assessments so that they knew their base level of general health and cardio fitness. Their doctors advised them of their current level of conditioning and how much additional stress they could safely withstand. After that, they talked to trainers or found other resources to give them a suitable program based upon their starting level of condition. They started out a little more slowly than the others, but they steadily progressed, and now they're much closer to their ultimate goal than those who rushed right in.

Meeting financial goals requires a similar level of preparation. Think of this chapter as your "financial physical" to see what kind of fiscal shape you are in today. You'll thoroughly assess your present financial condition so that later on in the book, you can devise the most suitable regimen to get to the ultimate $1 million goal.

For this reason, I refer to my overall investment program as FIT—the Farr Investment Technique. This six-step process breaks down into two phases: the Million-Dollar Groundwork and the Million-Dollar Maneuvers. Now that you understand the nature of the mission and the rationale behind it, it's important to prepare for that mission. Here again are the steps of the Farr Investment Technique:

MILLION-DOLLAR GROUNDWORK

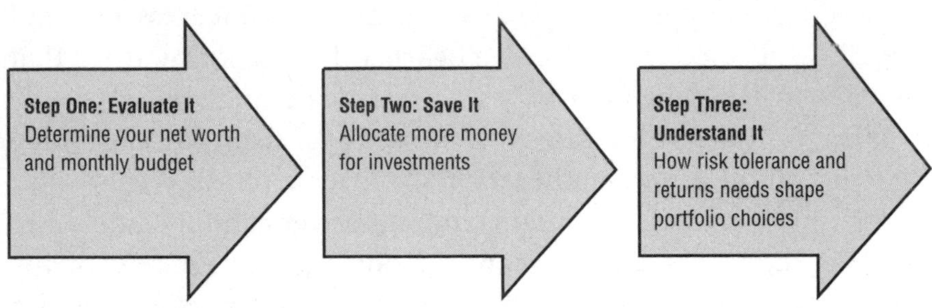

MILLION-DOLLAR MANEUVERS

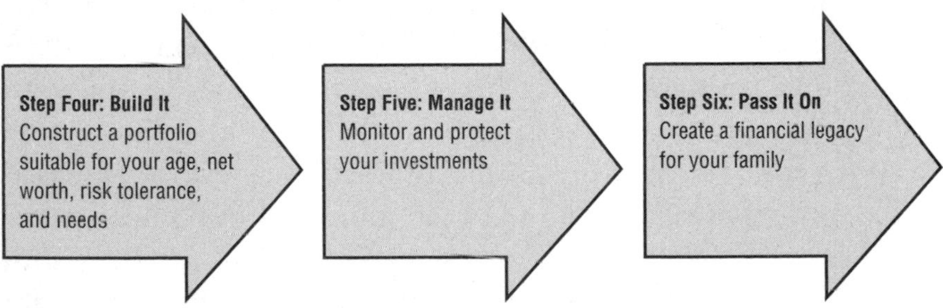

Step Four: Build It
Construct a portfolio suitable for your age, net worth, risk tolerance, and needs
Step Five: Manage It
Monitor and protect your investments
Step Six: Pass It On
Create a financial legacy for your family

In this chapter, we'll concentrate on the first of these steps: determining your true net worth—and getting a snapshot of your monthly expenditures (and savings) so you can execute your plan for your future.

Task 1: Calculating Your Net Worth

The first financial stress test is to figure out your present net worth. *Net worth* is the amount of financial assets (minus debt) you have accumulated. In a sense, it is a representation of all that you've done with your earnings over a lifetime. By determining this figure, you'll have a better understanding of where all the money from your paychecks has gone—toward purchases, savings, or investments. In some ways, you can think of this as a financial scorecard where you record your efforts, good and bad, birdie or bogey. The results may be surprising.

We all like to see our results and know how they compare to others'. Recall the kind of rubbernecking that went on when a teacher passed back a test in school. That's not the point of this exercise, though. Here is where the scorecard analogy falls short—there is no real target number that we are all shooting for. We must each design our own course and determine the relative values that we are aiming for. Magazines love to print features listing the most powerful people in Hollywood, the highest-net-worth individuals, and the like, but don't fall too deeply into that pit. Compare your own results solely with where you thought you might be or hoped to be. Of course, the number matters, but only in terms of what you're going to do with it next. What it tells you can be either a blow or a boost to the ego, but the key thing to keep in mind is that you're determining where you stand now in order to figure out how best to get to where you want to be. This is a key phase of your Million-Dollar Mission.

Calculating net worth can prove beneficial in other regards, too. When you take the time to really examine and analyze all of your assets and liabilities, you'll have a better sense of where your money has gone and where you've chosen to keep it. You can take this opportunity to reevaluate some of the decisions you made early on. Perhaps your financial circumstances have changed considerably since you first decided where and how to invest or save. Now is the time to take control. I know many people who've bought a new house and in the process of moving discovered a great deal about all that they'd accumulated and no longer needed. Calculating your net worth in anticipation of the Million-Dollar Maneuvers is like moving into a new financial house. You want to bring only the things that are most essential, valuable, and useful.

Determining your net worth should not be a time-consuming process. Everything you need should be readily available; no high-level mathematical or financial gymnastics are required. It is not necessary to account for every item in your house. The goal is to create liquid, usable value of $1 million by the time you retire, so we'll focus on those types of assets in this assessment.

You only need to set aside an evening to calculate your net worth. Begin by reviewing the following list of the information that goes into a determination of net worth. You may be able to fill in some items off the top of your head. You may need to dig through some files to find some of the less accessible bits and pieces. At the very least, you need to have access to:

1. Statements of bank and credit union accounts: checking, savings, and term accounts.
2. Statements of investment accounts, including any mutual funds or annuities held outside your brokerage account(s).
3. Statements of retirement accounts, including 401(k) plans, IRAs, SEP-IRAs, and any pension or profit-sharing plans.
4. Statements from your mortgage holder reflecting your current balance.
5. Credit card statements.
6. Statements from your auto loan(s) provider.
7. Life insurance policies.

Fill in as much of the Sample Net Worth Calculation Worksheet (page 62) as possible that first evening. Figure out what you don't know and create a plan to get that information. If you can estimate pretty closely, that will be sufficient for now, but it still is a good idea to verify any guesses and also figure out where and how to get the information when needed. When in doubt, always underestimate values; it'll be safer in the long run.

The Sample Net Worth Calculation Worksheet breaks assets down into four categories:

1. **Liquid assets.** Cash or other assets quickly convertible to cash.
2. **Savings and investments.** These can be converted to liquid (cash) somewhat easily.
3. **Nonmarketable assets.** These are holdings that are of some value but with a limited sale market.
4. **Tangible assets.** The everyday items that accumulate over the years—furniture, appliances, electronics, and so on. Think of tangible assets as those you can literally touch.

Of the four, tangible assets will likely present with the most problems in calculating. Not only do most of us have far more tangible assets than we do savings and investments, but their real-world value is more difficult to determine. Resist the temptation to overvalue these items here. What they are "worth" means what amount of money you could receive if you decided to sell them today as is. A professional appraiser could help you with certain kinds of items, and you could spend many days doing things like going to a car dealer to find out what your car is worth in trade or wholesale. You'll save yourself a lot of time and effort by researching wisely. A number of resources exist online that can help you determine the approximate value of your tangible assets—online auction sites have myriad prices, professional services like the *Kelley Blue Book* list the value of automobiles and other motorized vehicles, and newspapers frequently publish lists of homes sold in a particular time period. While an estimated value of a television set may not skew your results greatly, misassigning the value of your home can create real distortion. Homeowners' insurance includes a replacement-value figure that you can use on the worksheet, depending upon how recently it has been updated. In addition, having a professional appraisal of your home isn't a bad idea. Utilize all these and more in determining the dollar value to ascribe to these items.

Liabilities

The last part of the net worth calculation is determining what you owe others—your liabilities. Remember, your net worth is what's left over after you pay off all your debts and head to your missionary work. You're not fleeing creditors and heading to some remote Caribbean island. You're taking with you what you've earned. *Short-term debt* is the debt used to fund daily living expenses and due within one year. Charge cards, revolving store credit, unpaid medical co-pays, and other short-term bills fall into this category.

What if you always carry a balance on your charge cards? That debt can be called at any time by the card issuer. A couple of late payments or other misdeeds, and you'll have to repay immediately. Every financial planner and counselor of whom you have ever heard has railed against credit card debt for a reason. It's egregiously expensive and almost invariably stupid. Don't carry credit card balances. *Ever!* Heed this one bit of advice, and you'll be much closer to a comfortable retirement than you might imagine.

Longer-term debt such as car payments and mortgages makes up the remainder of your liabilities. A car may be worth $30,000, but you may own only a tiny fraction of it when you factor in the outstanding loan. In fact, don't be shocked if you actually own less than zero of your vehicle in the first few years. As we'll discuss later on in more detail, new cars are *not* a good investment. (Vintage collectibles may be a good investment, but that's another issue entirely.) In the first few years, they depreciate much more quickly than the loan balance declines, leaving you with a negative value. Many people are shocked when they realize that the car they are trading in won't cover their down payment on a new one; in fact, they will have to come up with more money to pay off the old vehicle's outstanding loan.

Hopefully, your home will not cause the same predicament. Unless you've bought very recently at the top of the market in one of the overheated housing areas and used a low-down-payment mortgage, you should have *some* equity in your home. Of course, if you did have to sell, sales and moving costs could wipe out a meager equity position.

Recently, one of my clients was forced to move back to his hometown to care for his aging parents. They were doing well, but went into a somewhat rapid decline after they were diagnosed with a debilitating disease. As the only child, he felt strongly obligated to assist in caring for them. Two years prior to making the move, Terry and his wife, Beverly, had purchased a new home in a high-end development in Vienna, Virginia. Prior to this most recent purchase, they'd bought and sold homes three times in six years, and with each successive move, their profit margin grew slimmer. They had thought that this last move was exactly that—the *last one*. They'd put little down on the Vienna house, the market slumped a bit, and they wound up having to sell quickly, so they were forced to accept the first offer they got. Their $50,000 gross gain was quickly eaten up by the Realtor's commission, the cost of movers, and assorted moving expenses. Buy-and-flip had them nearly flipping out.

I don't mean to scare you with these examples; I only want to alert you to the reality of the fact that you don't own anything completely until all the debt on it is paid, and miscellaneous debt that isn't secured by a vehicle, real estate, or other real property also must be subtracted in order to figure out what truly belongs to you. You don't own your car until that last payment is made and the lender mails you the title. You don't completely own your home until the mortgage is fully paid off and the lender sends a letter to that effect.

The Bottom Line

If you haven't guessed by now, the last step in the net worth calculation is merely subtracting the outstanding balances of all your debts from the value of all your assets, the remainder being the amount that you are financially worth. Again, if you were going to quit your job today, cash out your investments, and retire to some island, your net worth is the amount of money you'd have to take along from your financial life so far.

It's too early in the process to do any assessment of whether your net worth is good, bad, or sufficient. It's merely a starting point. Earning power, time to retirement, lifestyle, and retirement goals all play very important roles in structuring a plan to get to a great retirement.

SAMPLE NET WORTH CALCULATION WORKSHEET

	Value in dollars
ASSETS	
Liquid Assets	
Cash (money market)	
Checking accounts	
Savings accounts	
CDs	
Savings and Investments	
Stocks	
Bonds	
Mutual funds	
Options[1]	
Annuities[2]	
Other assets in brokerage accounts	
Cash value of life insurance	
Trust funds for which you are beneficiary or you can access	
IRAs	
Vested pension benefits	
Nonmarketable Securities[3]	
Ownership interest in businesses and assets	
Leases owed to you	
Loans owed to you	
Timeshares	
True collectibles	
Fixed Assets	
Home	
Other real estate	

Autos	
Boats	
Jewelry	
Furniture	
Other machinery, equipment, and "toys"	
TOTAL ASSETS	
LIABILITIES	
Short-Term Debt	
Charge cards	
Bank loans	
Lines of credit	
Margin debt to broker[4]	
Salary advances	
Medical co-pays outstanding	
Other debt due in less than 1 year	
Long-Term Debt	
Mortgage	
Home equity lines	
Student loans	
Car loans	
Partnership loans or other advances	
Other debt due in more than 1 year	
TOTAL LIABILITIES	
NET WORTH (total assets minus total liabilities):	

1. An *option contract* is an agreement in which one party (the holder or buyer) pays for the right (but not the obligation) to buy or sell an asset at a set price on or before a future expiration date. The other party (the writer or seller) has the obligation to honor the terms of the contract. At the expiration of the contract, the option is worthless to the buyer, but

the seller keeps the payment he or she received from the buyer. Here, I ask you to list any options you have apart from stocks.

2. A *variable annuity* is a contract between you and an insurance company, under which you make initial payment(s) and the insurer agrees to make periodic payments to you, beginning either immediately or at some future date.
3. *Nonmarketable securities* are financial instruments that are not traded on an exchange; their value and liquidity is less certain. For instance, you may own stock in a family business, have loaned money to a relative to buy a car, or have taken back a note in order to help someone qualify to buy your house. None of these is traded on an exchange or through your broker, although with some effort you may be able to find someone to buy them from you.
4. *Margin debt to broker* is money you owe to an investment broker who has loaned you money to buy additional stocks. Current SEC law allows you to borrow up to 50 percent of the current market value of your stock.

Documenting Your Life

Gathering the information you need to put together your net worth and current spending statements can serve another very valuable purpose. I can't tell you how many times I hear stories from friends and clients of the trouble they have had organizing the affairs of a parent who has died or become incapacitated. For one reason or another, their parents didn't keep very good records of all their financial dealings and didn't leave information so that anyone else could figure out what was going on. From insurance accounts that they didn't know about to safe-deposit boxes they were not co-owners of and thus unable to access, information was either missing or scattered about. As you go through these net worth and budget processes, you must write down the necessary information so that a spouse or other trusted person can carry on your affairs if need be. Make the information accessible to that person. It does no good to lock it away in a safe-deposit box that only you can open or a file on your computer that's password-protected. Plus, don't rely on just one person—remember, something might happen to that person, too. While I'm preaching, I may as well stress that it's also important to give someone your financial and health care power of attorney so that important decisions can be made if you are incapacitated. Most states make it very easy to do this yourself utilizing standardized forms; or you can contact an estate-planning professional if your situation seems unique. Here's a list of some of the information that will help someone else carry on your affairs for you:

General

Name: ______________________________

Phone: ______________________________

Alieses: ______________________________

Social Security #: ______________________________

Veteran service information: ______________________________

Parents' information:

Name: ______________________________

Phone: ______________________________

Children:

Name: ______________________________

Phone: ______________________________

Name: ______________________________

Phone: ______________________________

Name: ______________________________

Phone: ______________________________

Spouses:

Name: ______________________________

Phone: ______________________________

Name: ______________________________

Phone: ______________________________

Other important people:

Name: ______________________________

Phone: ______________________________

Name: ______________________________

Phone: ______________________________

Name: ______________________________

Phone: ______________________________

Legal Documents (to be kept in a designated place)

- ☐ Birth certificate
- ☐ Social Security card
- ☐ Passport
- ☐ Power of attorney
- ☐ Military discharge
- ☐ Marriage certificate
- ☐ Prenuptial agreements

- ☐ Postnuptial agreements
- ☐ Name change documents
- ☐ Divorce decree
- ☐ Divorce settlement agreement
- ☐ House title
- ☐ Car title

Death-Related Instructions

- ☐ Will and any codicils
- ☐ Announcement
- ☐ Service
- ☐ Burial/cremation
- ☐ Organ donation
- ☐ Other donations
- ☐ Other requests

Government Benefits

Retirement plans and pensions:

Holder: ______________________________

Account #: ______________________________

Holder: ______________________________

Account #: ______________________________

Employment

Name: ______________________________

Phone: ______________________________

Name: ______________________________

Phone: ______________________________

Name: ______________________________

Phone: ______________________________

Financial Obligations

Car:

Lien holder: ______________________________

Phone: ______________________________

Account #: ______________________________

Mortgage:

Lien holder: ____________

Account #: ____________

Issuer: ____________

Phone: ____________

Account #: ____________

Issuer: ____________

Phone: ____________

Account #: ____________

Promissory notes:

Holder: ____________

Phone: ____________

Account #: ____________

Alimony:

Name: ____________

Phone: ____________

Amount: ____________

Support:

Name: ____________

Phone: ____________

Amount: ____________

Name: ____________

Phone: ____________

Amount: ____________

Name: ____________

Phone: ____________

Amount: ____________

Lawsuits and settlements: ____________

Financial (names, amounts, account numbers, who to contact)

Bank:

Name: ______________________________

Phone: ______________________________

Account #: ______________________________

Type of account: ______________________________

Name: ______________________________

Phone: ______________________________

Account #: ______________________________

Type of account: ______________________________

Name: ______________________________

Phone: ______________________________

Account #: ______________________________

Type of account: ______________________________

Safe-deposit boxes: ______________________________

Payable-on-death bank accounts: ______________________________

Brokerage:

Name: ______________________________

Phone: ______________________________

Account #: ______________________________

Type of account: ______________________________

Insurance: ______________________________

401(k):

Name: ______________________________

Phone: ______________________________

Account #: ______________________________

Type of account: ______________________________

Trusts:

Name: ______________________________

Phone: ______________________________

Account #: ______________________________

Type of account: ______________________________

Promissory notes:

Name: ______________________________

Phone: ______________________________

Account #: ______________________________

Type of account: ______________________________

Small Business

Name: ______________________

Lawyer:

Name: ______________________

Phone: ______________________

Accountant:

Name: ______________________

Phone: ______________________

Medical Information

Doctors:

Name: ______________________

Phone: ______________________

Insurance company:

Name: ______________________

Phone: ______________________

Policy #: ______________________

Living will or other health care directive: ______

Day-to-Day Living

- ☐ Contracts with service providers
- ☐ Instructions for keeping the household running (unique issues)

Secured Places and Passwords

E mail:

Username: ______________________

Password: ______________________

Online banking:

Username: ______________________

Password: ______________________

Other online accounts:

Type: ______________________

Username: ______________________

Password: ______________________

Type: ______________________

Username: ______________________

Password: ______________________

Type: ________________________________
Username: ____________________________
Password: ____________________________

Obviously, with fears about identity theft a reality, it's important to keep this information as secure as possible. Keeping important documents in a safe-deposit box in a bank is a good idea. Any documents that you need to keep on hand in your residence should be placed in a safe or fireproof box in a secure location in the house. Make certain that the location of any of this information is revealed to as few people as possible.

The time you invest now can save your loved ones and you immeasurable time and pain down the line.

Task 2: Determine What You Are Spending Now

How were you able to accumulate the net worth you just calculated in task 1? It's simple—other than inheritance, winning the lottery, or some other windfall, the only way to create a positive net worth is to spend less than you earn. I cannot stress that fundamental truth enough. Sure, you might have made a killing on the sale of your home, but unless you have net worth in addition to your home equity you will not be in position to retire well. Your goal is to create a liquid net worth of $1 million by the time you retire. And the way to do that is through spending less than you earn, and taking the remainder and investing well.

At this point in the process, you are merely going to measure your current spending and saving behavior. I'll leave for a later section of the book the question of what you really need versus what you want or *think* you need. All you're trying to do here is create on paper and in numbers your monthly financial picture. When you determined your net worth in task 1, you were getting a picture of how much you've saved up to this point. In this step, you're closely examining your monthly expenditures to see how much of your monthly income you'll have left over to add to your current net worth.

Creating a budget doesn't need to be as complicated as it might sound. Yes, businesses have staff dedicated to creating budgets, and the government budget battles strike fear into many of us. This won't be so bad. In this step, you'll just pay attention to your spending for some period of time. Later on, you'll make some decisions about whether the way you're spending suits your goals.

What Do You Spend in a Month?

I like to suggest that clients take a month to review all the bills and other financial statements that they receive over that cycle and make sure that they are included in their calculations. It's easy to overlook some items that you don't deal with on a daily basis; going through a billing cycle helps jog the memory.

I know what you're picturing right now—sitting at a table with stacks of papers piled high around you. The documents seem to have no real connection to one another. Neither chronological order or alphabetical order is going to cut it for this task. Just as with the last worksheet, then, you're going to have to put this information into more meaningful and user-friendly categories.

Obviously, some of the information will reflect money coming in, and the rest will show the money going out. That's the first step—dividing up income and expenses. Next, look for categories where you can combine receipts and statements into similar piles. For example, all your grocery store receipts and restaurant bills can go in together—possibly to be subdivided later. By doing this sorting, you'll discover that some piles are bigger and some are smaller. Generally, a pile with a single artifact or document in it tells you that you could probably combine that receipt with another pile. For example, if during the time period that you're tracking expenses, you have a single bill for an old family photo that you had restored and reframed, you might want to create the category "photo restoration." Probably not—unless you regularly spend money on this. It's likely to be a one-off item, and there's no real sense in tracking that expense if it doesn't represent something that you do regularly. Good old "miscellaneous" can come in handy here.

Once you have your piles, look for similarities so that you can combine those smaller piles into bigger ones. Doing this is like putting together a jigsaw puzzle. My parents are big puzzlers, and I've often visited them and seen how they've taken the three thousand or so pieces and sorted them into several piles—the border pieces, pieces of sky (if it's a landscape they're working on), trees, flowers, and so forth. This sorting process sounds more complicated in explanation than it is in execution, so let's take a look at the Simple Budget Worksheet.

SIMPLE BUDGET WORKSHEET

	Actual	Budget	First Review
INCOME:			
Take-home salary/wages/ commissions/ bonus			
Interest/dividends			
Other income			
Total Income:			
EXPENSES:			
Rent/Mortgage			
Utilities			
Maintenance (dry cleaning, etc.)			
Automobile (gas, etc.)			
Clothing			
Medical/dental			
Entertainment			
Food			
Child-related			

Vacations			
Gifts/charity			
Misc. insurance			
Car loan payments			
Credit card payments			
Miscellaneous			
Other: List			
Total Expenses			
CASH SURPLUS (DEFICIT)			

This sheet is useful for those who don't keep detailed records because it gives a general look at the budget picture. For a quick shortcut to get the ball rolling toward an investment plan, this should suffice. The more detailed Family Monthly Budget Schedule will give a more precise picture.

FAMILY MONTHLY BUDGET SCHEDULE

	January	February	March	Monthly Average
INCOME DESCRIPTION				
Wages (take-home)—partner 1				
Wages (take-home)—partner 2				
Interest and dividends				
Miscellaneous				
TOTAL INCOME				

EXPENSE DESCRIPTION				
Housing				
Mortgage payment				
Rent				
Home repairs				
Insurance				
Utilities				
Electricity				
Gas				
Telephone				
Water				
Cell phone				
Transportation				
Auto insurance				
Auto payment				
Gasoline				
Auto maintenance				
Food				
Groceries				
Necessary outside meals				
Household				
Cleaning expenses				
Other upkeep				
Personal Care				
Beauty shop and barber				
Clothing				
Laundry and dry cleaning				
Children				
Tuition				
Child care				

School supplies				
Entertainment and Recreation				
Cable TV				
Internet access				
Club dues				
Subscriptions				
Movie rentals				
Games				
Activities				
Restaurants				
Vacations				
Health				
Health insurance				
Life insurance				
Medical and dental out-of-pocket				
Charity				
Gifts				
Debt Payments				
Home equity				
Credit card payments				
Other debt payments				
Miscellaneous				
TOTAL EXPENSES				
CASH (SHORT) EXTRA				

Keep in mind that what's here are merely suggested categories. You definitely should modify this worksheet to meet your own needs. For example, if you have a golfing habit and tend to spend a lot of money each month on that hobby, then create a specific subcategory for those expenses related to it. The same is true if you spend money fairly regularly at a particular retailer. I worked with one woman who tracked her Starbucks expenses to the penny.

Some expenses are likely to fit into more than one category. It's tempting to move these to an area you deem less "sensitive"—one where you spend fewer dollars. By doing so, you make it look as if you spend less on one of your "sinful indulgences" than is really the case. There are all kinds of creative accounting practices you might be tempted to resort to, but honesty is important if you want your worksheet to accurately portray your spending habits. Remember, you want to see what your budget *really* looks like, not what you'd like it to be.

How Long Should You Track Expenses?

To create that accurate picture, in a perfect world you'd track expenses for an entire year. Since your primary concern right now is tracking expenses so you can identify sources for saving or investing, you may not want to wait a year before beginning that program. In that case, three months of data will give you a solid foundation on which to base your conclusions. You may also wish to do an estimated annual budget, but the key to accuracy is recognizing that some expenses are seasonal and will vary by time of year. Utilities are probably the prime example of this cyclical phenomenon. For variable or seasonal expenses (such as heating costs, holiday gifts, or vacations), be sure to account for fluctuations or inconsistencies in the data. Your check register or other financial data tracker software like Quicken may be an aid in determining many of these expenses over a longer period of time.

While I suggest tracking those expenses for a year, it is by far easier and more efficient to convert that annual data into a monthly set of numbers. This big-picture versus smaller-picture issue is important. As I will discuss throughout the book, small changes can yield big results. It is also far easier to make those smaller, more incremental changes I'll discuss later on than it is to say, for example, "This year, I'm going to cut back on discretionary spending by $10,000." That's a staggering amount, and it would be easy to get discouraged if you aren't making progress toward it. In addition, if you think in terms of a full twelve months, there is always the temptation to think you can do the work you need to later.

To get to these monthly amounts, divide the total by the number of months you've been tracking it to get your monthly average. I recommend taking an additional step: determining what percentage of your total expenses each category represents. This will tell you what percentage of income you spent on each of the categories. You might see, for instance, that you spent 25 percent of your income on food. Every family's situation will be unique, and percentages are helpful in determining what kind of modifications you may want to make if any one category really surprises you.

For Core Boomers, the ideal scenario is to be completely debt-free—having your house paid off, and paying for all other big-ticket items in cash. At present, US Department of Labor statistics demonstrate that this ideal scenario is achievable: 36 percent of homeowners surveyed between the ages of fifty-five and sixty-four are without mortgages. That figure increases to 61 percent among those sixty-five and older. A worthwhile target may be to decide at what age you want to be mortgage-free. Once you hit fifty-five, you want to be in the master's good graces and letting that compounding magic do its thing for you.

As I've stated before, don't worry if you aren't at the ideal stage for your demographic group. You can still catch up. What's important is that you have a firm understanding of exactly where you stand and set some savings goals for yourself.

Extending Your Budget Time Line

Where will your current condition get you by the time you retire? Here's a quick-and-dirty method to figure out where you'll be. Let's assume that your income will rise with inflation—nothing more or less—and that your various windfalls (bonuses, inheritances, stock options, sale of your home, and other good fortunes) will exactly offset the various nonrecurring expenses you'll face (college, wedding, illness, vacations, and the like). And let's assume that they will also just keep up with inflation. Let's further assume that you can earn a respectable 6 percent after taxes on your assets and your future savings; however, inflation will take away half (3 percent) of your earnings. (I'll analyze these assumptions later on; for now, just use these figures.) Next, add up the value of all the liquid assets you now own—those that can be liquidated within a short period of time. Then multiply that value by the number in table 3.1 that corresponds to the number of years left until you retire.

Table 3.1
ASSET MULTIPLIERS

Years to Retirement	Compound Interest Multiplier at 3% Annual Increase
5	1.16
10	1.34
15	1.56
20	1.81
25	2.09
30	2.43
35	2.81
40	3.26

So if you have $100,000 saved up right now and you're thirty-five, the calculations will look like this:

Current savings:	$100,000
Multiplier for 30 years:	x2.43
Amount you'll have when you retire:	$243,000

Well, it doesn't look as if you'll be able to spend everything you make from here on out. What will your projected savings add to the pot? You were shooting for savings of $500 per month—$6,000 per year. What will that add? Use table 3.2 to figure out what your current savings rate will grow to at that same 3 percent rate.

Table 3.2
SAVINGS MULTIPLIERS

Years to Retirement	Multiplier at 3% Annual Increase Net Effect
5	5.31
10	11.46
15	18.60
20	26.87
25	36.46
30	47.58
35	60.46
40	75.40

For our example, the numbers work out like this:

Current savings rate:	$6,000
Multiplier for 30 years:	x47.58
Amount you'll have when you retire:	$285,480

Altogether, at your current budget, you'll have about $528,480 at the time you retire. If you'd like to go through the exercise with more precision, go to my company's Web site (www.farrmiller.com) and use the retirement tools section to create a year-by year budget to determine where you will be by the time you retire.

Now that you have a better idea of how to determine where you are, the next step is of course to figure out where you want to be and devise a plan for how to get there. In the chapter that follows, we will take a look at how you can better allocate your resources to reach your ultimate goal.

CHAPTER FOUR

Save It

Allocate More Money for Investing

As I started working on this chapter, I checked the Web site www.brillig.com to find the amount of our national debt. Here is the screen that stared back at me:

U.S. NATIONAL DEBT CLOCK
The Outstanding Public Debt as of
04 Jan 2007 at 09:23:57 PM GMT is:
$8,681,789,571,763.17

For those of you whose eyes glazed over once we got past the seven-figure mark, our national debt on this date and time was more than $8.6 *trillion*. Another article declared that the US population will reach three hundred million this year. I got my calculator out and determined that the national debt represents $28,989 of debt for every man, woman, and child who is a citizen of this country. The national debt has been growing at a slowing but still lofty pace of nearly 9 percent per year since Reaganomics took hold in 1980. We didn't hit $1 trillion until 1981; the second trillion took five years, but the latest trillion will take a little more than one year!

The national debt has continued to increase an average of $1.74 billion per day since September 30, 2005.

How the heck could this have happened? All we hear about are cuts in services, so where is all the money going? We've also heard about the Pentagon and its $400 toilet seat expenditures and the

Figure 4.1

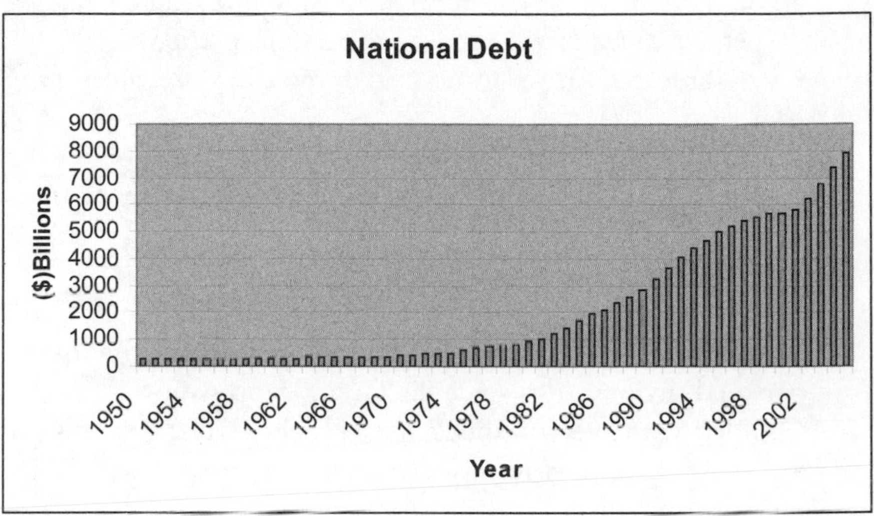

$300 hammers that would retail for $19.95, but how many toilet seats and hammers does it take to reach $8.6 trillion? I decided not to put my calculator to use on that one.

It's easier to understand how the government has become so bloated over its history when we look at the average American family and its debt orgy:

- According to the American Bankers Association, the average American family carries approximately $8,000 in credit card debt.
- Total nonrevolving credit in the United States, including loans for cars, tuition, boats, vacations, and so forth, increased to $1.36 trillion in 2005, and total household debt rose 11.7 percent to $11.5 trillion, marking the fastest growth since 1985.
- The household debt-to-income ratio reached an all-time high of 126 percent in 2005, up from 100 percent in 2000. To illustrate the pace of this rise, consider that the last increase of this size took fourteen years.
- Nonmortgage consumer debt is now $2.18 trillion, an average of $7,266 for every man, woman, and child in the United States. Factor in $8.68 trillion of mortgage debt, and that

indebtedness-per-citizen figure rises to about $36,200. The amount continues to rise at an increasing rate—an average of 10 percent since 1998, and 11.75 percent in 2005.

- Forty-three percent of American families *spend more than they earn.*

Not only are we spending at a record rate, we're actually disinvesting:

- The average personal savings rate in the United States was a negative 0.7 percent in December 2005, one of the lowest personal savings rates since the Great Depression.
- Coupled with the continued rise in debt levels, it seems we aren't using savings to pay down high-interest debt; we are instead using them to make more purchases.

Figure 4.2

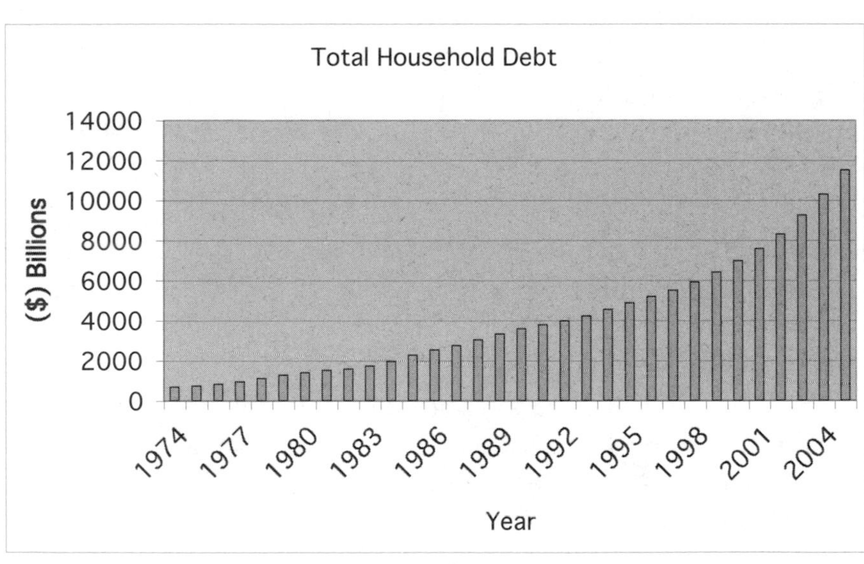

An Epidemic of Spending

In case the preceding statistics left you saying "So what?" or "Why does that matter?," consider that bankruptcies continue to be filed at a record pace, foreclosures have doubled in many regions of the country, and more families are behind in their mortgage payments or other debt payments than ever before. In short, we are piling on more debt than we can handle.

Several years ago, I handled the investments for the Brown family. The patriarch of the family was a prominent banker by the name of James. He'd done well for himself, and he wanted to turn his finances over to someone else so he could simply relax. When he died several years later, he gave each of his two children, John and Patty, $2 million each. That left his wife, Ann, with a tidy $4.5 million. Seeing the different ways the two siblings dealt with their windfalls was an eye-opening experience.

The older child, John, ran a small contracting outfit and earned a little over $100,000 per year. But unlike many contractors who drive a well-broken-in pickup truck, John tooled around in a Mercedes sedan, while his wife, Lizzy, drove a drop-top Mercedes roadster. They spent a great portion of their inheritance on an expansive landscaping project in their backyard, installing a running stream, a waterfall, a rock garden, an outdoor swimming pool with an attached whirlpool tub, and an adjoining sauna room. Nothing was too good for them. And soon, nearly nothing was left in their account. That is, until his mother died.

In contrast, John's sister, Patty, was frugal. She worked as an interior designer and pulled in about $60,000 a year. She lived simply, driving an old Honda Accord that she scrupulously maintained; when she received her inheritance from her father, little changed about her lifestyle. She loved antique books and bought them with less guilt than before, and she worried less about her frequent trips to Boston and occasional forays to London to find more treasures. By the time her brother had burned through $1.7 million of his $2 million inheritance, Lizzy's judicious spending and wise investments had in fact increased her account total to $2.8 million. Her net worth was even higher because many of her prudent purchases had appreciated in value very nicely.

I made every attempt to get John to curb his spending, but he kept telling me that he was soon to inherit everything from his mother and sister. He insisted that Patty was in ill health (she was) and that she would never marry (she eventually did, at age sixty). He also insisted that Patty didn't need the money and would gladly give it up for his sake. I don't know what kind of magic John worked on his sister, but his words proved prophetic. Not only did Patty give John the money, she did it in the most fiscally responsible manner possible—she disclaimed. This maneuver meant that she would not be taxed at all because she'd never received the money legally; nor would John have to pay a gift tax, since it wasn't his sister's to give—she'd never received it in the first place. A smart estate planner helped them work their way through this tangle. But within five years, John had worked his way through his latest inheritance, too. Without any money left for me to manage, John and I lost touch.

What sort of things do we require that are worth such astronomical levels of debt and a mortgaging of our futures? Think about the things you spend your money on every day or every month. I bet that most of us don't even really know where much of our money goes. That's another of the reasons you created a budget and tracked your expenses in the previous chapter. Things that once were splurges can quickly become daily routines. Without flinching, most of us can make purchases that have substantial consequences on our financial well-being—purchases based on emotions rather than logic.

Financial advances have made charge card debt easier to use and obtain, home equity has been monetized, and we have been marketed into a nation with unlimited wants. Look around your home at all the paraphernalia of everyday life. Do you need it all? Must you have it *now*? Is it all worth putting your retirement survival at risk? With some examination and planning, you can recapture much of that leakage, be a more savvy consumer, and put your invigorated savings to good use growing toward your retirement needs.

Control What You Can

Step Two of the Million-Dollar Mission is to save more money for investing, and, based on the statistics regarding household saving, it's the one thing most folks need to do immediately. Cost-cutting measures can really help you get to your goal of having a million dollars put away by retirement. Why? Because if you have accepted this as your target, you're going to have to fund the mission somehow. One of the reasons that risk is such an important concept in this book—and one I'll discuss more thoroughly in the upcoming chapters on investing—is that if you're at all like me, you like to feel in control. And when it comes to finances, the one single thing you have control over is where and how much of your money you spend. Certainly you don't have control over micro- and macroeconomic factors that determine the relative health of the economy, prices of durable goods and services, and the like, but you *do* have direct control over how much you spend. Let me repeat that: *You do have direct control over how much you spend.*

I know we'd all like to think that our careers and income streams are going to be on a constant, steady, if not spectacular rise. Certainly our performance will dictate to a certain degree the kind of compensation we receive, the number of promotions, and so forth—but how many of us know someone who earned excellent performance reviews, regular bonuses and raises, and was still laid off from a job? Again, it is a question of control, and we all live with a certain degree of uncertainty and certain degree of self-delusion. That's why you did your homework in the previous chapter to get a realistic look at your financial picture and goals. Wishing and hoping aren't going to make your Million-Dollar Mission a success. As you'll see in the pages that follow, some simple steps like altering your morning coffee and newspaper-reading habits can earn you big bucks in the long run.

I'm not suggesting that you need to make a drastic change in your lifestyle. No back-to-the-earth, Mother Jones commune mentality is needed; just some relatively easy tasks that won't have a dramatic impact on your lifestyle but will, through the power of compounding, have a dramatic effect on your retirement savings. I tell my clients to remember the Rule of 72—dividing the number

72 by the percentage rate of return gives us the number of years to double our investment. If you earn 10 percent a year on an investment or savings, it will thus take you about seven years to double your money. If you earn 6 percent, it will take about twelve years to double. Not a very long horizon.

How Much Should I Save?

The average US household income is just over $56,000 per year. The average household is also in debt, so we are spending more than we make. Conservatively assuming that the average household budget is then also roughly $56,000, if you can shave even as little as 10 percent off your spending you'll have an extra $5,600 per year to save. That might not sound like much in terms of accomplishing the Million-Dollar Mission, but as table 4.1 illustrates, appreciation and the magic of compounding can go a long way toward getting you to that magic number. Based on the assumption that you're going to want $50,000 per year to spend in retirement, if you save $5,600 per year, table 4.1 shows how much you'll have at retirement.

How much do you personally need to save? It all depends upon your age, your past spending habits, your future needs prior to retirement, and how well you've been able to invest your savings. We'll figure out specifics later in the book; for now let's just do some simple math. A typical working life is roughly forty years, and a retirement life is about fifteen years, meaning that every year of your working life you would need to cover four and a half months of retirement life, all else being equal. Of course, the earnings on your savings can reduce that ratio, as can a reduced spending pattern during retirement. And the earlier you begin to save, the more earnings on your savings and the less retirement cash you actually have to work nine-to-five for.

You can subtract your current liquid net worth from the million-dollar target to find out how much more you need to accumulate. For you Neo-Boomers and your remaining thirty-year career, that $5,600 in the example earning 8 percent would get you $634,000 by the time you retire. If you haven't saved any-

Table 4.1
WHAT'S $5,600 PER YEAR REALLY WORTH?

Years to Retirement	Rate of Return on Investment								
	2%	3%	4%	5%	6%	8%	10%	15%	20%
5	$29,143	$29,731	$30,331	$30,944	$31,568	$32,853	$34,189	$37,757	$41,673
10	$61,318	$64,198	$67,234	$70,436	$73,812	$81,125	$89,250	$113,701	$145,369
15	$96,843	$104,154	$112,132	$120,840	$130,345	$152,052	$177,926	$266,450	$403,397
20	$136,065	$150,474	$166,757	$185,169	$205,999	$256,267	$320,740	$573,684	$1,045,453
25	$179,370	$204,172	$233,217	$267,272	$307,241	$409,393	$550,744	$1,191,641	$2,643,094
30	$227,181	$266,422	$314,076	$372,058	$442,726	$634,386	$921,167	$2,434,573	$6,618,537
35	$279,969	$338,588	$412,452	$505,794	$624,035	$964,974	$1,517,736	$4,934,553	$16,510,710

thing yet, thus relying solely on future savings, you'd actually need to save about $8,800 per year in order to make the million-dollar mark. For Tail End Boomers, you have twenty years to go, but you may have some money already socked away. If you already have $100,000 in a retirement account, and it can also earn that 8 percent, it will grow to $466,000 by the time you retire. To make up for the difference, you'll need to save $11,700 each remaining year—about $1,000 per month. If you have $225,000 already saved, that alone can get you to the million-dollar level if you can earn 8 percent. Lastly, you Core Boomers who have ten years to go until retirement, a million dollars would be a daunting task if you haven't begun already. It would take nearly $70,000 per year to accumulate $1 million in ten years. If you have $250,000 saved by now, you're halfway home. Saving $32,000 per year would make up the difference. To reduce your savings requirement to the $5,600-per-year example in table 4.1, you'd need to have saved about $430,000 by now.

How Do I Get There?

As the old line goes about mental health—the fact that you admit you have a problem is the first step toward your recovery. Like many things that you may want to improve about yourself or your life, it all starts with becoming more self-aware regarding your spending habits. That means you need to think about every dollar you spend—that's why I suggested keeping track of expenses in the previous chapter. Also, keeping track of dates on which you spend might shed some light on spending habits you may have developed. Splurging the weekend after payday and then scrimping the rest of the month is a stressful way to exist and an unproductive way to try to save.

My father and mother were markedly different in their approaches to spending. Both were thrifty, but in comparison with my father, my mother was relatively impulsive. If she thought she needed or wanted something, she went out and got it. Not my father. He would contemplate, research, research his contemplation, contemplate his research, consider the origins of the universe, vacillate, pontificate, and hesitate before making any substantial purchases. Most often, he'd wind up talking himself out of his original need or desire.

Cate Taylor, the well-regarded and oft-quoted director of financial literacy for Money Management International—one of the legitimate nonprofit credit counseling institutions, which help consumers of all income brackets create workable budgets—reminded me that saving and budgeting aren't going to work if you just rely on tactics. She and her agency's Web site have hundreds of ideas for saving money, but they will only be effective if you first change your mind-set. Saving more money each month is much like dieting or quitting smoking. First, you need a specific goal or reason in mind as motivation. Without that point of focus, you run the risk of falling back on old habits when things get tough. Focusing on a goal of money for retirement or for your daughter's college tuition should get you back on the straight and narrow when you realize that new car is just a little out of your budget. Second, be realistic. Setting overambitious goals simply ensures that you're going to fail. Failure weakens motivation and leads to giving up altogether. You must know your needs and abilities and try to make marginal cuts that don't completely destroy your lifestyle. Lastly, Cate suggests communicating the goals and ideas to everyone over the age of eight in the family. If you're trying to do this alone, you'll receive a lot of pressure from your spouse and children because they won't understand what you're trying to accomplish.

There's a lot of budget and money-saving help out there. Google any phrase related to spending less and you'll find an astonishing number of Web sites devoted to living on less and cutting costs. You can pick up thousands of ideas for saving money, dealing with utilities and other daily-living service providers, and worksheets to help organize and plan your finances. Later on in this chapter, I'll provide some real-world daily cost-cutting measures and longer-term shrewd moves to make to help save more than ever before. Before we get to those nitty-gritty daily moves, though, let's take a look at some strategies you can employ to help alter the spend-now, pay-later mentality that may be getting you in trouble.

Take the Budget for a Test Drive

Try this for a period of three months: Make yourself wait a month before you make most big purchases. A month later, you might not want some things quite as much. That may sound unrealistic, but let's say you're in the market for a new car. The old one isn't creating any safety issues or facing major mechanical repairs, so you aren't under any great rush to get a new one. For big-ticket items like a car, it's a good idea to practice living on the revised budget that such a purchase would create. Will your new car payment take a $400 bite out of your monthly budget? Try taking that money out to see how it feels to live at that level and whether the purchase is really affordable and worth the sacrifice. That four-year-old, fully paid-off model you currently drive may end up feeling pretty good. If you experience no appreciable adaptation issues with the new $400 bite out of your budget and still want to proceed with the purchase, then you can do so comfortable in the notion that you've really done your homework and lived with the decision before committing to it.

Make All Your Transactions with Cash for a Month

One of the things that makes it difficult to stay focused on the here-and-now reality of our money is that we are becoming increasingly disconnected from it. Auto-pay agreements are a double-edged sword. In exchange for the convenience they provide, you give up awareness of where your money is going. You don't physically write the check and mail the payment each month, so it's easy to lose the feeling of actually giving up money that you earned. We get paid through auto deposit, pay our bills through auto debits, buy everything through charge cards, and get money out of the ATM when we need it. We end up feeling that the money is never really ours and there is an endless supply; we never know how much actually belongs to us. *If you can, make all your transactions with cash for one month.* Actually handing over money out of your wallet or purse is much more difficult than handing over a piece of plastic, and you'll think much harder about how you spend your money. I think you'll be surprised at where your money actually goes.

Write Down Every Expenditure

This is an even more detailed examination of where your money is going than your budget worksheet—a kind of real-time look at how you spend in the real world. If you buy a bottle of water and some chips when you stop for gas on your way home from work, pay cash, then get back in the car, open your handy expense notebook, and write down those expenditures—gas and snacks both. By doing this, you will have the answer to that proverbial question: *Where does all my money go?*

Obviously, we all have to buy things, and we've been doing it most of our lives. At this point, it may seem like the act is as natural and thought-free as walking. Well, now that you're not just walking but hiking toward a desired point and are entering unfamiliar ground, it makes sense to concentrate on some of the fundamentals you've taken for granted.

When you shop, shop well, and buy carefully. A little preparation can go a long way. Know what you are setting out to buy and stick to it. Shop around. Again, do your research for larger-ticket items. Check out *Consumer Reports* and other resources for best buys and suggestions.

Shop for needs rather than wants. I don't grocery shop a lot, but I do know that when I go to the market, if I'm thirsty when I'm in the store, I end up with a cartful of beverages. If I'm hungry, then I come home with all my favorites—from sweets to salty snacks. Not only does my waistline suffer, but so does our financial bottom line. Deciding what is a need and what is a want is always tricky—I have kids, so I can tell you for a fact that a cell phone is not just a need but has somehow been written into the Constitution as an inalienable right. Navigating this distinction is hard but worthwhile.

Spend Your Most Precious Commodity Wisely

I realize that time is one of the scarcest resources we all have, but maybe it's time to think about how you spend yours. Does how you spend your time get you closer to your goals—whether financial, relationship, or spiritual? This kind of assessment may also require you to change your attitude about money. One of the things that studies of people who have become millionaires reveal is that to them every dollar makes a difference. If you can shift your perspective from thinking of money in terms of dollars to thinking of it as your future, you're not likely to so cavalierly spend it. I agree that it's no fun to think about money all the time, all the way down to what the cost is long term if you go out to lunch instead of bringing food from home. Sometimes though, you have to consider the consequences. If you stop thinking of it as giving up something and start thinking about earning something in return, it's going to be easier to stick with any kind of savings plan. A lot of this is mental gymnastics, but the unexamined life isn't worth living—and the examined expenditure may not be worth making, either.

Finding $470 a Month

I hit you with a big number earlier—saving $5,600 per year, which works out to $470 a month. I still believe this is a doable and realistic goal. But cutting out one major expense won't usually get you there. You have to do it a little at a time with lots of small cuts. I don't think it's always feasible or preferable to make those major cuts anyway—you still want to enjoy your quality of life.

Here are a few simple ideas that can help you get to that baseline goal of saving nearly $500 per month.

Brew Coffee at Home

It's a cliché, sure, but it does make sense. If you can cut out even one cup of latte a day, the savings are considerable. A plain $1.99 cup of coffee every afternoon amounts to $500 a year. Throw in a scone, a cookie, or a muffin, and you can double or triple that.

Cost savings: $5 per day for coffee and muffin = $100 per month.

Bring a Brown-Bag Lunch

Sure, networking is important, and so is getting away from the office for a while during the day, but a brown-bag lunch out on the plaza or a quick lunch in the office and a walk afterward a couple times a week can be very effective, enjoyable, and economical—and just as effective as a networking tool. Depending on your location and lunch buddies, lunch can set you back anywhere from about $7 for a sandwich up to $20—or more—for a nicer business-meeting lunch.

Cost savings: $7 per day three times a week = $82 per month.

Don't Pay for Free Information

Magazines and newspapers are usually available in some fashion online. Most are also available at the library. Unless you refer to them over and over, it probably isn't necessary to own the hard copy. Web portals provide access to a multitude of news providers. You can even set up an e-mail service to keep you informed of news in any particular subject of your choosing so you don't have to cull through the day's entire output of irrelevant news.

Also, compare the newsstand price with the subscription charge. If you must read newspapers or magazines in hard copy, you are far better off subscribing than you are purchasing at a newsstand or in a retail outlet. These kinds of impulse purchases are real money drains as well. Just to give you a general sense of how subscriptions can save you money, consider that the newsstand price of the daily *New York Times* is $1.25 Monday through Saturday; the Sunday edition costs $4. That means it costs you $11.50 per week to purchase the *Times*. For a full year, that comes to $598. The price of a full week's subscription delivery, however, is $10.20, or $530.40 a year, a savings of $67.60. Not a whole lot of money on the face of it, but you'd be paying $67.60 less a year *and* receiving the convenience of having the paper delivered to your door. Of course, you'd save that entire amount, $598, if you simply read the online edition. Magazines also have online editions, and you can find past articles more easily on the Web than by poring through hard copies stored in your basement.

Cost savings: Reduce your subscriptions by one paper and one magazine = $50 per month.

Mow Your Own Lawn

How often have you heard someone say, "Time is money. My time is more valuable than the X number of dollars I could have saved." While it's good to think about that time-money equation, some people have a misshapen decision tree they use to evaluate the worth of their time. If you make $100,000 per year and work a normal two-thousand-hour year, you probably assume your time is worth $50 per hour. So you evaluate the effort you put into things—say, researching the costs of a purchase or mowing your own lawn instead of hiring a landscaper or a neighbor—by whether it costs less to hire someone than it does to do it yourself at $50 per hour. That's the proverbial apples and oranges, though. If the choice is whether to work another hour and earn another $50, such an analysis would hold true. But the real choice is usually whether to mow the lawn or to watch TV or to do something else that doesn't put cash in your pocket. You can earn/save $40 for an hour of mowing the lawn, plus get some exercise that will keep you healthier and may reduce your medical bills over the long run. The same applies to washing your car or any number of other household maintenance jobs.

Cost savings: $40 per week = $160 per month.

Your Communications Bills Are Negotiable

What with cable TV, satellite TV, landline phones, cell phones, DSL, VOIP, satellite radio subscriptions, GPS navigation, Netflix, Movieline, and all the other entertainment/communications services available, you can end up spending a fortune. How much do you really use each of them? How much do you really *need* to use them? And what are they really costing you per unit of use? What are you really paying per minute of long distance? What are you paying per hour of cable? Does every member of your household need his or her own cell phone? Don't some of these services overlap? It pays to rationalize these expenditures every once in a while. Get a plan that fits your needs and budget. Have the kids share a phone to be used at activities or other times they need to be in contact with you. Don't pay for a lot of minutes that you won't use. We're all afraid of the large overage charges, so we build in a needless and expensive cushion just in case.

Most rates are negotiable. It costs these providers a considerable amount to attract new customers—upward of $400 goes into marketing, advertising, and equipment for every new cell customer, plus continuing maintenance costs. They really don't make any money until you've been on board for a while. Threatening to leave scares them to death, so they'll usually come up with a better deal, whether new equipment gratis or a lower monthly charge, just so they won't lose their upfront investment in you. If an Internet-only or new-customer rate is available, always call and ask for it. You'll usually get it as an incentive to stay.

Don't sign up for bundled services or long-term contracts. Prices continue to drop for new technologies as scale rises and more competitors enter the market. A long-term contract with cancellation penalties will lock you in at today's higher rates. Bundled services do save you a little in the short term, but providers know that if you have two services from them, you are caught in their clutches. Rarely do such customers leave. If you have three or more products, studies show that you're a customer for life, and they'll keep your rates higher than the market average. The flexibility of no or short contracts allows you to take advantage of falling rates.

Cost savings: Delete a couple of premium channels ($9.95 each); reconstruct your phone bill for a $20-per-month savings; drop one cell phone ($15); and get the Internet-only price to new customers on your high-speed DSL ($15 savings), and you can put away another $70 per month.

Eliminate a service (do you really need Sirius?) or substitute a similar service (Netflix versus satellite), and you can save even more.

Total savings: $457 per month.

In addition to these four sample cost-cutting measures that I've quantified for you, you can take many other steps to help you make up that shortfall and get to your $470-per-month savings goal. Here are some other savings measures and issues for you to consider.

Don't Use Credit

This is one of those ideals that we all should strive for but is very hard to accomplish. I've used many examples to show how compounding will build a minimal savings into a quite substantial amount in a number of years. Try thinking about saving as actually deferring a wanted item. If you can hold off for a while, your money will grow enough to allow you to afford it—plus have money left over. When you borrow, however, the laws of compounding work against you. The money you spend now becomes a larger amount that you need to pay back. Did you look at the disclosure statement when you applied for a mortgage? If you borrow $300,000 for thirty years at a 7 percent rate, you will be paying $714,359.60. The interest alone will far exceed the original principal amount. This is an extreme example because of the high amount of principal, but think about charge card debt that carries a high interest rate and low payments. At a 12 percent interest rate with no principal reduction, it would take only eight years, three months, to pay out interest equal to the amount you originally borrowed. And you'll still have the original principal outstanding and continue to pay interest on it. If you hadn't made the purchase, instead saving the payments you made to the card company, at the end of that period you would have enough to make the purchase with over 40 percent more left over (if you had earned 8 percent on your monthly payment).

It helps to pay off existing debt with savings. Sure, it's a comforting feeling to have savings socked away, but it's really a no-brainer to pay off 13 percent or higher charge card debt with savings that are earning 5 percent. That 8 percent difference on the average household's nearly $10,000 of debt adds up to $800 a year. Over a thirty-year period, that savings can amount to $53,000.

Debt is acceptable for appreciating assets. If you can earn more after taxes on the investment you make than you pay after taxes on the debt used to carry the investment, you are wisely using debt. But most of our purchases are for depreciating household items. Look at a car purchase. You not only pay 7 or 8 percent interest on the purchase, but the car loses 23 percent of its value in the first year you own it. It's a losing proposition. You need transportation, but the idea is to cut your losses.

If You Must Charge, Be Aware of the Hidden Pitfalls

Careless charge card usage costs users billions of dollars per year, especially those who carry a balance from month to month. Rates are rising, payment percentages have increased, fees upon fees have been added, and—as if the new bankruptcy laws haven't given card companies enough protection—they've written their contracts so that they can pretty much do whatever they want to you whenever they want for virtually no reason at all. They can raise their rates on a "fixed-rate" card even if you've been a model citizen and never even returned a library book late.

Federal regulators recently pressured credit card companies to boost the required monthly minimum payment to 4 percent of your outstanding balance– which could more than double many people's monthly payment. It does force the cardholder to pay off more quickly, which is a good thing, but the immediate pain is harsh.

Ask for a lower rate. If your FICO credit score is above 720, you are an excellent credit risk. If you carry balances, credit card issuers love you even more. As with your phone and cable providers, they don't want to lose you, and they're willing to negotiate. Call your current card issuers and advise them that you're forced to move your balances to another card unless they reduce your interest rate. If you decide to move anyway, shop around. If you go for a low intro rate, make sure the rate you'll be paying after the intro period is still a good deal.

The Massachusetts Public Interest Research Group reported that it found that many customers with good credit were able to significantly reduce their annual percentage rates with a simple call to the credit card company. Volunteers participating in the PIRG survey called their credit card issuers, saying they would switch to another company unless given a lower interest rate. With one five-minute phone call, 56 percent of the volunteers were able to lower their APR.

Those who were successful reduced their APRs by an average of more than one-third. That translates into real savings. For example, if you had a credit card balance of $5,000 and you were able to reduce your current rate from 16 to 10.46 percent, you could realize an annual savings of $278 (assuming you made only the 2 percent minimum monthly payments many credit card companies require), according to PIRG.

Some cards are eliminating the grace period. In the past, no interest was charged on the purchases in the most recent month. Now some cards let interest accrue from the moment you swipe your card at the checkout counter.

It is absolutely essential to make at least the minimum payment on time. Don't mail your check on the due date; make sure it arrives before that date. The average fee for a late payment is now more than $30. Pay late and your rate might go up. Many card companies have universal default clauses, too. Miss a payment on one (or even a utility bill) and the others using such a clause can also raise their rates to their highest default rate. Default rates are usurious, if you haven't checked your card agreement lately. Rates as high as 30 percent are common.

Good credit card management is a major way to cut your expenses. Shop around, read the fine print, make your payments on time for everything, and protect your excellent credit score—it's the key to lower interest rates.

Don't Get a Tax Refund

It feels good to get a fat refund check from the IRS sometime after April 15. It makes us feel as if we've somehow beaten the system and received money back. Unfortunately, that feeling is misplaced. We've really given Uncle Sam a free loan. When you get a refund, you have effectively loaned the money out to Uncle Sam interest-free for the year. You could be paying off your 18 percent credit card debt or investing the money rather than giving a gift to Uncle Sam. In addition, that big check at the end of the year creates a lot of temptation to splurge. You're probably more likely to productively use smaller amounts spread throughout the year. Plan better so you reduce your refund or owe only a little in April. Adjust your W-4 to reduce the withholding from your regular paycheck. Even if you've been good about saving that refund check, by reducing your withholding instead you would earn an additional $4,400 of interest at 4 percent over a twenty-year period.

Still, be cautious and know thyself. If you know that the only way to stop yourself from spending the money is to keep it where you can't get at it, by all means let Uncle Sam act as your piggybank. Don't make a tough situation tougher.

Buy a Home

But be sure to watch out for all the hidden costs incurred in buying a home. Lawyers, agents, title insurance, inspections, appraisals—they can really add up. Shopping around can pay off. One particular item that can save a great amount of money is PMI—private mortgage insurance.

When home prices rise quickly, many home buyers find they don't have the full 20 percent down payment that lenders usually desire. Without that, they need private mortgage insurance, an added monthly charge that protects the lender if you ultimately can't keep up with your mortgage payments.

Traditionally, lenders would just tack on the monthly PMI as an added cost to your mortgage. More recently, the piggyback loan—taking out a home equity line of credit to cover the difference between your down payment and the 20 percent—has become a popular way to sidestep PMI. But the problem with a piggyback is that as rates rise, the home equity line of credit becomes even more expensive. I suggest skipping both the traditional PMI and the piggyback and instead asking your lender to roll your PMI into the cost of the mortgage.

The cost of rolling the PMI into the mortgage is typically 1 percent of the mortgage amount. On a $200,000 thirty-year fixed-rate mortgage charging 6 percent interest, your monthly payment would rise from $1,199 to $1,211—$12 more a month. If you instead paid the PMI as a separate cost, you would be looking at about an $86-a-month charge. And when it's rolled into your mortgage, the interest payments are deductible—reducing the cost even more. Using a $25,000 home equity line to get to the 20 percent level would cost you $312.50 per month at an 8 percent interest rate.

Avoid loans with negative amortization. A lot of creative financing took place as everyone tried to get in on the recent real estate boom. In order to afford more house than they had cash flow to cover, many people chose a loan that capped the payment for a year or so. The payment wasn't enough to cover the interest charge, so it got rolled into the loan. The loan actually increases as you make your initial payments. You end up paying interest on top of interest and actually losing equity in your home unless prices are rising more quickly than the rate on your loan.

Don't Pay Off That Mortgage so Quickly

While I generally extol the virtues of reducing debt, I think that fifteen-year mortgages or making extra payments on your thirty-year mortgage don't always make sense. It depends upon your available alternative investments for the money. If you can make more after taxes than you are paying after taxes on the mortgage, then you should invest the money rather than paying down your mortgage. And if you still have availability on your tax-advantaged retirement plan, it makes even more sense to put the money there instead. A further benefit applies to those applying for college aid. Having less of a mortgage improves your net worth and reduces your aid. On the other hand, assets in retirement accounts are not used in the aid calculations. And if you have pre-college-aged children, the same comment that applies to tax-advantaged retirement accounts applies to tax-advantaged college savings accounts. It likely pays to max out both retirement and college accounts before you consider paying off your mortgage early.

Be Smart with Your Insurance

As with everything else I've mentioned, it pays to be informed and to shop around. Accomplishing both of those for your insurance is becoming easier and easier. Life, health, auto, homeowner's, and renter's insurances quotes and policies are all available on the Internet or from mass agencies, so shop around. Some services even provide side-by-side comparisons. Don't buy just on a broker's recommendation. Ask what you are getting for your money and what adjustments to your deductible might significantly reduce your premium.

Your level of deductible has a major impact on the cost of your insurance. If you have a low deductible of just a few hundred dollars, find out how much your premium will fall if you increase it to either $1,000 or $2,000. Insurance is best used to cover big-time accidents. I realize we all see insurance as money down the drain, and we want to get some of it back no matter how small the claim. But making small claims aggravates insurance companies. In turn, they will boost your premium or even deny you coverage altogether. So raise your deductible to a level that would be manageable. In return, you can see your premium cost drop 10 to 20 percent or more.

Check into an umbrella rider policy. For pennies on the dollar, your insurance agent can increase your overall, general liability coverage to as much as $5 million.

Go for all the discounts you can. Bundle your needs with one company and get major savings. Good driving, good student, AARP, and many other discounts are out there for the asking.

Medical coverage riders on your auto and home policies might overlap your own health insurance, so you might want to eliminate them. On your homeowner's insurance, you want enough to cover the replacement cost of your home and possessions. You don't need to cover the value of the land the home sits on. So don't use an appraisal or sales price to determine the insurable value.

Insurance companies will reimburse you for the lost value of your car—even if they pay to have it fixed. The diminished-value clause in your policy allows you to receive the value you've lost when your car is damaged. Even after being repaired, your car is worth less than if the accident never occurred. You are entitled to receive compensation for that. In all states, you can receive reimbursement from the responsible party's insurance company. In some states, you cannot claim compensation from your own insurance company—the theory being that if you caused the accident, then it's your loss to bear. But in many states, your policy covers your car even if the accident was your fault. Check with your agent.

If your car is totaled, you can lose a substantial amount of money. Insurance companies initially offer you an amount based on a survey of dealers and the value they are willing to sell the car for. Traditional valuation sources, such as Edmunds and the *Kelley Blue Book,* look at actual sales prices, which are often higher. You are entitled to get your own valuations and go through an appraisal arbitration process to fight for more money. You can also appeal the insurance company's decision to total the car—a decision insurers are more and more prone to make to save themselves money. They turn around and sell the wreck to a salvage yard for a decent profit on the usable parts.

Consider Term Life Insurance

It's nearly always best to buy term life insurance rather than the more expensive whole life insurance and invest the difference in an S&P 500 Index fund. Whole life insurance has its place in estate planning; it can help pay estate taxes without dipping into the estate. But most of the time, whole life insurance doesn't make financial sense, since the cash value that accrues almost never equals the rate of return you can earn by investing. You can compare and buy your life insurance online or through a broker to save even more. When you are first starting out and you have one or more dependents, it is essential to have life insurance coverage. Your death could be financially devastating to your young family, and you need to ensure that housing, education, and everything else will be provided for. As you age, become empty-nesters, and see your financial position strengthening, life insurance is less essential. But if you are fifty-five and still struggling to save for retirement, by all means maintain your life insurance. If you should die, your spouse would have difficulty preparing for retirement.

Avoid credit and mortgage life insurance policies. Sure, you want enough insurance to protect your heirs by covering your liabilities, but credit and mortgage insurance are grossly overpriced. You are much better off increasing your existing term life insurance policy.

Save Money on Teen Drivers

Auto insurance for your teenage drivers can cost more than the monthly payment on the vehicle. It usually turns out to be cheaper to buy an older car for teenagers and name them as the primary drivers on it. Keep them off your main car, which carries the higher premium. If their car is old enough, go with just comprehensive insurance and forgo collision to save even more money. You'll be covered for repairs if another driver is at fault, but not if your teen is responsible.

Coordinate and Maximize Your Employee Benefits

If you are a dual-income couple, you both likely have access to employer health plans and retirement plans. Make sure that you understand how to most efficiently utilize the combined choices you have. Given the composition and health needs of your family, decide which of the two plans to use. Likewise, the retirement plans may have different investment alternatives or match rates.

Use a Flexible Spending Arrangement for Your Health Care Costs

Health care costs have been the fastest-growing expense categories over the past several decades—far eclipsing inflation. According to the Bureau of Labor Statistics, the medical services price index had risen 3.5 times its level in 1982 as of the end of 2005, while the overall Consumer Price Index had risen to 2.05 times its 1982 level. And health care rate increases are accelerating, particularly the burden put on the employees as employers cap subsidization levels. While you certainly don't want to skimp on health care to the point of putting your health in jeopardy, you can still save money. In fact, you can save 25 to 28 percent or more, depending on your tax rate, by setting up a flexible spending arrangement. FSAs are accounts that allow you to pay your medical expenses with pretax dollars (a similar account exists to pay for dependent care). You agree to have an amount taken out of your paycheck and set aside to be used only for such expenses. By reducing your salary, you avoid federal and state (except New Jersey and Pennsylvania) income taxes and Social Security taxes on the money.

There are two added benefits. First, when you itemize deductions in the standard way, you must exceed a 7.5 percent of adjusted gross income floor before you can take any medical deductions; with the FSA, you avoid that. Second, the courts have ruled that FSAs can pay expenses beyond the normal definition the IRS uses to judge whether something is a valid deduction. For instance, over-the-counter medical expenses can be paid with FSA funds.

The downside is that at the beginning of the year, you declare the deduction you wish to take from your salary to fund the FSA. If you need more, you cannot adjust the amount. If you don't use the full amount, you lose it. You do have two and a half months after the end of the year to use up the excess, but after that it is forfeited.

Job Search Expenses Are Deductible

If you look for a new job in your current field, you can deduct your search expenses. That holds even if you don't end up getting a new job. Make sure to keep track of your search expenses.

Don't Cheat Yourself on Charitable Contributions

If you volunteer, you can deduct a mileage charge for the travel required to get there as well as any travel you do on behalf of the charity.

Drive Your Car Longer

I talked earlier in this chapter about ways to reduce your vehicle cost without giving up much. You can buy a previously owned car or a comparable new but less pricey vehicle. In the same vein, if you keep your car longer, you can save money. The depreciation curve on autos starts off very steeply, but by the third or fourth year it starts to slow down. If you get past that point, your annual cost to own the car can drop significantly.

Trick yourself into saving money by owning the car longer than the term of the loan used to purchase it. After the loan is paid off, you can take the monthly car payment amount and put it into your savings. You'll be used to sending that $300 or more to the

Table 4.2
AUTO DEPRECIATION

Year	Depreciation Rate	Lost Value on a $25,000 Car
1	23%	$5,760
2	12%	$2,888
3	10%	$2,454
4	8%	$2,086
5	7%	$1,773
6	6%	$1,508
7	5%	$1,281
8	4%	$1,089
9	4%	$926
10	3%	$786

lender every month, so you should be able to live without it. If you can do that for two years, you'll accumulate $7,200. If you invest the $7,200 at 8 percent, in twenty years you'll have almost $34,000—enough to purchase a car after you retire.

Collect Free Money

More than half of all eligible employees aren't taking full advantage of their company's 401(k) matching program, according to Employee Benefit Research Institute. That's unfortunate: It's free money, and a great incentive to save. If at all possible, max out your 401(k) by electing to contribute at least as much as your company requires to get the full employer match, usually between 3 and 6 percent of your salary.

A 401(k) is a form of retirement savings plan that takes pretax salary deductions made by you and allows you to defer tax on the deduction and create a tax-free buildup of earnings. The contributions are pre–income tax but are subject to Social Security and Medicare taxes. Income taxes are paid when withdrawals occur after retirement. In 2006, you could contribute up to $15,000 and receive tax-preferred status; if you were older than fifty, you could contribute an additional $5,000 if your employer's plan allows. The laws governing the plans have strict guidelines about the structure of the plan, especially safeguards so that highly compensated employees do not get preferred treatment. For that reason, sometimes the legal limits are not available for some employees.

Again, your savings should go into your 401(k) before anything else. By taking advantage of the tax deferral benefits of the plan, you can supercharge your retirement savings. In addition, any match your employer provides greatly enhances your returns. Table 4.3 illustrates the difference in savings for a simple example. Assume you are forty-five years old and you get a $10,000 bonus. You have three options. You can put the money in XYZ mutual fund, which earns 6 percent per year. You can make contributions this year to your 401(k) plan amounting to $10,000, and the money goes into the same mutual fund earning 6 percent. The third option adds a 50 percent match funding by your employer, up to a $3,000 match. Assume that you are in the 28 percent tax bracket and will be when you retire at sixty-five and that you take all the funds and pay all taxes at that time.

Table 4.3
FREE MONEY IN ACTION

	Direct Invest	401(k)	401(k) with Match
Initial investment	$10,000.00	$10,000.00	$10,000.00
Matching funds	$ 0	$ 0	$ 3,000.00
Less upfront taxes	–$ 2,800.00	–$ 0	–$ 0
Actual investable funds	$ 7,200.00	$10,000.00	$13,000.00

Appreciated amount in 20 years	$23,091.38	$32,071.35	$41,692.76
Less taxes owed at distribution	–$ 2,383.71	–$ 3,310.70	–$ 7,943.91
Retirement nest egg	$20,707.67	$28,760.65	$33,748.85
Difference	—	$8,052.98 (39%)	$13,041.18 (63%)
Overall Return on Initial Investment	**107%**	**188%**	**237%**

An amazing difference. By deferring taxes, you are able to save 39 percent more than if you had merely put the money in the same investment vehicle but in a taxable way. In fact, the difference is even more pronounced, since you would be paying some amount of taxes every year on the mutual fund's earnings, depending on its turnover and other factors. The $3,000 free money adds nearly $5,000 to your total and 49 percent to your total return. And that's looking at just a single year's 401(k) contribution.

Consider College for Kids Versus Your Retirement

We all want the best for our children. And giving them the best education possible is a way to ensure their success in life. Or is it? Several cohort studies of Ivy League grads show that a degree from such prestigious schools is really no guarantee of success. In one recently published study, only four out of nineteen grads who finished in the top tier of their school could by any stretch of the imagination be considered successful a decade or so later. With the steep price of private institutions, it doesn't seem rational to borrow against your future, and many times their futures, for something that might not pay off. According to the College Board, in 2004–2005 the average tuition and other costs of a four-year private college added up to $27,677; at a four-year public college, $12,841. Really weigh the added expense of the finest schools against the better public institutions before committing.

Also remember that your student can attend the better private schools through scholarships or earning a portion of the cost. Of course, individual circumstances vary. A superb student who has her heart set on some unique field of study only offered at higher-priced schools and can earn back the cost of the education over the extent of her career might have a good case for cajoling Mom and Dad into helping with the expenses. But if it puts you in the poorhouse, will she be able to support you in your dotage?

The same argument can be made for private primary and secondary schools, and even day care.

Explore Cheaper Ways to Pay for College

Given the skyrocketing cost of higher education, Uncle Sam has come up with some generous programs to help us pay. Of course, *Hope and Lifetime Learning Credits* continue to be available to offset your current income tax bill, *savings bonds* can accrue tax-free income if applied toward college tuition, and *IRA withdrawals* are not fully penalized if used toward college expenses. (Exceptions exist to each of these statements, so investigate with a tax professional before assuming you qualify.) In addition, some savings programs give you benefits for prepaying your college bills—sort of a layaway program—or setting up a saving account earmarked for college bills. They are full of rules, but if followed properly they can make a large dent in your college costs.

QTPs (qualified tuition programs), also named Section 529 plans, allow you to either prepay a specified beneficiary's future education expenses or to establish a savings plan that will pay those expenses in the future. As with a Roth IRA, after-tax contributions are made into the plan, but it grows in the account tax-free. When the money is taken out, it is tax-free as long as it doesn't exceed the eligible expenses. The prepayment-type plans don't have that problem since they strictly prepay directly to the school. Prepaying usually freezes costs at today's level, which could save a potential huge cost escalation by the time the beneficiary reaches college age. Another benefit of these plans is that anyone can establish one for a student—it's not limited to parents. Grandparents, aunts, uncles, godparents, or other benefactors can create such an account. But be aware that the contribution is considered a gift, and the tax rules regarding gifts apply. If your student goes elsewhere, or doesn't attend school at all, you can get your money back or transfer the benefits to another child. One downfall continues to be the fact that financial aid calculations include the money in these accounts as an available family contribution, thus reducing need and eligible financial aid. In addition, if distributions exceed expenses, taxes will be imposed. And you don't have the option of directing your own investments. There are significant differences from plan to plan on how they work and are administered, so you'll need to do a lot of homework to decide on the appropriate vehicle. Prepay plans used to lock you in to a certain school or state, but they are now joining forces, with groups of schools offering the program together so that you have more flexibility in where your child ends up.

Coverdell ESAs, sometimes called Education IRAs, are another savings instrument with tax benefits. Coverdells aren't limited to use for college; they can be used for elementary and secondary school, too. You can have both a 529 plan and an ESA for your student, although the benefits cannot exceed the eventual expenses. Distributions also must be coordinated between the two plans. Like a 529 plan, ESAs take after tax income, allow it to grow tax-free, and provide for tax-free distributions for qualified education expenses. Unlike the unlimited contribution to a 529 plan, ESAs max out at $2,000 and fall further at higher income levels. More than one ESA can be set up for each individual (grandparents and others can also create one for a student), but the total annual contribution per *beneficiary* still can't exceed $2,000. ESAs allow you to direct the investment of the account. Any money in the account must be distributed by the time the beneficiary reaches age thirty, and taxes are paid on any distributions not used for eligible education expenses.

Maximize Elder Care Tax Breaks

If you're financially supporting your parents, a number of tax breaks may be available for you. The dependent care tax credit isn't just for child care—it also applies to adults who are unable to care for themselves. The credit can be used even if the person has income above the normal limit of $3,200 (in 2005). Some care costs may not apply to the dependent care tax break, but could be deductible medical expenses. If you provide more than half of the support costs for a parent, you can claim him or her as a dependent on your tax return.

Do Your Homework with Brokerage Accounts

If you decide to use a brokerage rather than a fee-based money manager, there are many different factors to consider in selecting your brokerage. Most relate to the amount of hand-holding you will require in achieving your investment objectives. Experienced investors generally like to do their own research and make their own decisions, whereas novices obviously feel more comfortable with a financial professional leading the way. Unfortunately, the hand-holding that novices need (and they generally don't have as much money to invest) can be quite expensive. In this section, I will attempt to demystify the brokerage industry.

At opposite ends of the spectrum containing all brokerage firms are the full-service or traditional brokerage, and the discount brokerage. As the name implies, a full-service brokerage will provide you with a range of services that you may or may not find valuable. These include investment ideas, recommendations and advice, performance reports, proprietary products (such as mutual funds), broker accessibility, tax counseling, research, estate planning, professional referrals (accountants, lawyers, tax advisers), asset allocation models, and enhanced order execution. While these services can all contribute to the success of your investment objectives, some broker promises should be taken with a grain of salt. For example, if you are a small investor seeking to buy blue-chip stocks and hold them for a long period of time, should you really be overly concerned about achieving the best possible execution price for a trade? I would argue that the emergence of electronic trading platforms has significantly reduced the risk involved in getting unfavorable trade execution in the larger and more liquid blue-chip stocks—especially if you are just buying a hundred shares! Determine which services are important to you, and avoid paying for anything that isn't.

The full-service brokerage option comes at a price. In general, these brokers earn hefty commissions on each trade made in your account. If you are a small investor and can only afford limited amounts of stocks or bonds, these commissions can sometimes run as high as 4 to 5 percent of the total value of the trade. While these commission costs can be helpful in discouraging excessive trading, they can also significantly reduce your portfolio returns. I encourage you to do a cost-benefit analysis to determine whether you are receiving commensurate value from these services before paying the commissions. Make sure you request a commission schedule and that you understand all the ancillary fees you will be paying for the maintenance of your account. Also, make sure your broker has no conflicts of interest that will lead him to recommend a product that might benefit him more than you. My biggest problem with retail brokers is that they get paid more each time you make a trade in your account. This incentivizes them to constantly "churn" your account, cutting into your portfolio returns over time. Even the most ethical and honorable have to reconcile this conflict with their clients' interests.

Pure discount brokerages, on the other hand, simply execute orders for you after you have made a trade decision on your own. The employees generally aren't permitted to provide investment advice to customers. Furthermore, you generally won't work with the same "broker"; rather, you will either place trade orders over the Internet or on the phone with whoever answers. Due to their complete lack of ancillary services, commission rates charged by these brokers are much lower. I would add that commission rates are likely to continue decreasing as the number of automated trading platforms and industry competition increase.

Pure discount brokers generally compete on factors such as execution speed, ease of use, and frequency of account errors. These errors could include jammed Internet servers, long wait times on the telephone, or lost checks or correspondence. I would argue that the biggest risk of trading with a discount broker may be the inability to execute a trade during a period of high volatility. Given their efforts to keep costs low, many discount brokers simply do not have the capacity to deal with huge spikes in trading volume such as those that occur during a sharp market sell-off. However, because you are a long-term investor who does not panic at such market gyrations, I don't want to overstate this risk.

Commission rates at the discount brokers generally run from about $5 per trade on up to as much as $15 to $20. The more expensive discount brokers usually provide added services and benefits. For instance, some online discount brokerages now offer elaborate portfolio analysis tools or fast execution guarantees. Again, you must determine which features are most important to you when choosing your brokerage. Avoid paying for anything that is not important in helping you achieve your goals.

Hybrid brokerages have also emerged over the past several years to address individual investor demand. Discount brokers have begun to offer research and advisory services, for instance, while full-service brokers have started offering online trading capabilities and paring service offerings in an effort to become more competitive. I suspect that you will find your ideal brokerage within this group of hybrids. While I acknowledge that your experience level may be low, I also do not believe that full-service broker commissions are worth the money. Most, if not all, of their services can be acquired elsewhere for a lower price, to say nothing of the conflicts of interest inherent in getting paid by the trade. In my view, the full-service broker is a dying breed that must adapt to survive. Furthermore, I'm hoping that this book will empower you to take control for yourself without complete reliance on a full-service broker.

The most important lesson to take away from this discussion is that the line between full-service and discount brokerages is rapidly blurring. Competition for new brokerage accounts is extremely fierce, and you could be the beneficiary. It is increasingly likely that you will be able to find all the services and features you need or want while still paying low commission rates. Do your research!

Know What You're Paying for with Your Mutual Funds

The expense ratios and sales charges that managers of a mutual fund get from you can make a big difference in your results. A one-hundred-basis-point difference in expense ratios or sales charges can add up to 22 percent more money in your account over a twenty-year period. Be sure you are getting quality performance if you are paying premium prices. If you're using plain vanilla index funds or something that closely tracks a given category, there is little reason to pay extra for performance that won't vary from the index. In other words, many mutual funds are requiring you to pay for research work and management of an account that requires little or no research or managing. Those charges add up and subtract from what you could be earning.

Ignore Found Money

Or rather, *save* found money—don't spend it. Gifts of money, rebates, raises, bonuses, garage sale proceeds, and the like should be socked away rather than used to splurge. It's very easy to view such items as a reason to indulge—they're not part of your normal routine. By now I hope that the examples presented in this section have driven home the fact that paying off debt or putting the money into a savings instrument will lead to better results over time.

Outsmart the Marketers

Companies love to find consumers who buy based on ego or status. They throw a few little items in or put obvious branding on the item so that purchasers can display their good taste to the world. In return, sellers are able to charge a premium price unjustified by the actual utility of the item. Here's a case in point—automobiles. A 2006 Cadillac Escalade all-wheel-drive SUV, fully loaded, lists at $56,405. This edition has a Bose sound system, OnStar vehicle assistance, rear heated seats, power adjustable pedals, an entertainment system, a stability enhancement system, a road-sensing suspension, and ultrasonic rear parking assist. The 2006 Cadillac Escalade ESV Platinum Edition has a list price of $70,175. Essentially, the two look and perform the same. The Platinum Edition does have upgraded sound and entertainment systems (the base system itself is extraordinary), special alloy wheels, and a sunroof. It also carries special badging that informs everyone it's an ESV Platinum.

The difference in price between the two vehicles: $13,770. If you were to buy the lower-priced model and invest the money you saved in the stock market for fifteen years, a conservative stock return of 7 percent would mean you earned nearly $38,000! By making smart decisions and erring on the side of modesty, the interest alone on your investment would pay you over $24,000. What's to feel guilty about or deprived of when you make that decision? Cost savings: A $13,770 price difference, along with an 8 percent sales tax, at 7.9 percent for five years, means an additional $301 monthly payment.

Putting Savings Plans into Practice

Let's take a look at Rick and Sally Taylor, a forty-five-year-old couple with two kids. Rick is an administrator in the parks and recreation department; Sally, a branch manager at her local bank. They're doing a good job with their budget. With no charge card debt and no car loan, they feel that they're living within their means. Unfortunately, they realize they're running out of time to save for retirement and the upcoming college bills for their three children—ages sixteen, fifteen, and eleven. So they've taken a look at their budget and tried to find additional ways to save even on their seemingly frugal lifestyle:

- Sally really feels the need to continue being in the loop with her co-workers, so she doesn't want to replace both coffee and lunch with substitutes from home. Instead, she and her contacts have found that coffee breaks are much more convenient and productive than the crowded and expensive lunch meetings they used to rely on. She already took a coffee break, so the $2 she spent was not an incremental cost. She's eliminated the nearly $7-per-lunch, three times a week habit. Cost savings: $7 lunch x 12 lunches = $84 per month.
- Rick and Sally had been with their cell provider since they bought their first cell phones. They kept their same high-minute plan even though they never came close to using all the minutes. As their two oldest children entered high school,

they just added them to their plan without shopping around. When their long-term contract expired, they finally shopped around for a new cell provider. They've found a cheaper plan that allows free calls to each other—their main reason for having the phones—and reduces their anytime minutes. They've even received updated phones. The only stipulation is that they sign a one-year agreement, which they feel still offers them the ability to benefit from better rates or features later. Their monthly charge has fallen $30 based on lower minutes, and the family package doesn't require a per-phone fee ($9.95 per phone). Cost savings: $44.90 per month.

- At one time, their oldest son, Rob, was really into online gaming. So he talked Mom and Dad into industrial-speed DSL. At $49.95, it was expensive, but it was Rob's part of the entertainment budget. High school sports and academics have now reorganized his priorities and interests, so the super DSL really isn't as necessary for homework and instant messaging. They've moved down to the still-speedy residential DSL, and since they've done so through their provider's Web site, they're able to get the preferred rate of $12.99 per month for the first year. They've marked the anniversary date on the calendar so that next year they'll make sure they revisit the Web site to lock in the assuredly lower rate offered at that time. Cost savings: $37 per month.
- College tuition for their three children is a real concern for the Taylors. They started a college savings plan for each of their children. Although the accounts were small, they hoped this might be a way to keep up with the pace of tuition increases. After reviewing their situation, they've decided that since they're certainly going to need financial aid to send all three to college, the Coverdell plan isn't the best for them. The way the aid formulas work, Coverdell plan moneys reduce available aid. Instead, the Taylors have started maxing out their IRAs, which they were previously scrimping on in order to set aside money for college. While this change doesn't result in a change to their monthly budget—they continue to set aside the same amount, simply putting it in a different vehicle—they feel more comfortable that between savings

and financial aid, their children will have a wider choice of schools to attend.

- Rick and Sally never set up a health care FSA account. Healthy and with three children, they've been worried that their bills are so unpredictable, they might not use their full contributions and therefore forfeit that money. But with a $4,500 bill for braces looming for their youngest, they decide to review their past bills and come up with a safe amount they're sure they'll use. Because of the braces, they settle on $8,000 as their amount for this year. They'll likely exceed that amount, but they want to be sure they don't forfeit any of their contributions. Handling their medical expenses this way, they do not have to exceed 7.5 percent of their income in order to claim a deduction. As a result, that 7.5 percent of their $86,000 income ($6,450) is now deductible. Cost savings: At their effective tax rate of 13.6 percent, the Taylors' additional $6,450 deduction will save them $877 per year, or $73 per month.
- While they investigate the tax issues of their health care FSA, Rick and Sally decide to rationalize the withholding payments on their paychecks. The average American got about a $2,400 refund in 2006. Thinking that withholding more would be a good way to save, the Taylors haven't used all the W-2 exemptions to which they're entitled, so they've actually received a $3,100 check from the IRS. After submitting new W-2s, they feel their payments will be pretty close to their actual tax bill. While this strategy does not reduce their tax bill or create more money to spend, it does allow them to get the money earlier and invest it. Cost savings: Conservatively assuming that they'll take home $240 per month more than before ($2,880 per year), the Taylors will earn $53 the first year at a 4 percent interest rate. If they had credit card debt to pay off, they would earn (save) at whatever interest rate their card charged.
- Rick's car has reached an age and a value at which it probably doesn't make sense to keep the expensive replacement and collision coverage that seemed necessary when the car was new and they were still making payments. He and Sally

decide they might as well have their entire insurance package reviewed. After talking with their insurance agent, they find that they need more coverage on their highly appreciated home, but could save money by moving their auto and home insurance to a different carrier. In addition, their auto insurance needs higher medical limits, but overall the premium will drop because of the comprehensive-only policy on Rick's car and the new carrier's lower rates. Cost savings: $45 per month.

I hope by now you recognize just how valuable little steps can be in getting you down the path to success in your Million-Dollar Mission. By adding these savings tactics and better understanding your relationship with money to your existing savings activities, you should be well on your way to accumulating a critical mass of wealth for retirement. As much as you may need to change some of your behaviors, though, it is probably just as crucial that you change your mind-set. What you might have once considered a sacrifice, you can now look upon as a profit-making enterprise. When you defer gratification until a later day, you reap even greater rewards. By becoming more conscious of your financial life and responsibilities, recognizing your tendencies, strengths, and weaknesses, you develop skills that will serve you throughout your lifetime. I'd venture a guess that once you develop the habit of examining your spending while thinking of new ways to cut costs and keeping your standard of living high, you'll get as hooked on the idea as you are to that second cup of coffee.

In the next chapter, we'll move to the next FIT step—understanding how risk and reward play an essential role in the successful completion of the Million-Dollar Mission.

CHAPTER FIVE

Understand It

How Your Risk Tolerance and Return Needs Shape Your Portfolio

I have a friend named Tom who does a lot of traveling by motorcycle. He doesn't just take trips around town; he heads off on true cross-country, time-zone-changing jaunts that take him all over the United States, Canada, and Mexico. Tom takes one extended three-week tour each year, and spends the other forty-nine weeks preparing for that trip—doing maintenance on his bike, planning routes, securing campground reservations, finding backup accommodations at hotels and motels, and dreaming of the open road. I tell him that all that work makes it sound more like a second career than a vacation, but he simply laughs. In true Boomer fashion, he reminds me that getting there is only a small portion of the adventure. He also likes to point out that over the years, he's developed a method for planning and executing his travels; once he throws a leg over his bike, the rest is relaxing and enjoyable.

In much the way my friend Tom has done over the years in refining his trip planning, you've been using the Farr Investment Technique to reach your financial destination as easily and comfortably as possible. As you've seen so far, the planning stages involve some work, but once you get your plan into gear, the remainder is easy.

As a reminder, the six steps of the FIT are:

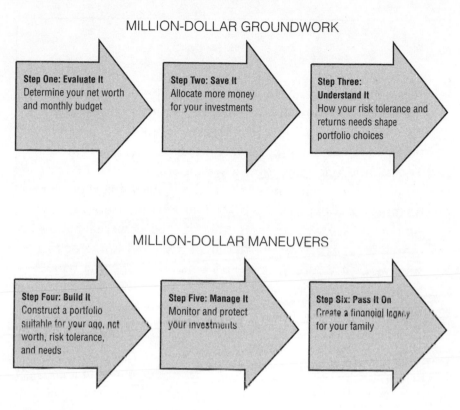

MILLION-DOLLAR GROUNDWORK

Step One: Evaluate It
Determine your net worth and monthly budget

Step Two: Save It
Allocate more money for your investments

Step Three: Understand It
How your risk tolerance and returns needs shape portfolio choices

MILLION-DOLLAR MANEUVERS

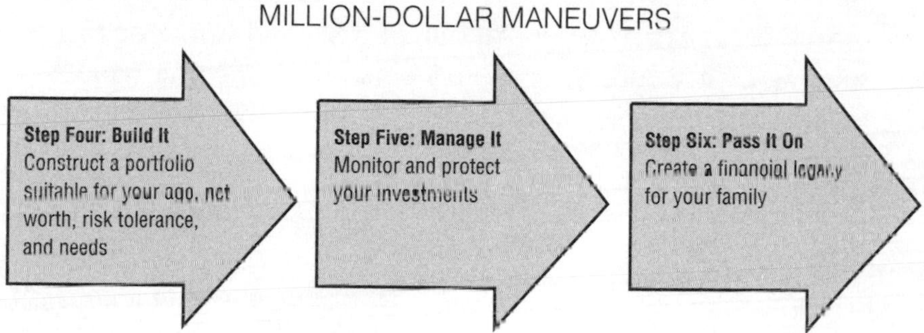

In this chapter, we'll concentrate on the third of these steps. In it, we will undertake four tasks:

Task 1: Understanding your risk tolerance.

Task 2: Understanding the inherent risks of investing.

Task 3: Determining your returns expectations.

Task 4: Determining the asset classes that match your returns and risk profiles.

Taking Chances

So far, we've spent a good deal of time off the road. We've decided on a destination and determined our present and future prospects

> ## BEFORE WE BEGIN
>
> Based on your work in chapter 3, you should now have a budget projected out on a yearly basis until your expected retirement age, making all necessary adjustments for anticipated changes in income and expenses. Remember: You should take care to always be conservative in your estimates for income increases, while also leaving room for unanticipated expenses. Also, be sure to incorporate any significant known expenses that will be incurred before retirement, such as the purchase of a second home or the funding of a wedding or child's education. Income windfalls such as inheritances should also be incorporated into the model.

for getting there. I know you're eager to fire up the engine and get some miles under your belt. Before you do that, though, you have to take another few steps. I know that one of the reasons I think my friend Tom is a bit crazy is that motorcycling is a risky venture. I've said this to him, and Tom's aware of the statistics that support my claim. He understands what his chances are, so he does everything he can to minimize the prospect of getting hurt. He always wears protective clothing and a helmet; he's made modifications to his bike so that it and he are as visible to others on the road as possible. He also knows a lot about motorcycles mechanically and can do most repairs and maintenance himself. He's willing to take on the risks involved because the returns are so great. Based on my guidance, Tom applies the same thought process and steps to his investing strategy.

Investment Basics

Investing can simply be defined as committing money with the hope of achieving a financial return on it. Implicit in this definition is the assumption that we would like to generate the highest possible return for the least possible amount of risk. Therefore, the next step in the process of creating your financial plan is to establish your individual tolerance for risk, understand the kinds of risk you'll face, and determine the type of returns you'll need to meet your financial goals. We have to consider risk and reward together because they are inextricably linked. Most of us understand that we have to take on more risk to lead to higher returns over a long-term horizon, and vice versa. Your return expectations need to be realistic relative to the amount of risk you are willing to assume. And while the amount of risk you can accept should largely be a function of your investing time horizon, there are other factors to consider, which I'll discuss later in this chapter.

How low can you go? How much can you lose and still be financially secure? How much risk you should incur is also determined by your ability to lose money without sacrificing your living standards or life goals. Risk tolerance has two components: how much you're *willing* to lose and remain comfortable, and how much you're *able* to lose and remain comfortable, while retaining the ability to recover. A loss *you* might be willing to sustain is likely to be different from one that I am willing to sustain. Also, whenever investing, be sure to take into account how time, quality of investments, and discipline will mitigate risk that you, the investor, are willing to take. As far as I'm concerned, a potential investment loss that could threaten my financial security is unacceptable and inappropriate. However, for every individual investor, what is unacceptable and inappropriate depends on a number of factors. The first is what kind of financial personality you possess. How do you feel about taking risks? Remember that long-term investors have to overcome their emotions to be successful over the long haul.

A Case in Point

Back in 2002, just before the start of the Iraq war, the market was down 22 percent. We were all still feeling the post-9/11 economic aftershocks, and I had been dealing with more than a few panicky clients. As a result, I was bracing myself for a lunch that

I'd scheduled with one of my clients, a fifty-five-year-old lawyer named Jeff. Jeff had recently made partner in his firm, and I knew him to be a very smart, shrewd guy. Over the years, my firm has served him well. But this particular year, during the notorious 2002 slump, I didn't expect to find him dancing in the streets about his personal portfolio.

True, I hadn't heard a word of complaint from him. And realistically, he hadn't done too badly. His portfolio was a few percentage points better than the overall decline. Still, I was worried. I knew that Jeff was not one to fling his monthly statements, unopened, into the nearest file drawer. He was thoughtful. He studied. And I knew he would not hesitate to tell me if he was unhappy with the way I handled his investments.

Lunch turned out to be comfortable—we chatted about the Redskins, his recent acquisition of a vintage Corvette, and the new log home that was under construction in rural North Carolina. When we started to review the details of Jeff's portfolio, he quickly moved on to strategy.

"Michael, the way I look at it," he said, "the stock market has lost about 44 percent over the past three years."

"Yes, that's true."

"And we're about to go to war."

"All signs point to it."

"Well, so, I've been thinking. Isn't this a prime opportunity to step in and buy more stocks?"

"Yes, I would say so. The trouble is," I added, "I would have said the same thing a full year ago. But there hasn't been a rebound. I think we're probably right, but a lot of folks right now need a whole lot of assurance and data to back up that proposition. I can't say it'll be easy to provide."

"Further proof of the right idea," he replied.

Now, is Jeff just a contrarian—someone who automatically jumps into stocks when everyone else is getting out?

Sure, that's part of his makeup. But the point is, he was able to think quite clearly about strategy *apart from emotional factors*. Like any other investor, I'm sure he got that queasy sinking feeling when he read his statements and discovered that his portfolio was worth nearly 20 percent less than it had been a year before.

Maybe, like so many investors, he had a vision of early retirement that became more distant with each downtick of the market. In a moment of panic, he might even have dealt with the really catastrophic thoughts: *What happens if this recession continues?* Or: *What am I doing wrong?* Or: *What if the market doesn't ever recover?*

Whatever emotional reactions he might have had, Jeff was able to deal with those feelings, put them aside, look at the long-term performance of the market—perhaps weighing his own experiences against my investment advice—and come to the sane conclusion that the best time to buy stocks is when they were undervalued.

Much to my relief, *that's* what we talked about over lunch. By the end of it, we'd worked out a strategy that eventually netted him above-market gains.

Besides showing how emotions play a part in our investment decisions, Jeff's story also illustrates the three issues of risk and return that all of us must grapple with to become good investors. First, we need to know ourselves—what our risk tolerance is. Jeff was not a nervous investor. He slept well at night. He realized that ups and downs occur, but in the long run he would come out ahead. He could live with some risks because he knew that the market pays those who take intelligent ones. Second, we know how much risk and potential loss our personal financial situation allows us to reasonably absorb. If Jeff had not been in as good a financial position to begin with, I probably would not have developed as aggressive a plan as we eventually ended up with. Lastly, investors need to understand the market risks inherent in any investment decision. Within the stock market, different stocks and different strategies present varying levels of risk. When we move into other asset categories—real estate, hedge funds, derivatives, commodities, and so on—we assume even wider levels of risk. Matching a client's risk tolerance and ability to the proper strategy is a fundamental task of an adviser, and in this chapter that's what I'll show you how to do for yourself. Remember, all investments involve some form of risk.

Task 1: Understanding Your Risk Tolerance

Time for a show of hands. How many of you got totally caught up in the New Economy tech craze that brought the NASDAQ up to 5,000? Okay, I bet nearly all of us put at least a little money into it, or at least wished we had when the trend shot upward with no signs of leveling off. Some of us may have put a lot into what at the time appeared to be a no-brainer investment category. Next question. When the NASDAQ started its fall, at what point did you pull out? 4,999? 4,000? 2,500? All the way down to 1,300? Next question. When the NASDAQ hit 1,300, did you jump back in or have you sworn off the tech market for good?

If you rode the NASDAQ monster up but jumped off quickly, you're like the majority of us. Behavioral economists—a sort of cross among economists, psychologists, and sociologists—study why we do the things we do with our money and why economic theories that assume we will behave rationally sometimes crumble in the real world. One of their seminal findings is that we humans are loss-averse. In other words, we hate (or fear) to lose a lot more than we like to win. Studies of real individuals indicate that most people require nearly a two-to-one ratio of gain to risk to balance the scales. Put another way, if we're going to increase our risk, we need twice as much possible reward to make that risk acceptable.

So our pre-millennium reaction to a "riskless" NASDAQ rise followed by panic as it went into a free fall makes us human—emotional rather than rational. Only years of market experience and much self-knowledge can overcome this tendency, if it can be overcome at all. Even professionals fall prey to the emotions of the market.

What can help us overcome our tendency to deal with money emotionally rather than intellectually? Knowledge. If we properly assess the situation and have a clear understanding of the underlying risk profiles of various investments, we can probably sleep better at night. If we think investing is nothing but a floating craps game that the house will always win, and—even worse—our brother's friend has an uncle Frankie who lost it all in buying shares of Boondoggle.com, then we will wake up red of eye and weak of heart.

Knowledge lets us know that we are in control of some factors and not others. So why sweat the things we can't control? For instance, at my lunch with Jeff we spent a lot of time going over the facts of the situation and trying to handicap the various possible scenarios. From there, we detailed the possible risk profiles of the various investments that might make sense for each scenario. While we didn't have perfect information—we never will—we were comfortable with our assessment of the situation and the strategy we would employ. A good adviser can provide you with a risk assessment of any strategy she proposes. If a look at the hard facts doesn't convince you that you can sleep well at night knowing that you're doing the right thing for your future, then it is a good idea to reduce your risk level to a point that allows a manageable stress level. Good information and diligent research should help you reduce your level of risk aversion.

Some folks, of course, are on the other end of the spectrum, willing to take a flier on the next big thing—whatever the eventual payoff. I have had clients who thoroughly enjoyed the thrill of a big against-the-odds win. Others accepted risk a little more reluctantly in an attempt to impress friends and neighbors or to reach financial goals when they had fallen behind. Some clients thought that the downside of risk only happened to others. They had been lucky before or felt that they had an innate ability to pick winners. Whatever the reason, the more risk was involved, the better they felt. No two individuals have the exact same level of risk tolerance.

So how do you know where you fit on this sliding scale from highly risk-averse to risk-tolerant to risk lover?

Here's a brief questionnaire that will give you a better sense of your investment risk comfort zone. Choose one answer for each question.

RISK TOLERANCE

1. Which statement best matches your attitude toward investment risk?
   a. I am very comfortable with and willing to take more risk to pursue maximum growth.
   b. I have a moderate appetite for risk as long as I feel I am being compensated over time.
   c. I am uncomfortable with risk, and short-term volatility in my investments makes me nervous.

2. At what level of loss in a single year would you start to feel very uncomfortable about your investment decisions and start to question your willingness to continue investing?
   a. More than 20 percent.
   b. 6 to 20 percent.
   c. 5 percent or less.

3. How did you react when an investment suddenly dropped by 20 percent?
   a. Nothing, as long as I still believed my investment had good long-term potential.
   b. Worry a little, reassess the situation, but take no action.
   c. Bail out and go to cash.

4. Which alternative would you prefer?
   a. A 50 percent chance of winning $2,000 but a 50 percent chance of losing $500.
   b. A 75 percent chance to gain $1,000 but a 25 percent chance of breaking even.
   c. A sure gain of $750.

5. Which of these alternatives would you prefer?
   a. A 50 percent chance of losing $2,000 but a 50 percent chance of gaining $500.
   b. A 75 percent chance of losing $1,000 but a 25 percent chance of breaking even.
   c. A sure loss of $750.

Give yourself 2 points for each a answer, 1 point for every b answer, and 0 points for every c answer.

If you scored 7–10, your risk tolerance is *high*. You want high returns, and you're willing to take risks to get them.

If you scored 4–6, your risk tolerance is *moderate*. You prefer to strike a balance between risk and reward. You don't want to risk it all, but you do want high performance.

If you scored 0–3, your risk tolerance is *low*. You don't like risk; you believe slow and steady wins the race.

In addition to investment knowledge, understanding the nature of your risk personality is essential to becoming a better investor. It's vital that you know your own issues and blind spots so you can compensate for them. I strongly suggest you read more of the burgeoning literature about behavioral finance as well as emotions and money. What I can tell you is that an investor with a moderate risk tolerance will likely be more successful than those at either end of the spectrum.

Ability to Absorb Risk

Ideally, willingness to accept risk should coincide with financial wherewithal. If you can't afford to lose, then you shouldn't be too aggressive. The inverse is also true: If you can afford to lose, then you shouldn't be too conservative. I'll talk more specifically about what that means in the pages to come.

Having a high personal tolerance for risk but little money to put at risk or a very short time frame to reap the potential benefits doesn't work well. Certain situations call for more or less restraint than usual. Several of the more important factors to consider when determining how much risk you should bear are:

- **Your investment time frame**. The more time you have to allow your savings to grow, the more risk—to a point—you can absorb. For example, if you know you'll need the money you've invested in one or two years to start a business or pay for a child's college tuition, it's not a good idea to take too many chances with it. If you're approaching retirement, too,

Figure 5.1

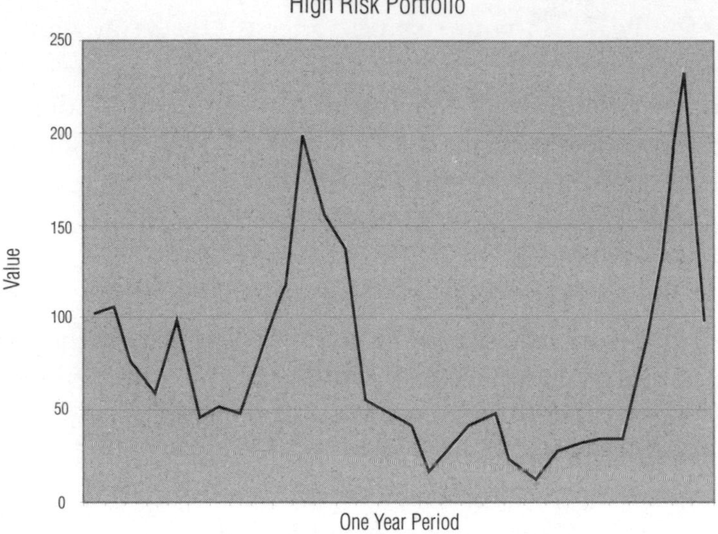

less risk is prudent. More risk means wider fluctuations in returns, and if you only have a three- or five-year time horizon, you might be caught in a downturn just when you need the money the most. Figure 5.1 takes real stock market risk-return statistics and plots a simulated but possible scenario. As you can see, on its way to a 10.4 percent compound annual return over the long run, much volatility can occur, with negative returns for the first few years not out of the realm of possibility. Of course, positive returns are also possible.

- **Your overall financial condition.** Putting away money for your retirement and other long-term goals is essential, and the rest of your investment house needs to be in order so you can put your portfolio to optimal use. If you have adequate coverage of the following items, you can lengthen your investment horizon and become a little more adventurous with your portfolio. If any item is lacking, you should shore it up by allocating additional funds to it and viewing your needs as near-term until the situation is resolved.
    - Do you have three to six months' worth of living expenses set aside for emergencies?

- Do you have sufficient insurance—health, life, home, and liability—to assure that you'll weather those issues?
- What is your current earning power, and what would a loss do to your current lifestyle or investment goals? Would you be able to recover in time to reach that goal? Do you rely on a single, tenuous source of income or do you have two incomes or other income streams?
- Aside from retirement fund and emergency fund, do you have other savings? If you're putting your entire financial life on the line, extreme risk isn't warranted.
- Are our other assets diversified? Are you very concentrated in real estate, your employers' stock in your 401(k) plan, collectibles, or other asset classes?
- Are your debt levels manageable? Are you able to manage your debt payments as well as pay them down, or are you struggling?

- **Other risk factors.** What other existing or potential financial demands might you be facing? Do you own a personal business that may need funding? Are you now or will you possibly in the future be financially responsible for children or parents? Any number of other needs may come up before your intended retirement day. While you can't fully prepare for or even contemplate them all, if certain issues appear likely it's a good idea to fold them into your investment scheme.

Three Phases of Boomers and Risk

Knowing your own personal level of comfort with risk is just one factor in determining a wise investment strategy. Knowing which of the three Boomer phases you're in and the advantages and disadvantages of those age ranges (thirty-five, forty-five, fifty-five) will also influence some of the investment decisions you make. It's not possible for me to account for every individual circumstance, so what follows are broad guidelines and observations based on most individuals who fall into the Neo-Boomer, Late Boomer, and Core Boomer categories.

• **Neo-Boomers (investors in their thirties)** have one advantage over the other two categories—time till retirement (TTR). All other things being equal, TTR is in many ways the most important factor in determining your investment position and strategies. Why? As I've mentioned before, the magic of compounding is in your favor over the long haul. Let's say you invest safely and earn a 5 percent return. If you're thirty years from retirement, that 5 percent return will serve you fairly well—particularly if you are able to invest a substantial amount of money each year. One of the disadvantages that Neo-Boomers face is that, for the most part, they earn less in salary per year than their counterparts in the other two groups. Also, Neo-Boomers spend at nearly the same dollar amount level as their Tail End Boomer counterparts, but since their income is lower, they are spending a great portion of their income. As a result, they tend to have less money to invest. That tends to negate the advantages of being able to invest in safer, lower-return products such as bonds, CDs, saving accounts, mutual funds, and the like. Slow and steady won't be effective if you aren't investing enough money.

One additional time advantage that thirty-five-year-olds have is that if they should invest aggressively and end up losing that money, they have more time to catch up. The market will inevitably go up and down but trend upward over the long term. The joke about falling behind as soon as possible to give yourself more time to catch up has a grain of truth in it. Neo-Boomers, in terms of *time,* can afford to be more aggressive. However, in terms of income and savings, they can least afford to take on high-risk ventures because they tend to have less capital to begin with.

• **Tail End Boomers (investors in their forties)**, unlike their younger counterparts, are in the prime earning years of their careers. Generally, they have a clearly established career path, have been in a chosen industry for a longer period of time, and by virtue of their seniority tend to earn more than their younger colleagues. Depending on their situation and lifestyle choices, they should have more money to invest, have a larger nest egg of savings and investments already in place, and have weathered some of the turbulence of spending and career shifting to give them added security. Of course, they have less TTR than Neo-Boomers, but that accumulated nest egg could allow them the space they need to be more aggressive in their investments. They will have less time to catch up, but they may have more of a financial cushion to absorb the blows from a loss.

• The same is true of **Core Boomers (investors in their fifties),** but to a greater degree. They have even less time to recover from a loss, but should have deeper pockets to draw from. Of course, for Core Boomers, TTR is a major factor in determining strategy. Because they will have relatively high incomes and a longer history of investment, and therefore more time for compounding to have done its work, Core Boomers have the largest nest eggs of all three groups. Given that they can best endure a loss of money, we may think that they can be the biggest gamblers of the bunch. Time to catch up after a loss is at a premium for Core Boomers, however, and as a result, most investment counselors recommend that they play it safer at this stage.

Also as a general rule, our ability (and possibly our willingness) to accept risk will decline as we get older and our time horizon becomes shorter. Therefore, if you are not close to retirement and can afford to take a longer-term view of your investments, you're at a distinct advantage. Again, regardless of the risk profile of my clients, I often tell them that two things mitigate the risks inherent to investing more than anything else: time and the quality of investments.

Figure 5.2 illustrates the kind of returns necessary for you to get to a million dollars, depending upon the annual amount of money you're able to set aside for retirement. As you can see, if you are able to put away $10,000 a year starting at age thirty, you only need a 5 percent return on investment to get to that $1 million mark. On the other hand, if you are only able to invest $500 per year, then you need an annual return of 20 percent in order to reach the goal. At $1,000 per year, you still need a 15 percent return. Given that the rate of return represents a higher-risk investment, those 15 to 20 percent returns represent a level of risk that very few of us could tolerate—even if you were able to find something to invest in that offered such returns.

No matter which group of Boomers you're in, you don't want to be forced into taking a position that doesn't sit well with your financial temperament, income and savings level, and TTR. For

Figure 5.2

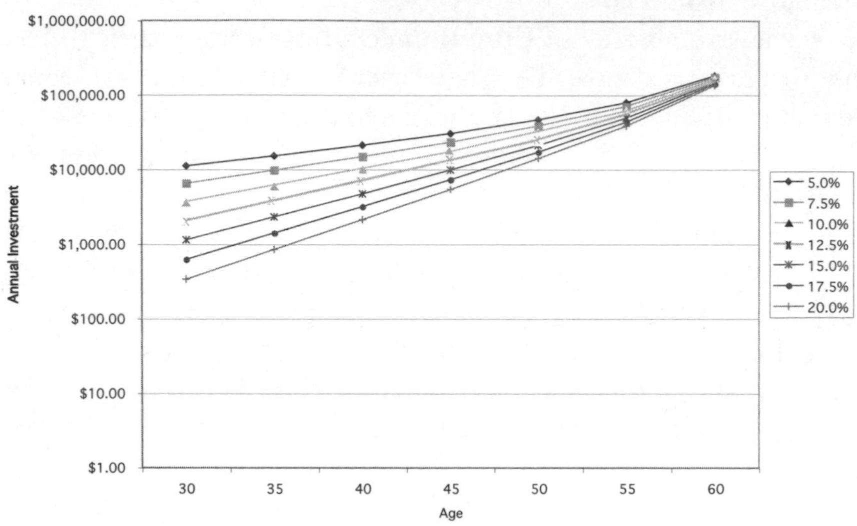

me, risk is always about what degree of control I perceive myself to have. I want to be able to make choices and not have them thrust upon me. I also understand that some of life's inevitabilities and surprises can force us out of our comfort zones. That's why I will present to you both best-case scenarios and worst-case scenarios for each of the three groups.

I love football, and I've used this analogy with a number of my clients. The best offenses in football use both the more conservative ground game and the more aggressive air game to move the ball downfield. It is always best to get a lead, build on it conservatively, and then stay aggressive enough to keep scoring without taking real chances on high-risk plays. When you fall behind early and have to become much more aggressive as the clock winds down at the end of the game, that's when you take chances and can make mistakes. You don't want the opponent to dictate your strategy. For the vast majority of investors out there, the main opponent is lack of time. Investment procrastination may force you to venture where you don't want—and may not have the ability—to go. As is true in a lot of football games, in investing, you don't want to beat yourself. How do investors beat themselves? Primarily by not understanding their own risk-related tendencies, not having realistic returns expectations, and not understanding the market forces that determine the relative risk or safety of their investment options. In the next section, we'll turn to the second of these points.

Task 2: Understanding the Inherent Risks of Investing

To this point, we've concentrated on factors that are more or less directly in our control—our own financial temperaments. The next factors to consider are those that, to a far greater degree, are out of our control. These include the risks inherent in investing in the stock market, and those that are related to a specific investment itself—a particular company's stock, a bond, et cetera.

The first type is referred to as *market risk*. Such risks are common to all members of an asset class. The three major asset classes are stocks (US and international), bonds (US and international), and cash. Any other valuable items that we can hold for investment purposes could be included as a separate asset class (real estate, commodities, and art, for instance). To keep things simple, and because this is where the majority of people choose to invest, I will confine our discussion to the three major asset classes: stocks, bonds, and cash.

Market risk is due to trends in the entire economy, tax policy, interest rates, inflation, and so on, and affects all securities. It can also be attributed to unfavorable trends in product prices, interest rates, exchange rates, raw material prices, or stock prices. To varying degrees, market risk affects all securities, and, as you can see, it's something over which we have no real control. There is a new type of market risk that you may hear the talking heads discuss: exogenous risk. This is essentially a pseudonym for terrorism or some other type of world crisis. Market risk, of all types, is in a sense, the price of admission to investing in the various asset classes.

THE THREE MAJOR ASSET CLASSES

• **Stocks**, sometimes referred to as common stocks, are securities representing equity ownership in a corporation; they provide the holders with voting rights and entitle them to a share of the company's success through dividends and/or capital appreciation. There are many types of stocks that corporations can issue besides common stock, but we'll confine our discussion to common stock.

• **Bonds**, unlike stocks, don't entitle the holder to any kind of ownership; instead, they represent funds loaned to a corporation or the government for a defined period of time at a specific, fixed income rate. Since these institutions tend to be very stable, and because the amount we are to be paid back on the "loan" is set at the time of purchase and does not vary, the level of risk associated with them is low. The main types of bonds are the corporate bond, municipal bond, Treasury bond, Treasury note, Treasury bill, and zero-coupon bond.

The higher the rate of return a bond offers, the riskier the investment. There have been instances of companies failing to pay back bonds (default), so to entice investors, most corporate bonds offer a higher return than do government bonds. It is important to research a bond just as you would a stock or mutual fund. The bond rating will help in deciphering the default risk.

• **Cash** is defined much as you'd expect: legal tender or coins that can be used in exchange for goods, debt, or services. Sometimes it also includes the value of assets that can be converted into cash immediately, as reported by a company. Just as in determining your net worth, you look at liquid (easily convertible) assets as cash. This usually includes bank accounts and money market funds.

Cash May Be King, But Stocks Rule

Ibbotson Associates, Inc., is an organization that has done extensive analysis of the various asset classes and their performance. It breaks down stocks into subcategories; figure 5.3 represents its analysis of data from 1926 through 2005, revealing which of the asset classes are associated with the highest and lowest risks as well as returns. As you can see, small-company stocks have generated the highest returns while experiencing the most volatility. As you'd expect, cash equivalents posted the lowest return with the least volatility.

The data Ibbotson Associates compiled provide evidence for earlier assertions regarding risk: The higher the risk, the higher the return.

Some (but not all) of the volatility, or variation in returns, associated with these asset classes is due to the forces that constitute market risk. The other risk factors that you should be concerned with refer to a security's individual volatility—how much its price varies over a given period of time. We look exclusively at its price at different points in time to compare how it has varied from its mean—the average of all the fluctuations in the price. We quantify this variation (and therefore risk) using something called a standard deviation. This risk specific to an individual security, and the comparison of its price over time is known as absolute risk.

Figure 5.3
ASSET RISKS AND RETURNS

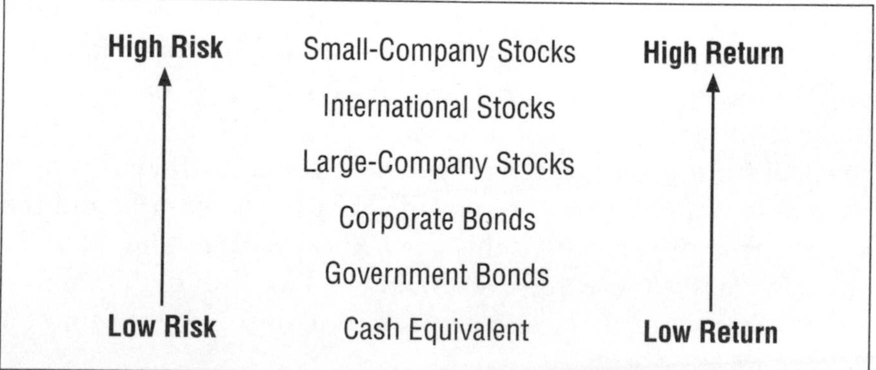

Source: Ibbotson Associates, Inc.

For example, when we were students, we took tests all the time. We earned a score on those tests. If we were to plot our test scores on a graph, we could see the highest and lowest number of points we earned, and we could also determine our overall average. Once we knew what our average score was, we could also determine how far any of our individual test scores were from that average. How much that individual test score varied would be its standard deviation.

If you're like me, you probably weren't content to know your own score; you also wanted to know how it stacked up against how other people had done. In looking at a security, we often do the same thing. Instead of simply comparing an individual stock's price to itself, we compare it to how the stock market as a whole (or a particular segment of the market) has done. Going back to our school testing metaphor, this would be like your physics instructor posting your score in comparison with the average score of all other sophomore nonphysics majors. In other words, how did your score relate to those of others who took the same test?

It's important to realize that market risk, absolute risk, and relative risk are all determined by analyzing historical data. All of them are subject to change—sometimes rapid, other times glacial.

Task 3: Determining Your Returns Expectations

So far we've been talking about risk. Now it's time to return to the other side of that equation. Just as it's important to have an understanding of your risk tolerance, it's equally important to understand and determine necessary and realistic expectations for your returns on the dollars you've invested. Different people have different expectations and tolerance levels for risk, and the same is true of returns. In this case, instead of looking at what you can stand to lose and reasonably endure losing, I'm talking about what you can expect or need to gain to get to a million dollars.

Finding the annual return you'll need to reach your million-dollar goal takes a bit of calculating, but it is important to know where you stand. Knowing whether you can reach your goal by safely earning a paltry 2 percent per year because you have a substantial nest egg already—or if you have to be a bit more aggressive to make up for lost time—is one of the million-dollar questions. Of course, the other side of the equation and the more prudent method to improve your retirement nest egg is to save more money and invest it each year. The magic of compounding certainly helps, but the more you save, the more it can help you reach your goal. In the next sequence of calculations, you'll figure out what your current plan will provide.

Please note that if you want us to do the calculations for you, you can go to www.milliondollarmission.com/returnexpectationscalulator and follow the instructions there to determine this number. What follows is a method you can use as a do-it-yourself means of getting the answer. In most cases, an 8 percent rate of return should get you close to where you need to be. We will use that estimated 8 percent return to begin our calculations. If, at the end, you arrive at a figure above or below one million, you can redo the calculations using either a higher or lower rate of return.

First, What Will Your Current Savings Be Worth by the Time You Retire?

Take your current retirement savings from your net worth statement and multiply it by the factor in table 5.1 that corresponds to the years you have left to retirement and, for starters, the 8 percent annual return we're estimating.

Let's return to Rick and Sally Taylor, the forty-five-year-old couple we met in chapter 4. With twenty years before they need their retirement savings and an initial guesstimate of an 8 percent return, we would multiply their $200,000 nest egg by a factor of 4.7.

Current retirement savings:	$200,000
Growth multiple from table:	x 4.7
Value at retirement:	**$940,000**

Table 5.1
WHAT YOUR CURRENT SAVINGS WILL BE WORTH

Years Remaining	Annual Return												
	2%	**3%**	**4%**	**5%**	**6%**	**7%**	**8%**	**9%**	**10%**	**11%**	**12%**	**15%**	**20%**
5	1.1	1.2	1.2	1.3	1.3	1.4	1.5	1.5	1.6	1.7	1.8	2.0	2.5
10	1.2	1.3	1.5	1.6	1.8	2.0	2.2	2.4	2.6	2.8	3.1	4.0	6.2
15	1.3	1.6	1.8	2.1	2.4	2.8	3.2	3.6	4.2	4.8	5.5	8.1	15.4
20	1.5	1.8	2.2	2.7	3.2	3.9	4.7	5.6	6.7	8.1	9.6	16.4	38.3
25	1.6	2.1	2.7	3.4	4.3	5.4	6.8	8.6	10.8	13.6	17.0	32.9	95.4
30	1.8	2.4	3.2	4.3	5.7	7.6	10.1	13.3	17.4	22.9	30.0	66.2	237.4
35	2.0	2.8	3.9	5.5	7.7	10.7	14.8	20.4	28.1	38.6	52.8	133.2	590.7
40	2.2	3.3	4.8	7.0	10.3	15.0	21.7	31.4	45.3	65.0	93.1	267.9	1,469.8

Second, How Much More Can You Save by the Time You Retire?

Rick and Sally are also going to be adding to their retirement savings every year, so we need to find out how much that will amount to. This gets pretty complicated in real life if the amounts vary each year, so for this exercise let's use an average or even the lowest amount that their projections show. Rick and Sally are good savers and have a goal of setting aside 10 percent per year, but remember they haven't yet funded college tuition for their three kids.

Rick and Sally determine that they will be able to put $6,000 per year into their retirement savings. With twenty years to accumulate at our 8 percent guesstimate, they will accumulate 45.8 times their annual contribution.

Annual savings:	$6,000
Growth multiple from table:	x 45.8
Value at retirement:	$274,800

Third, Add the Two Results Together

Next, we combine the two sources of their retirement nest egg—current savings and future annual savings.

Value of current savings at retirement:	$940,000
Value of future annual savings at retirement:	+ $274,800
Total:	$1,214,800

It looks as if Rick and Sally should celebrate—they've exceeded the million-dollar goal. Unfortunately, they shouldn't go dancing in the streets just yet: They have to account for two other factors. Inflation and taxes will reduce the value of their savings, thus increasing the amount they will need to save.

Fourth, Adjust for Inflation

Inflation is a bitter pill to swallow—it's basically a hidden tax that reduces the value of the money we've already saved. For calculating

Table 5.2
WHAT YOUR FUTURE ANNUAL SAVINGS WILL BE WORTH

Years Remaining	Annual Return												
	2%	**3%**	**4%**	**5%**	**6%**	**7%**	**8%**	**9%**	**10%**	**11%**	**12%**	**15%**	**20%**
5	5.2	5.3	5.4	5.5	5.6	5.8	5.9	6.0	6.1	6.2	6.4	6.7	7.4
10	10.9	11.5	12.0	12.6	13.2	13.8	14.5	15.2	15.9	16.7	17.5	20.3	26.0
15	17.3	18.6	20.0	21.6	23.3	25.1	27.2	29.4	31.8	34.4	37.3	47.6	72.0
20	24.3	26.9	29.8	33.1	36.8	41.0	45.8	51.2	57.3	64.2	72.1	102.4	186.7
25	32.0	36.5	41.6	47.7	54.9	63.2	73.1	84.7	98.3	114.4	133.3	212.8	472.0
30	40.6	47.6	56.1	66.4	79.1	94.5	113.3	136.3	164.5	199.0	241.3	434.7	1,181.9
35	50.0	60.5	73.7	90.3	111.4	138.2	172.3	215.7	271.0	341.6	431.7	881.2	2,948.3
40	60.4	75.4	95.0	120.8	154.8	199.6	259.1	337.9	442.6	581.8	767.1	1,779.1	7,343.9

purposes, what we need to do is take the result in step 3 and find out what it is worth in today's dollars. To do this, we go back to table 5.1 and divide the result in step 3 by the appropriate factor for the number of years until retirement and the inflation rate percentage. In chapter 3, I noted that inflation has averaged 3 percent since 1926, so we'll use that as the future inflation rate. Since Rick and Sally have twenty years to retirement, go down the 3 percent column to the twenty-year row to find the appropriate factor to use: 1.8.

Final result from step 3:	**$1,214,800**
Divided by 3% at 20-year factor:	÷ 1.8
Retirement funds in today's dollars:	$674,900

All that savings and inflation eats away $539,900! So the 8 percent rate we targeted isn't going to be enough. We'll need to go back and try a higher rate of return. Before we do that, there is more bad news—we also need to factor in taxes.

Fifth, Pay the Tax Man

What ends up in our retirement pocket is further reduced by taxes. I'll talk about ways to reduce the tax bite in chapter 7, but it will be very difficult to completely avoid taxes. You *can* pay them up-front. For instance, if you use a Roth IRA to save for retirement, you're putting after-tax money into the account; thus, you don't pay taxes on the money when you eventually take it out. If you use a traditional IRA, you're saving on taxes now, but you'll pay them later when you take the money out. The theory is that you'll be in a lower tax bracket, so there will be some marginal savings if that hold true. In any event, you will pay taxes.

Let's assume that Rick and Sally were able to use a Roth IRA to save for retirement; therefore, their withdrawals after they retire are free of taxes. The only adjustment they need to make is for their annual contribution to their retirement savings. The number we used in the above calculations represented an after-tax contribution, so we'll have to calculate what amount of pretax money Rick and Sally would need to save in order to end up with our after-tax requirement.

Table 5.3
TAX RATES 2007

	INCOME	
RATE	***Single***	***Married Filing Jointly***
10%	Up to $7,825	Up to $15,650
15%	$7,826–$31,850	$15,651–$63,700
25%	$31,851–$77,100	$63,701–$128,500
28%	$77,101–$160,850	$128,501–$195,850
33%	$161,851–$349,700	$195,851–$349,700
35%	Above $349,700	Above $349,700
	LONG-TERM CAPITAL GAINS	
5%	Income up to $31,850	Income up to $63,700
15%	Income above $31,850	Income above $63,700

In step 2, Rick and Sally estimated that they would be able to put $6,000 into their retirement account each year. To end up with that amount after taxes, they would need to actually save:

Roth contribution:	$6,000
1 + tax rate:	x 1.28
Actual pretax savings required:	$7,680

That's one possible scenario. A more favorable one is for Rick and Sally not to pay taxes up front but to wait. It's always wise to defer taxes. In most situations, the longer you can defer this, the more your money can grow and the better off you are. You'll end up paying your taxes later with dollars reduced in value by inflation instead of with today's more valuable dollars. So if you use a traditional IRA or a 401(k) that accumulates tax-free until you take the money out, your calculations will be a little different. Here's how to figure out what your tax liability will be:

What amount of your nest egg will you withdraw each year?

Annual withdrawal: $50,000

What are the taxes on your annual withdrawal?

Annual withdrawal:	$50,000
Tax rate for married filing jointly:	x 28%
Taxes paid:	$14,000
Life expectancy:	20 years

The reduction in value of your nest egg by deferring taxes until retirement is equal to the present value of the taxes you pay during retirement. This is calculated using table 5.4. In this guesstimate, we assumed an 8 percent return. With a life expectancy of twenty years, the factor from the table is 9.8. For our example couple, this works out as follows:

Annual tax bill during retirement:	$50,000
Multiple factor from table:	x 9.8
Total reduction in retirement account value:	$137,200

What this means is that paying taxes over twenty years is equivalent to paying $137,200 on the day you retire. This number also represents the amount that taxes reduce the availability of your retirement savings. The next step is doing the subtraction:

Pretax retirement savings (step 4):	$674,900
Value of taxes paid:	–$274,400
Real value of retirement savings:	$400,500

As you can see, taxes and inflation take an unhealthy bite out of our forty-five-year-old couple's investment savings. What can Rick and Sally—and, more important, what can *you*—do about that? Either earn a higher rate of return, save more money each year, or get started investing sooner. Obviously, our forty-five-year-old couple can't do anything about the past, so only the first two options are available to them. How can they—or you—earn a higher rate of return?

My answer is partly a confession. I asked you to use an 8 percent return rate knowing that unless you were a high earner with a lot of

Table 5.4

WHAT IS THE VALUE OF THE TAXES WE PAY IN RETIREMENT?

Life Expectancy	Annual Return												
	2%	**3%**	**4%**	**5%**	**6%**	**7%**	**8%**	**9%**	**10%**	**11%**	**12%**	**15%**	**20%**
5	4.7	4.6	4.5	4.3	4.2	4.1	4.0	3.9	3.8	3.7	3.6	3.4	3.0
10	9.0	8.5	8.1	7.7	7.4	7.0	6.7	6.4	6.1	5.9	5.7	5.0	4.2
15	12.8	11.9	11.1	10.4	9.7	9.1	8.6	8.1	7.6	7.2	6.8	5.8	4.7
20	16.4	14.9	13.6	12.5	11.5	10.6	9.8	9.1	8.5	8.0	7.5	6.3	4.9
25	19.5	17.4	15.6	14.1	12.8	11.7	10.7	9.8	9.1	8.4	7.8	6.5	4.9
30	22.4	19.6	17.3	15.4	13.8	12.4	11.3	10.3	9.4	8.7	8.1	6.6	5.0
35	25.0	21.5	18.7	16.4	14.5	12.9	11.7	10.6	9.6	8.9	8.2	6.6	5.0
40	27.4	23.1	19.8	17.2	15.0	13.3	11.9	10.8	9.8	9.0	8.2	6.6	5.0

savings to allocate to your investments, you would fall short of that million-dollar mark. Why did I do that? To reinforce the idea that the best way to earn high enough returns to overcome inflation and taxes is by being in the stock market. Even allowing for the Great Depression and the significant drops in value of the market as a result of the tech stock bust of 1999 and the post-9/11 doldrums, stocks have historically averaged a little over a 10 percent return on investment. Nothing else, including real estate, offers as much promise as the market. That is why, despite those market risks and absolute risks, the market is where you need to be.

Table 5.5 puts some hard-and-fast numbers to the asset classes studied by Ibbotson. As I mentioned earlier, risk is measured using standard deviation, which is the standard measure of volatility.

As you can see, the higher the standard of deviation, the greater the volatility, and consequently the higher the risk—but also the higher the return.

Remember that we have to subtract the inflation rate from the above returns to arrive at a real rate of return for each of the asset classes. Doing so leaves just a +0.7 percent compound annual return for Treasury bills from 1926 to 2005. Also note that the standard deviation of inflation exceeds the standard deviation of Treasury bill returns. In fact, the range of average inflation-adjusted Treasury bill returns over twenty year periods was –3.0

Table 5.5
ASSET CLASS HISTORICAL RETURNS

	Compound Annual Return	**Standard Deviation**
Small-Company Stocks	12.6%	32.9%
Large-Company Stocks	10.4%	20.2%
Government Bonds	5.5%	9.2%
Treasury Bills (cash equivalent)	3.7%	3.1%
Inflation	3.0%	4.3%

Source: Ibbotson Associates, Inc.

to +2.9 percent. This suggests that when you consider real returns, you would have lost money on Treasury bills for much of those seventy-nine years! The same is true, although to a lesser extent, for longer-term government bonds. The range of average inflation-adjusted returns over twenty-year periods for government bonds was –3.1 to +8.6 percent. Only stocks posted positive inflation-adjusted returns in all twenty-year periods from 1926 to 2005. Large-company stocks posted a range of +0.8 to +13.3 percent, and small-company stocks +4.0 to +17.2 percent.

What this analysis tells us is that holding stocks instead of bonds for long-term investors is the more attractive option, especially since this analysis doesn't even include the erosion of returns due to taxes! At least historically, the only taxable financial asset that has consistently provided a positive inflation-adjusted return over long periods of time has been common stocks. Yes, we do have to factor risk into this equation, but returns tell the better part of the story here. In my mind, a so-called safe investment like bonds that produces a real return that is no return at all when adjusted for inflation turns out to be riskier than we usually think. That's why we have to look at risk and reward together, as a kind of equation.

In the next task, you'll determine how much of your money should be in each of the asset classes discussed.

Task 4: Determining the Asset Classes That Match Your Returns and Risk Profiles

This bears repeating: Investing in the stock market is risky. This also bears repeating: Not investing in the stock market is risky. If you don't, you may not be able to achieve the rate of returns necessary to reach the million-dollar mark that will help you maintain your lifestyle in retirement. So the next question is: What can you do to lower your risk level and raise your returns?

You can reduce the effects of these risks by investing your money in different places, or asset classes. This spreading of the wealth is known as *diversification.* To offset some of the risk of investing in stocks, I suggest, particularly if you are risk-averse or don't have the financial strength or time to recover from losses, that you also place some of your money in bonds and cash equivalents.

Here are my very general, unscientific asset allocation recommendations for each of the three age groups:

Figure 5.4

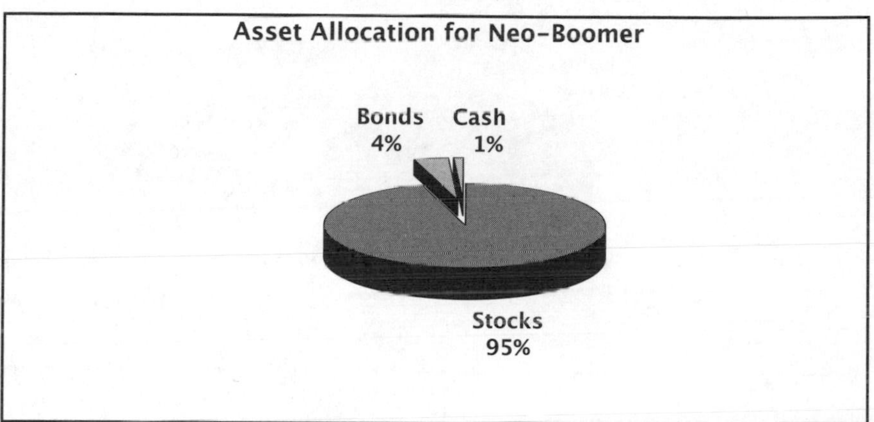

For all the reasons I've discussed, a thirty-five-year-old can, and often must, be more aggressive. With the vast majority of their money invested in stocks, Neo-Boomers can take advantage of:

- The greater number of years available to play catch-up if rewards don't equal risks.

With this asset allocation plan, Neo-Boomers can also compensate for:

- The smaller amount of money they have available to invest because of generally lower salaries.
- The erosion of earnings due to taxes and inflation.

If at all possible, Neo-Boomers should allocate 100 percent of their retirement funds to stocks. Figure 5.4 represents the most conservative position I recommend for Neo-Boomers.

Moving further along the time horizon, it makes sense for nearly every Tail End Boomer to have some money in bonds and cash.

Figure 5.5

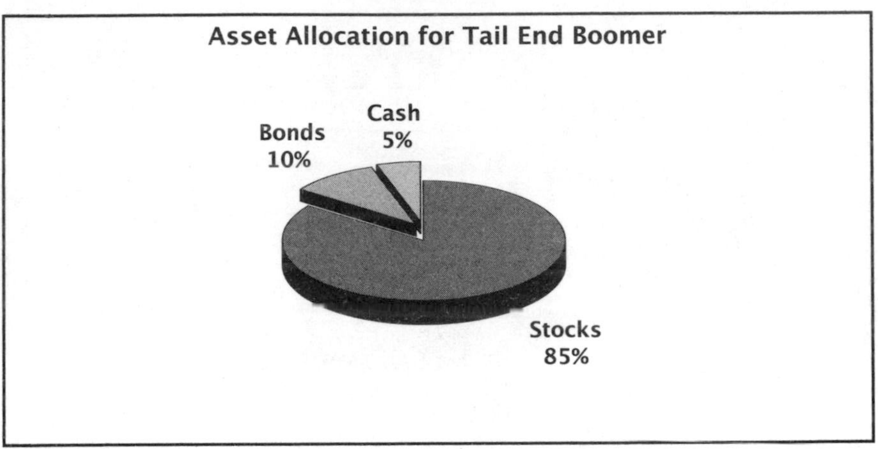

The moderately aggressive asset allocation scheme in figure 5.5 helps Tail End Boomers take advantage of:

- Their ability to absorb risk due to greater income and savings.
- A reduced risk level that doesn't offset returns because of greater savings available to invest.
- The approximately twenty-year TTR still available to them.

This scheme also helps compensate for:

- The slightly reduced TTR that will allow for them to catch up from any losses.
- Any delays in getting started in investing for retirement.
- The erosion of earnings due to taxes and inflation.

Finally, in the best-case scenario, Core Boomers should have a greater percentage of their funds in bonds and cash than the other two groups.

Figure 5.6

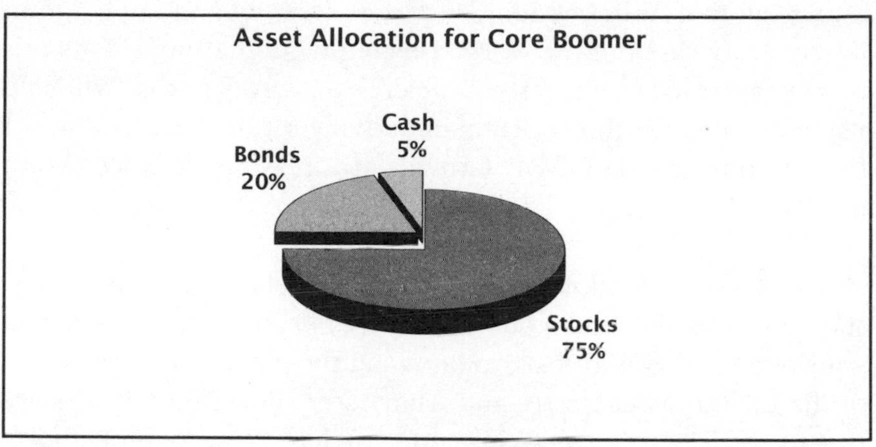

The slightly more conservative asset allocation scheme in figure 5.6 helps Core Boomers take advantage of:

- The lower returns needed due to the number of years that they have spent saving and investing.
- The lower returns needed due to the high levels of income available for investing thanks to many years in the workforce.
- The lower returns needed due to the magic of compounding.

It also helps Core Boomers overcome:

- The potential for substantial losses due to market and absolute risk.
- The erosion of earnings due to taxes and inflation.

These allocation models are just guidelines. Please consult with a professional investment adviser or CPA before committing to the plan that is right for you.

At this point, you're only concerned with the percentage of your total investment you should have in each of the larger asset classes. In chapter 6, we'll look at asset allocation—what percentage of your money should be within each subset of the individual asset classes—how much you could allocate, if necessary, to (say) small stocks, international stocks, and large-company stocks. As a preview to that discussion, let me say this. By and large and in nearly every case but the worst, I recommend that my clients primarily invest in large-cap stocks. Here's an acronym that will help you remember the fundamental underlying rationale I recommend for selecting stocks: GARP. Growth at a reasonable price. More on that in a moment.

We've covered a lot of territory in this chapter. From understanding yourself and your money personality, to recognizing your relationship with risk, to knowing the real risks and rewards of the various asset classes and what asset allocation schemes are best for your position as an investor, you have a lot to think about. Investing your hard-earned dollars isn't a task for which a sink-or-swim approach will work. Like my motorcycling friend Tom, you need to, if not love, at least tolerate the research and preparation process. Also like Tom, I'm sure you're eager to get on the road and make some specific investment decisions. In the next chapter, we'll review more detailed guidelines about specific stocks to invest in, so you don't make any wrong turns.

PART THREE

The Million-Dollar Maneuvers

Building a Healthy Portfolio

CHAPTER SIX

Build It, Part One

Investment Plans for Core Boomers, Tail End Boomers, and Neo-Boomers

I know. You've highlighted a lot of material in the book, done a lot of calculations, and now you're eager to get started immediately. But do you really want to go back over all your notes? Ideally, you will do so to make investment decisions that best suit your particular needs. If you think you're going to be happy with a more general approach, this chapter offers some easy-to-use data sheets that correspond to the three types of Boomers I've talked about in the book and the three situations you might find yourself in—behind in your retirement savings, on track, or ahead. Suggestions for marginally altering the risk and return profiles up or down are also included. Find your situation and the recommendations for that particular scenario. The portfolios give you the percentages of each asset class you should have your money invested in. Remember, though: Everyone's situation is unique, and these general guidelines are not meant to be a one-size-fits-all approach. Consult with a professional financial adviser if you have questions.

After you've reviewed this asset allocation information, you can move on to the specifics of my Million-Dollar Stock Selection Strategy to see suggestions about what stocks are right for you and how to select others on your own.

A BRIEF GUIDE TO TERMINOLOGY

- Market capitalization: This is a somewhat highbrow term for what a company is worth—the market value of its outstanding shares. To determine this number, take the stock price and multiply it by the total number of shares outstanding. For example, if Farr's Fairway Wood Corporation (FWC) was trading at $20 per share and had 1 million shares outstanding, then the market capitalization would be $20 million ($20 x 1 million shares).
- Large-cap(italization) stocks: These are companies that have a market capitalization of between $10 billion and $200 billion. In other words, these are the biggest fish in the pond. Also known as blue-chip stocks.
- Midcap(italization) stocks: These have a value of between $2 billion and $10 billion.
- Small-cap(italization) stocks: Those with a value between $300 million and $2 billion.
- Growth stocks: The stock in companies whose earnings are expected to increase at a rate greater than the market as a whole. They generally don't pay dividends to shareholders, but are reinvesting money in the company for expansion projects and the like. Many are not yet industry leaders—but they're on their way to becoming so.
- Value stocks: The stock in companies whose price is lower than their business fundamentals (dividends, earnings, sales, and so forth) merit. They are therefore *undervalued* by investors.

Neo-Boomer Starter Portfolio

This is a great portfolio for starting off when your level of investment income is low. Use mutual funds to provide professional management.

Asset level:
Up to $50,000

Risk level: Average

Effort level: Low

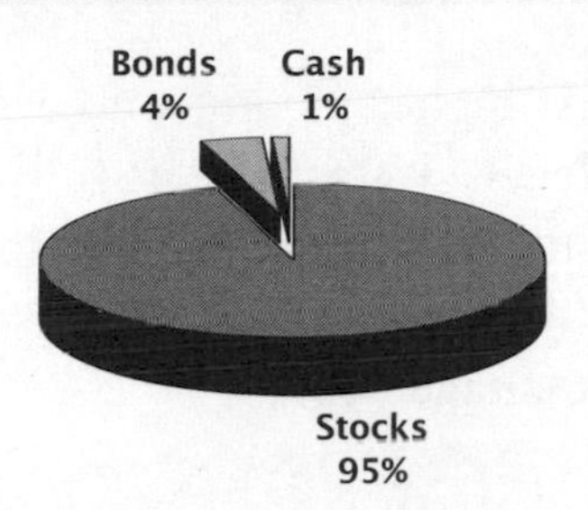

Stocks (95 percent):
Use one or more of the Farr Core Portfolio large-cap growth mutual funds.

Bonds (4 percent):
Use low-cost corporate bond mutual funds.

Cash (1 percent):
Use a brokerage sweep account or low-cost money market mutual fund for your cash allocation.

Neo-Boomer Intermediate Portfolio

At higher income and asset levels, it's safe to be fully invested in stocks. Use mutual funds to provide professional management.

Asset level:
$50,000–$200,000

Risk level: Average

Effort level: Low

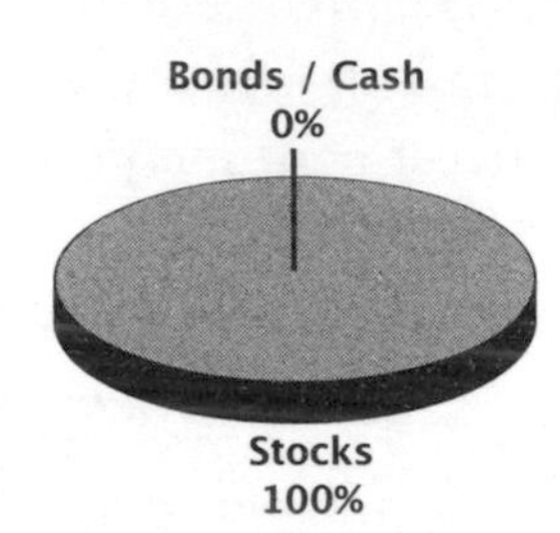

Stocks (100 percent):
Continue to use one or more of the Farr Core Portfolio large-cap growth mutual funds.

If you're willing to do research, begin moving some of your portfolio out of mutual funds and into some of the Farr's List stock when prices are favorable. Completely using stocks rather than mutual funds is okay if you maintain a good mix of industries.

Increased risk and return:
Allocate up to 25 percent of your stock portfolio to midcap or multicap growth mutual funds if the timing is appropriate.

Reduced risk and return:
Move 5 to 10 percent of your funds into one of the corporate bond funds suggested in the Neo-Boomer Starter Portfolio.

Neo-Boomer Large-Cap Portfolio

Once your asset levels grow strong and you still have many years to retirement, it's safe to be fully invested in stocks. This is the position I hope all Neo-Boomers will be in. Professional management is recommended.

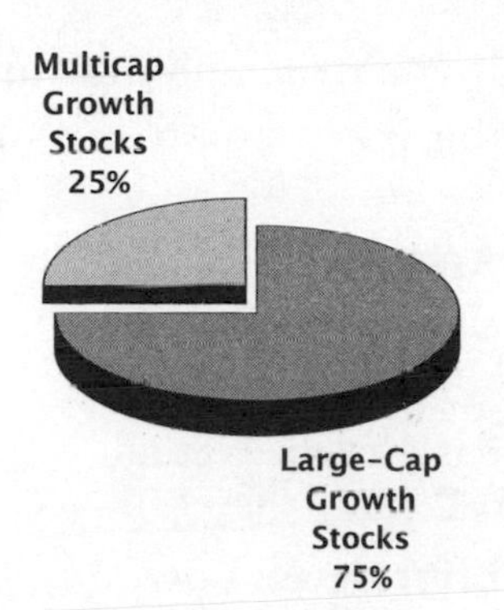

Asset level:
Above $200,000

Risk level: Average

Effort level: Individual stocks or individual management make sense

Stocks (100 percent):
Use Farr's List to populate your portfolio when prices are favorable. Maintain a good mix of industries. Funds will work for this, too. If your portfolio exceeds $300,000, I recommend owning individual shares.

Increased risk and return:
Allocate up to 25 percent of your stock portfolio to midcap or multicap growth stocks and special situations (dogs of the Dow and the like). Focus on out-of-favor quality companies.

Reduced risk and return:
Move 5 to 10 percent of your funds into one of the corporate bond funds suggested in the Neo-Boomer Starter Portfolio.

Core Boomer Starter Portfolio

If you're behind in your savings, this portfolio provides a boost.

Asset level:
Up to $50,000

Risk level: Average

Effort level: Low

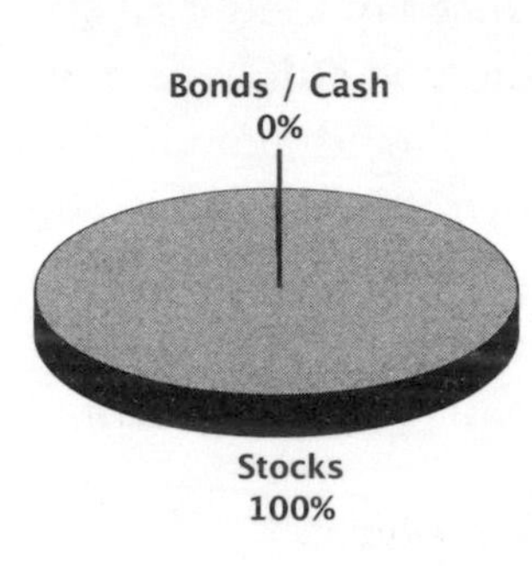

Stocks (100 percent):
Use one or more of the Farr Core Portfolio large-cap growth mutual funds.

Increased risk and return:
Allocate no more than 10 percent of your stock portfolio to midcap or multicap growth mutual funds if the timing is appropriate. Good funds include:

- Legg Mason Opportunity Trust
- BlackRock U.S. Opportunities Svc
- Bridgeway Aggressive Investors 2
- Royce Premier Inv
- Touchstone Mid Cap Growth
- Baron Growth

Reduced risk and return:
Allocate no more than 10 percent of your portfolio to a low-cost, high-quality corporate bond fund.

Core Boomer On-Target Portfolio

This asset allocation scheme is designed to keep you to your plan if you invested on time.

Asset level:
$50,000–$300,000

Risk level: Average

Effort level: Medium

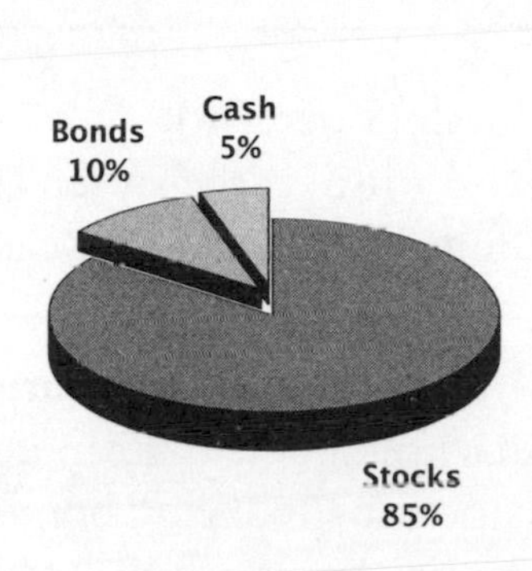

Stocks (85 percent):
Continue to use one or more of the Farr Core Portfolio large-cap growth mutual funds.

If you're willing to do research, begin moving some of your portfolio out of mutual funds and into some of the Farr's List stock when prices are favorable. Completely using stocks rather than mutual funds is okay if you maintain a good mix of industries.

Bonds (10 percent):
Use one or more of the following low-cost mutual funds.

- Vanguard Intermediate-Term Investment Grade
- Vanguard Short-term Investment Grade
- Dodge & Cox Income
- Harbor Bond Fund
- T. Rowe Price Corporate Income

continued

Core Boomer On-Target Portfolio
(continued)

Cash (5 percent):
Use a brokerage sweep account or low-cost money market mutual fund for your cash allocation.

Increased risk and return:
It's acceptable to keep up to 95 percent of your portfolio in stocks by reducing bonds and cash. If you're picking stocks, retain some cash to stay prepared in case a stock investment opportunity arises.

Reduced risk and return:
Go as low as 75 percent stocks and as high as 25 percent bonds to reduce risk, particularly after a strong run-up in your stock portfolio.

Selecting Specific Stocks

I want to keep heavy-duty stock analysis discussion to a minimum here: You can implement my Million-Dollar Stock Selection Strategy without it. At the same time, however, good information can help offset the risks of investing. So here's the Farr five-minute version of the Million-Dollar Stock Selection Strategy.

The principle that underlies all of my stock selection advice can be summarized with the acronym *GARP.* That stands for "growth at reasonable prices." This is my investment mantra and the approach I have settled on after decades of trial-and-error experience. Buying and holding undervalued large-cap growth stocks is the most effective way for investors to generate great returns adjusted for inflation, taxes, and risk. I believe that over the long

Core Boomer Large-Cap Portfolio

If you are ahead of schedule on your savings, it's appropriate to take on a little more risk with part of your portfolio.

Asset level:
Above $300,000

Risk level: Slightly above average

Effort level: Individual stocks and individual management make sense

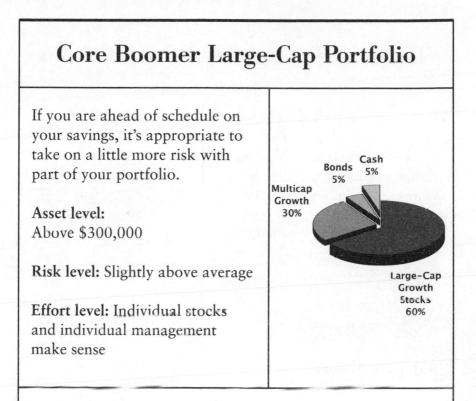

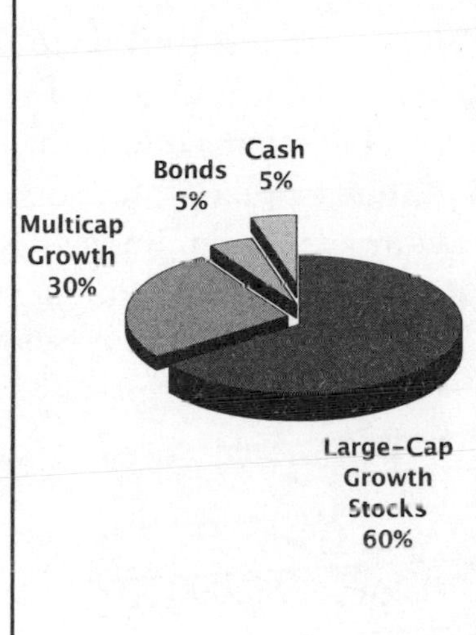

Stocks (90 percent):
Allocate two-thirds to three-quarters of your stock portfolio to the Farr's List large-cap growth sector. The remaining stock allocation can go into small and midcap growth or special-situation stocks through appropriate mutual funds or individual stock choices from the secondary Farr's List.

Increased risk and return:
At this stage, moving fully into stocks is still acceptable, using the same allocation of large cap to multicap.

Reduced risk and return:
Stick to large-cap growth and/or allocate more to bonds.

Tail End Boomer Catch-Up Portfolio

If you are just starting to invest, lack of time and lack of savings combine to make this the most difficult situation for someone in your age group. Budget issues (eliminating debt and increasing savings every year) are vital. Deferred retirement may be required.

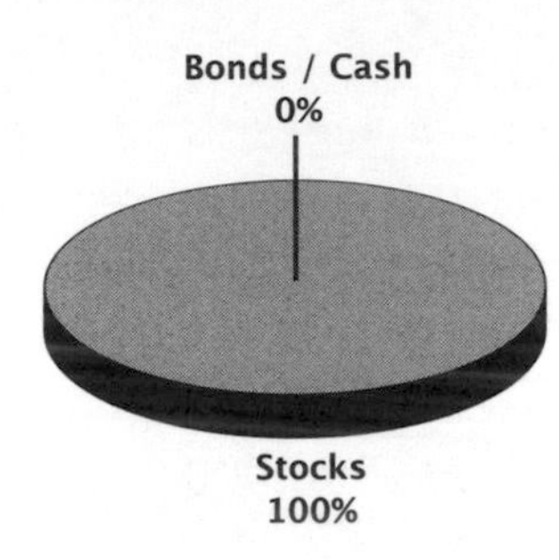

Asset level:
Below $250,000

Risk level: Average

Effort level: Low

Stocks (100 percent):
Use one or more of the following large-cap growth mutual funds:

- The Bill Miller-managed Legg Mason Value Trust fund
- Legg Mason Partners Aggressive Growth
- American Funds Growth Fund of America
- Fidelity Capital Appreciation
- T. Rowe Price Growth Stock
- Transamerica Premier Growth
- Janus Adviser Forty S

continued

Tail End Boomer Catch-Up Portfolio

(continued)

Increased risk and return:
I wouldn't suggest any additional risk at this point. Your short time horizon and low fund levels leave little room for added risk.

Reduced risk and return:
There's not a lot of room on the other side, either. At most, allocate 10 percent of your portfolio to corporate bonds.

term, the risk-return profile of the large-cap growth segment of the market is superior to the others. In general, I find that larger companies offer superior track records, higher market share, more pricing power, stronger balance sheets, superior management teams, and increased liquidity relative to small caps. I prefer growth stocks over value stocks because I am a long-term investor, and I believe that earnings growth is the single biggest determinant of stock price performance over time. However, unlike more momentum-oriented growth managers (*momentum* refers to watching for price movement—rather than the nature of the company's business—to indicate a buying opportunity), I pay very close attention to valuation when making my purchases. I try never to confuse a great growth company with a great growth investment. And finally, growth companies tend to pay lower dividends, making them more tax-efficient investments than high-yielding value stocks (all else being equal).

I look for places where the market has undervalued a great company's stock. I hold those stocks for an average of four years. I try to limit the realized capital gains taken in my clients' portfolios to less than 5 percent of the total account value per year.

Tail End Boomer On-Target Portfolio

You've done a good job of investing on time, so this portfolio is designed to keep you moving forward. You're almost there.

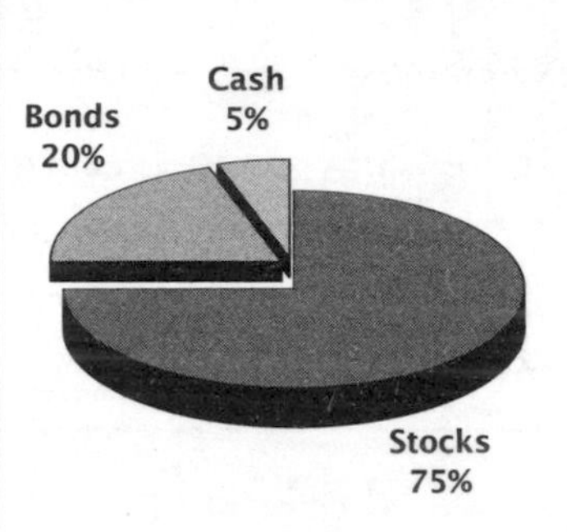

Asset level:
$250,000–$1,000,000

Risk level: Average

Effort level: Individual stocks and individual management make sense.

Stocks (75 percent):
Maintain a large-cap growth emphasis.

Increased risk and return:
Increase stock allocation to no more than 85 percent. Allocate up to 20 percent of your stock portfolio to multicaps.

Reduced risk and return:
Reduce stock holdings as low as 60 percent. You still have a way to go, so you can't alter much.

Tail End Boomer Large-Cap Portfolio

You've made it. Protect it. Enjoy the flexibility and peace of mind.

Asset level:
Above $1,000,000

Risk level: Low

Effort level:
Professional management and individual stocks are appropriate at this level

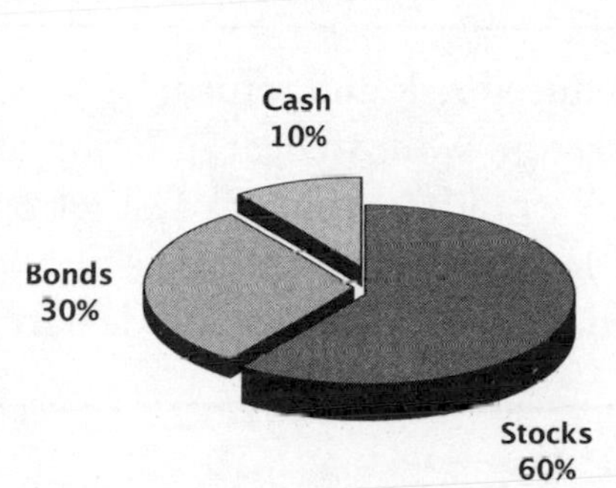

Stocks (60 percent):
Continuing growing your account while reducing risk appropriately. Maintain your large-cap growth focus.

Bonds (30 percent):
Move a little more of your portfolio into good-quality corporate bonds—the lower risk-return profile is appropriate for your situation.

Cash (10 percent):
A high-quality money market mutual fund or government bond fund is appropriate. A municipal bond fund can provide tax benefits.

Increased risk and return:
Protect what you've built, but you can increase stocks to 75 percent or move one-third of your stock portfolio into multicap positions if you feel the need.

continued

Tail End Boomer Large-Cap Portfolio
(continued)

Reduced risk and return:
You still want to beat inflation and improve your portfolio, so I wouldn't suggest a full retreat to bonds. A fifty-fifty mix of large-cap growth stocks and quality corporate bonds can reduce risk and still provide acceptable returns.

By focusing on growth companies, you limit taxable dividend income, and your focus on large-cap companies reduces risk in volatile markets. The large-cap growth approach has allowed my clients to beat the S&P 500 Index (which is a hybrid of large-cap growth and value) by 3 percent per year on average over the past ten years. My clients have also bested the Russell 1000 Growth Index, which is a more apples-to-apples benchmark for large-cap growth managers, over the past nine years. Note, however, that past performance may not be indicative of future results.

I like to exploit the inefficiency of time for my clients—making money from the mistakes of investors who focus too much on the short term. I believe that investors have become too obsessed with quick profits, creating volatility that can very often lead to bad decision making. Successful investors need to be able to ignore all the noise and maintain conviction in the face of overwhelming pressure to do otherwise—a virtue known as *sticking to your discipline*. I buy reasonably priced stocks in industry-leading companies with solid track records, superior management teams, and above-average earnings growth expectations. I care more about the next five to ten years than the next one or two quarters. I don't base my investment decisions on a view of the short-term economic outlook, because I am likely to hold my stocks through several different economic cycles. Start with the premise that you cannot predict short-term market gyrations or key economic variables such as interest rates. Therefore, the goal is to create a portfolio that will outperform the market whether it goes up or down. This generally entails selecting companies that will benefit from some long-term secular trend in the economy.

I am a buy-and-hold investor. As long as your original rationale for owning certain companies does not change, stay the course through market peaks and valleys.

MORE TERMS YOU'LL NEED TO KNOW

Earnings per share (EPS): A measure of the value of a firm. Higher is better.

Return on equity: Earnings divided by capital. This measure shows how efficiently a company uses its investments to generate earnings.

Debt-to-total-capitalization ratio: This measure shows how highly leveraged a firm is. More debt is more risk, and debt holders get paid before stockholders. The measure also reveals whether a firm's cash needs exceed what it is able to earn in income.

Price-to-earnings ratio (P/E): This measure shows how much a dollar of earnings costs; it's a traditional indicator of the reasonableness of the stock's price. The more you have to pay for each dollar of current earnings, the more the company needs to grow and produce additional earnings. If it doesn't, you're paying too much.

As part of the Million-Dollar Stock Selection Strategy, I use the following "screens" to generate a list of approximately a hundred new companies per year:

- Market capitalization greater than $1 billion (roughly two thousand stocks)
- A ten-year average earnings-per-share growth greater than 10 percent.

- A ten-year average revenue growth greater than 7 percent.
- Return on equity greater than 15 percent.
- A debt-to-total-capitalization ratio of less than 50 percent.
- Projected EPS growth greater than 10 percent.
- A price-to-earnings ratio of between 10 and 30 times earnings.

Anyone with an Internet account can use these screens. What sets my approach apart is the additional factors I search for:

- A history of superior performance and consistency.
- A company that is a leader in its market, with a competitive advantage its counterparts can't easily match.
- A healthy balance sheet and great income to generate strong cash flows.
- Sustainable growth markets that don't require mergers and acquisitions for growth.
- Strong, proven management.
- Not overpriced, with below-market P/Es.
- Not overly risky—a stock with financial leverage more conservative than its peers.
- Large enough for trading to be liquid and information to be available. Market capitalization of $20 billion is average; $1 billion is a minimum.

Follow this strategy to retirement success. I know of no other strategy that offers a risk-reward profile that suits a retirement portfolio as well.

Investment Recommendations

I hope that I've made it clear by now that I think the best risk-reward possibilities for a retirement portfolio come from the large-cap growth sector of the stock market. Mixing in a small amount of high-quality corporate bonds as your portfolio grows is acceptable as a buffer against temporary swings in the stock market. I don't believe hedge funds, derivatives, commodities, collectibles, precious metals, and other exotic investments belong in a retirement portfolio. If you have the means to take a chance on these types of investments outside your retirement savings, please take a tiny dip in the water *after* you've ensured that your retirement is protected.

Here are some further tips on your portfolio—and especially its structure.

- Be as fully invested in large-cap growth stocks as possible.
- If you have less than $50,000 to invest, using mutual funds is acceptable. You'll get professional management and more diversification than you could achieve yourself, at a reasonable price. A well-run large-cap growth fund is best, but a sector index fund or even a marketwide index fund will work if you're really low on funds. Remember to heed my fund-buying caveats in the chapter 4 budget suggestions. Basically, cost is the factor distinguishing the various index funds.
- The overall large-cap growth sector goes through a cycle of favor and disfavor, as all sectors do, but great nuggets are usually found here. I believe that Bill Miller at Legg Mason is one of the finest stock pickers—and he happens to operate in my favorite sector. All the Legg Mason Funds run by Bill adhere to the same guiding principles as I do, and if you feel the need to remain in mutual funds, you can't go wrong with him. Given the size of his fund, he has lost a little of the ability to be as selective as I can, but he still has a keen eye for value. Another option is the Torray Fund run by Bob Torray and Doug Eby—a great investment team. The Torray Fund's goals are to build shareholder wealth over long periods (ten years or more) and to minimize shareholder capital gains tax liability by limiting the realization of long- and short-term gains. The manager's strategy is to buy and hold stocks of quality companies for long-term investment. Investments are made only when it is believed that a company's long-term outlook is sound and the shares are fairly priced.
- The invest-it-and-forget-it fund. If you're starting early, don't want to put much effort into investing, and want to incur little risk, a marketwide index fund would be a good low-

cost, low-effort, average-risk way to get started. You won't set the world on fire, but you will track the market.

- I don't care for lifecycle funds. These funds are targeted to retirement accounts. They have an asset allocation mix that someone decided is suitable for your age, and you move from one to the other as you move closer to retirement. My problem with them is their cost for the lackluster performance you get. Plus, they don't factor in all the other criteria that an adviser would use to construct a suitable portfolio. Some fund providers have even taken them a step further by creating cohort funds, which are managed toward a specified target retirement or need date. For instance, if you are forty-five in 2006, you will presumably retire at sixty-five in 2026. You buy the cohort fund with the target date closest to 2006, and managers do all the allocating and reallocating for you. All the issues I have with lifecycle funds apply to cohort funds as well.
- As you move up from $50,000, it makes more sense to buy individual stocks or hire a professional manager who can better manage your tax and overall investment situation.
- The only way I believe you can prudently improve your returns and keep risk manageable is to look at the midcap and multicap growth-stock segment. I believe the risk-adjusted results are much better in my large-cap growth world, but sometimes you can apply my philosophy to smaller firms. Heed all of my analysis and decision-making processes save the size criteria, and I think it can be acceptable to put up to a third of your stock portfolio into these categories—under certain conditions.
- Remember GARP—buy *growth at reasonable prices.*

Farr's Lists

So far, I've given you a lot of information about how I go about, and how I recommend you go about, selecting stocks. Now it's time to get to the nitty-gritty and demonstrate to you this method in action. I know the following sounds obvious, but I have to say it: I'm writing this in December 2006, at the peak of a great end-of-the-year run-up. By the time this book is published, the landscape may have altered greatly. The stocks recommendations given here are to illustrate my points. You need to do your own careful research to protect your investments.

Stock prices change. They go up and down. Excellent companies and not-so-excellent companies both enjoy and endure periods of over- and undervaluation. Another way to say this is that the price pendulum has a habit of swinging too far in either the up or the down direction. As a result, there are times when the greatest companies are overpriced. Thus, there is *no* stock that I recommend owning at all times.

That being said, what follows is a list of great companies that I have felt in the recent past would be great in a core portfolio, at the right entry price. Watch these companies and look for opportunities to purchase. Every quarter, my Web site highlights these and other stocks that I find interesting.

Farr's List of Core Holdings

Here are some companies that have been strong for many years. There is no way to determine if they represent good buys right now unless you do your research and develop an independent valuation. In fact, now may be the time that you should be *selling* any number of these names. Get the message? Do the research!

Large-Cap Growth Stocks

- **Microsoft (MSFT)** is the eight-hundred-pound gorilla of the computer software world, with fiscal 2006 sales of more than $44 billion. The company's operating system has a virtual monopoly on the market, while its ancillary products span a wide range of computing applications. The company's balance sheet and financial flexibility are unsurpassed, creating numerous competitive advantages relative to its competition.
- **Medtronic (MDT)** engages in the development, manufacture, and marketing of medical devices for a worldwide market.

The company specializes in implantable cardiac devices but has become increasingly diversified over the past several years. I expect this company to be a primary beneficiary of the aging of the Baby Boomer population in the United States and the increased access to advanced medical treatments throughout the world.

- **Wal-Mart (WMT)** is an American success story whose prowess in technological innovation and tight focus on the bottom line have accrued countless benefits to the American consumer in the form of lower prices and greater convenience. Recently, the company has been caught up in a firestorm of controversies ranging from allegations of gender discrimination, to forcing employees to work off the clock, to a failure to provide adequate health care coverage to its employees. As a result, the stock price has been flat over the past five years despite double-digit EPS growth annually.
- **Johnson & Johnson (JNJ)** is a diversified health-care company with a strong presence in the pharmaceutical, medical device, and consumer markets. I view the company as another way to gain exposure to demographic trends not only in the United States but also in less developed countries throughout the world.
- **PepsiCo (PEP)** manufactures and markets various snacks and beverages for the global market. As consumer staples, PepsiCo products are unlikely to suffer serious demand declines in even the most trying economic environments. Given this stability and high earnings visibility, the stock tends to trade at a higher valuation relative to the market. Nevertheless, I view the company's growth prospects as compelling for long-term investors.
- **American International Group (AIG)** is a diversified financial services company heavily concentrated in insurance and retirement-planning products. The company's presence in high-growth, emerging Asian economies is unsurpassed. This presence, along with steadily growing operations in the United States and Europe, should enable AIG to post earnings growth rates well in excess of the market for several years into the future.

- **General Electric (GE).** I view GE as a carefully constructed and diversified portfolio of industrial and financial businesses, all run by a world-class management team. The company has outstanding exposure to high-growth emerging markets, an outstanding portfolio of highly stable service businesses, and a collection of high-return financial businesses operating in niche markets. Furthermore, CEO Jeff Immelt is my kind of manager—aggressive and straight talking, with plenty of skin in the game. Immelt recently decided to forgo his 2005 cash bonus in favor of "GE performance shares," half of which can be redeemed only if GE shareholder returns meet or exceed those of the S&P 500.
- **Procter & Gamble (PG)** is another producer of consumer staples that should perform relatively well in periods of slow or negative economic growth. The company's products meet a wide range of everyday consumer needs. Historical performance has been outstanding, the management team is very strong, and the company's brand is highly recognizable across the world.
- **Staples (SPLS)** is a top-shelf retailer by any standard. The company has consistently taken share in both the United States and Europe while growing earnings at a 20-percent-plus annual pace for the past several years. I believe the company has simply created a better mousetrap in its domestic retail, delivery, and international segments. I expect continued market share gains and margin expansion in the United States, with longer-term growth coming from its immature international operations.
- **Dell Computer (DELL).** Michael Dell pioneered the commoditization of the personal computer market. The company's direct-sale model allowed it to strip major costs from the marketing process, resulting in lower prices to the consumer and increased value to shareholders. While competitors are beginning to catch on to the new paradigm, I believe that Dell will continue to lead the way with continued operation innovation and entry into new product lines such as printers. While the company is currently out of favor with investors, I would not count it out by any means.

- **Sysco** (SYY) is a distributor of food and related products to the food service industry in the United States and Canada. While offering consumer staples, the company nevertheless generates huge returns on equity. While growth prospects at the company (and the industry as a whole) are not especially exciting, I'm attracted to its stability of earnings and high returns.
- **Waters Corporation** (WAT) is a global manufacturer of analytical instruments used to detect, identify, monitor, and measure the chemical, physical, and biological composition of materials, as well as to purify a range of compounds. Other company products are used in drug discovery and development, including clinical trial testing, the analysis of proteins in disease processes, food safety analyses, and environmental testing. The company sells to a number of end markets with strong secular growth prospects due to demographic shifts.
- **Stryker Corporation** (SYK) is a manufacturer of orthopedic products and medical specialties. Yet again, this company stands to benefit from the aging of the US Baby Boomer population, as well as the increased access to advanced medical technologies worldwide. Historical earnings growth rates have been very impressive, and I see little reason why growth rates cannot continue well into the future given the company's small relative size and presence in its end markets.
- **Oracle** (ORCL) engages in the development, distribution, servicing, and marketing of database, middleware, and application software. I believe the software segment of the technology universe has especially compelling growth prospects, particularly given the apparent need for consolidation within the industry. I expect Oracle to continue absorbing its smaller and less successful competitors, resulting in the opportunity for continued market share penetration and status as a "one-stop shop" for software solutions.

Large-Cap Growth Mutual Funds

- Legg Mason Value Trust
- Torray Fund

- T. Rowe Price Institutional Large-Cap Growth
- Janus Twenty
- Fidelity Advisor Fifty
- Fidelity Advisor Dynamic Cap App
- Any low-cost, large-cap growth index fund that acceptably tracks the sector performance

Farr's List of Corporate Bond Funds

(Listed in order of credit quality—AAA to A)

- Managers Fremont Bond
- Dodge & Cox Income
- Vanguard Interm-Term Bond Index
- Calvert Income A Load Waived
- Loomis Sayles Bond Ret
- Templeton Global Bond A Load Waived
- Oppenheimer Strat Income A Load Waived

Strategies to Add Incremental Risk/Return

If you determine that you are able to withstand more risk in search of higher returns, there are many ways to add a little "octane" to your portfolio. I would caution, however, that each of these strategies is likely to lead to more short-term volatility in your portfolio returns. Furthermore, there is no guarantee that reallocating into higher-risk classes will ultimately lead to better performance over the longer term. With these disclosures, I would suggest any of the following to help you reach your investment goals:

1. My first suggestion would be to increase your allocation to stocks at the expense of bonds and cash. As I have discussed at length, the expected returns on stocks over the long term is well above that expected on stocks and bonds. Therefore, if your portfolio contains a 70 percent weighting in stocks rather than 60 percent, you are likely to earn higher returns *over the long term.*

2. Second, I would suggest adding an allocation, or increasing your allocation, to small-capitalization stocks (those companies with a market cap less than $2 billion). While it is very possible to find attractive small-cap stocks on your own, it takes a lot of time. Small-cap stocks are less widely followed by Wall Street analysts, which means quality information can be hard to find. I would suggest using an exchange-traded fund or a highly-rated mutual fund to get your exposure. The market can be very punitive on smaller-cap companies that do not meet performance expectations, so it is probably wiser to buy into a basket of these highly-volatile issues rather than buying individual stocks.
3. Third, I might suggest a higher allocation to growth stocks over value stocks. While much of the empirical historical data suggests that the value style of investing has outperformed growth over time, I believe that earnings growth is the single-best predictor of stock prices over time. Therefore, if investors are able to identify high-quality growth stocks (or identify professional managers adept at identifying these types of stocks) at reasonable valuations, these stocks will likely outperform the market.
4. Next, I would suggest increasing your allocation to international equities. I would caution, however, the many international and emerging economy stocks are quite volatile. Also, sharp increases in many international stocks in recent years have made it much more difficult to identify compelling values. And finally, understanding the different tax, accounting and regulatory laws in different countries can be quite a challenge. Therefore, as with small-cap stocks, I would suggest using an ETF or high-quality mutual fund to limit volatility when investing internationally. Also note that you get a large amount of exposure to international economies through investing in large-cap multinational companies with significant international operations.
5. And finally, many individual investors are increasing their allocation to relatively new investment products like hedge funds, venture capital funds, and private equity funds. However, many of these funds are simply not accessible to the

small investor due to regulatory restrictions designed to protect the little guy from losses. I would defer using these types of investment vehicles until you have more investing experience and your investment portfolio has grown to a relatively large size.

Small- and Midcap Growth Mutual Funds

- Fairholme. If you want to own Berkshire Hathaway—basically have Warren Buffett and his crew manage your money—you could purchase Fairholme, which has a sizable position in it plus some good stock pickers of its own handling the rest. It's a riskier proposition since Fairholme searches for special situations, but its track record and view regarding buying companies rather than stocks suits me.
- Legg Mason Opportunity.
- Dreyfus Founders Mid-Cap Growth.
- Fidelity Advisor Leveraged.
- Alger Small Cap and Mid Cap Growth.
- Any low-cost, mid- or multicap growth index fund that acceptably tracks the sector performance.

The Million-Dollar Stock Selection Strategy is just one tool that you need to successfully complete your Million-Dollar Mission. I've taken you through various stages in this process, and some of you may be ready to move on to the next step—managing your portfolio. If so, you may want to skip right to chapter 8. For those of you who'd like to see how all this works together, the next chapter revisits each of the essential steps by following some specific case studies.

CHAPTER SEVEN

Build It, Part Two

Analyzing Real-Life Investment Scenarios

In chapters 5 and 6, you got an education in some basic and advanced investing concepts. What follows is a practical application of those ideas to the specific cases of some people you've met previously in the book, and others whom you will be meeting for the first time. In analyzing these scenarios, we will be reviewing many of the concepts that make up the Farr Investment Technique. These case studies of typical thirty-five-, forty-five-, and fifty-five-year-olds are meant to give you a solid understanding of the process involved in creating your own personal financial plan for retirement. Obviously, your own situation may differ dramatically from the scenarios I present. However, the case studies should provide you with more tools to evaluate your unique situation and proactively resolve potential conflicts that may be many years out in the future.

We will start by reviewing each individual's balance sheet, budget, and retirement goals. Then I'll present a road map toward achieving the goals with the least amount of pain and sacrifice. Finally, in chapter 8—the next step of FIT—I'll cover the ongoing maintenance of your financial plan once you implement it.

I cannot stress enough that goals must be realistic, and they must be prioritized. These hypothetical case studies are meant to demonstrate that difficult choices and sacrifices are inevitable in the quest for financial independence. Relatively young investors in their thirties have the advantage of time, but even a long time horizon cannot work miracles. One of the most difficult aspects of my job is managing the expectations of my clients. Investing should not be viewed as a sprint toward riches but rather as a marathon ending in financial independence and security. Patience and perseverance are imperative. Now let's get into the details.

In each case, we will follow much the same process:

1. Establish where you are through determining your net worth.
2. Determine how aggressive you need to be based on net worth and your working budget.
3. Factor in your risk tolerance.
4. Run the numbers to see what you need to make the Million-Dollar Mission, establish returns expectations, and so forth.
5. Build an investment portfolio suitable for your age, net worth, risk tolerance, and needs.

Let's begin by taking a look at a Neo-Boomer.

The Thirty-Five-Year-Old Neo-Boomers

Henry Rollins is a thirty-five-year-old man living in the Washington, DC, suburbs. He is married to a woman named Lisa (also thirty-five) and has two children, ages one and three (Jeff and Alex). Henry and his family live in the house they purchased five years ago for $250,000. They put a $25,000 down payment on the house and acquired a thirty-year fixed-rate mortgage for the remaining $225,000. Henry currently makes $80,000 per year as an accountant for a large corporation. Lisa stopped working as a dental hygienist after the birth of their older child, Alex. Henry would prefer that Lisa not go back to work, but Lisa may decide to do so when the boys "are old enough to look out for themselves." Lisa's salary as a dental hygienist was $40,000 per year. She now gets her health insurance through her husband's company plan.

Establishing Net Worth

Henry and Lisa's major assets include their house, which is now worth $300,000, two cars, their 401(k) accounts, and a small amount of savings. One of the cars, a Honda Accord, was purchased in 1999 for cash. The second car is a Chevy Tahoe that Henry and Lisa bought after the birth of their second child in 2005. They owe $20,000 to the local bank for the Tahoe. Henry and Lisa have a combined $60,000 in mutual funds through company-sponsored 401(k) plans, and Henry currently contributes $500 per month to his 401(k) on an ongoing basis. Neither spouse expects to receive any pension benefits. The Rollinses also have cash savings totaling roughly $10,000 (a checking and a savings account, each containing $5,000). Lisa's father, now sixty years old, has promised the couple a $50,000 inheritance upon his passing. He is currently in relatively good health.

In terms of liabilities, the Rollinses have a $210,000 principal balance on their mortgage, the $20,000 car loan, and $1,000 in credit card debt. Henry has just finished paying off his college loans after fifteen years. The family has no other outstanding debt.

Their balance sheet shows that the Rollinses have $403,000 in assets, $231,000 in liabilities, and a net worth of $172,000. However, the couple is a little short on liquid assets right now, because Henry's income isn't currently high enough to enable any savings after accounting for expenses. The couple will need to run a tight ship over the next few years as Henry works toward advancement at his company. The good thing is that the family's mortgage payment will not increase even as Henry's income and all other expenses likely will. This is a benefit to using a thirty-year fixed-rate mortgage as opposed to an adjustable-rate mortgage. It is much easier to create a budget when your single biggest expense is known for certain.

Henry and Lisa's goals are relatively straightforward. Most important, they would like to fund their children's college education when the time comes. Although they have not started saving yet, they are confident that time is on their side. Second, the Rollinses would like to someday purchase a condominium on the Florida coast. This would serve as a second residence to be used by the

Table 7.1
THE ROLLINSES' BEGINNING NET WORTH

ASSETS	
Liquid Assets	
Cash & money markets	
Checking accounts	5,000
Savings accounts	5,000
Certificates of deposit	
Savings and Investments	
Stocks	
Bonds	
Mutual funds	
Options	
Annuities	
Other brokerage assets	
Cash value of life insurance	
401(k)/IRAs	60,000
Fixed Assets	
Primary residence	300,000
Other real estate	
Automobiles	23,000
Jewelry	
Furniture	10,000
Other assets	
TOTAL ASSETS	**403,000**
LIABILITIES	
Short-Term Debt	
Charge cards	1,000
Bank loans	

Other debt due in less than one year	
Long-Term Debt	
Mortgage	210,000
Home equity loan	
Automobile loans	20,000
Other loans	
TOTAL LIABILITIES	**231,000**
TOTAL NET WORTH (ASSETS LESS LIABILITIES)	**172,000**

whole extended family. And finally, they would like to add a deck and expand the kitchen at their primary residence. This final project would be undertaken only "as resources permit." Both Henry and Lisa (if Lisa should return to work) would like to be retired by the age of sixty-five.

Setting Returns Expectations

Having been an accountant for nearly ten years, Henry is relatively knowledgeable about the financial markets. Therefore, he knows roughly what to expect in terms of returns on the various asset classes. Recently, however, Henry has been hearing a lot about how some of his co-workers have earned huge sums of money by flipping condos in the local Washington, DC, market. These investors made small down payments on condominiums in construction and sold them before project completion for large gains. Henry wonders whether or not this type of investing could work for him.

Henry and Lisa's experience in stock investing has been limited to their 401(k) plans. During the stock market correction of 2000–2002, both became uneasy at losing significant portions of their accounts. Their accounts have since rebounded somewhat, but both believe they have been dealt a large setback in their long-term savings plans. Still, neither Henry nor Lisa stopped contributing to their 401(k)s at any time since starting their jobs. Henry believes he may be able to make up for lost time by getting involved in real estate.

Determining Risk Tolerance

From what we have learned about Henry, he has an above-average *ability* to take risk. He and Lisa are relatively young, and they have some critical goals they need to accomplish, such as funding their retirement and their kids' college education. While the size of their current savings isn't large, the couple has nearly enough income to meet their everyday expenses. They believe they are in good health and do not foresee any large, unusual expenses in the near term. However, the Rollinses don't currently have a sizable amount of liquid assets in case of emergency. A good rule of thumb is to always have three to six months' salary put aside in cash or cash equivalents (savings account, money market funds) in case of emergencies. An emergency might take the form of job loss or major medical expense. The couple's low level of liquid savings will limit their ability to take risk in the near term.

Henry's *willingness* to take risk, on the other hand, is probably only about average. His job as an accountant suggests he has a basic understanding of investing, but accountants are generally not known as big risk takers. He works for a large corporation with a bureaucratic structure, and he has never taken any entrepreneurial risk. Furthermore, both Henry and Lisa became somewhat uneasy as their 401(k) portfolios lost value during the market downturn of 2000–2002. Finally, Henry is a man of modest needs and tastes. He is satisfied with his standard of living and simply wants to maintain his lifestyle through retirement. Therefore, the preponderance of evidence suggests that the Rollinses would be more comfortable limiting the risk they assume.

Fortunately, Henry's goals are somewhat realistic given his appetite for risk. However, he feels he has fallen behind and wants to consider getting involved in real estate to bolster the lost returns on his 401(k). Should he consider real estate as an investment alternative?

Hopefully your answer was no. Henry and Lisa already own a house with an estimated value of $300,000. This is by far their largest asset, and it appears that neither Henry nor Lisa has the time required to actively manage investment properties. Their investing time horizon is very long, and all the historical data suggest that stocks have outperformed the other major asset classes—including real estate—consistently over long periods of time. Therefore, it is clear that the Rollinses will need a large allocation to stocks when creating their asset allocation.

Running the Numbers

Table 7.2 shows the first five years of the Rollinses' budget. I've assumed that Henry will get a 3.5 percent pay raise each year, and that all expenses (with the exception of the mortgage and car payments) will grow at the rate of inflation, which I assume to be 2.5 percent. I also assume that Henry's $500-per-month 401(k) contributions grow at the rate of his pay increases (3.5 percent). For this example, I have presented Henry's income net of both taxes and the 401(k) contributions.

The first thing you may notice is that Henry and Lisa are not making enough money to cover their expenses in the first year. The Adjusted Surplus/Deficit line item in table 7.2 shows a $418 deficit, assuming no contributions to the kids' education funds. In year two, however, the family begins running a surplus, enabling them to contribute $500 to a tax-advantaged 529 savings plan for college. Things get even easier by year five, when the couple is able to increase the 529 contributions to $3,500 and still be left with $926. I've assumed that each annual budget surplus (after education funding) is deposited into a taxable "surplus" account.

The Cumulative Values listed at the bottom of the table represent running balances for the family's various accounts. The education fund represents the tax-advantaged 529 accounts, the retirement fund is Henry's tax-advantaged 401(k) account, and the surplus represents a new taxable account that the family will open to enable them to invest their leftover income. In the first five years, I assume that these accounts will be 80 percent

Table 7.2
THE ROLLINSES' BUDGET—FIRST FIVE YEARS

	Year 1	Year 2	Year 3	Year 4	Year 5
INCOME					
Salary					
Husband (net)	60,120	62,224	64,402	66,656	68,989
Wife (net)	-	-	-	-	-
Interest/ dividends	150	150	150	150	150
Total Income	***60,270***	***62,374***	***64,552***	***66,806***	***69,139***
EXPENSES					
Mortgage	17,520	17,520	17,520	17,520	17,520
Utilities	5,300	5,433	5,568	5,708	5,850
Real estate taxes	1,800	1,845	1,891	1,938	1,987
Homeowner's Insurance	1,200	1,230	1,261	1,292	1,325
Home maintenance & repairs	2,000	2,050	2,101	2,154	2,208
Automobile loan	4,400	4,400	4,400	4,400	4,400
Auto insurance	2,700	2,768	2,837	2,908	2,980
Gas, maintenance, & repairs	2,600	2,665	2,732	2,800	2,870
Medical/dental	480	492	504	517	530
Food	7,800	7,995	8,195	8,400	8,610
Clothing	2,400	2,460	2,522	2,585	2,649
Entertainment	2,400	2,460	2,522	2,585	2,649
Activities	1,800	1,845	1,891	1,938	1,987

Vacations	3,000	3,075	3,152	3,231	3,311
Health insurance	2,400	2,460	2,522	2,585	2,649
Life insurance	288	295	303	310	318
Miscellaneous	2,600	2,665	2,732	2,800	2,870
Child care					
Total Expenses	***60,688***	***61,657***	***62,651***	***63,669***	***64,713***
SURPLUS/ (DEFICIT)	**(418)**	**717**	**1,901**	**3,137**	**4,426**
Education funding		(500)	(1,500)	(2,500)	(3,500)
Vacation home					
Inheritance					
ADJUSTED SURPLUS/ (DEFICIT)	**(418)**	**217**	**401**	**637**	**926**
Retirement funding (netted out of income)	6,000	6,210	6,427	6,652	6,885
CUMULATIVE VALUES					
Education fund	-	500	2,039	4,695	8,557
Retirement fund	70,620	82,268	95,030	108,999	124,277
Surplus	(418)	(233)	150	782	1,683
STOCK ALLOCATION					
College fund	80.0%	80.0%	80.0%	80.0%	80.0%
Retirement fund	80.0%	80.0%	80.0%	80.0%	80.0%
Surplus	80.0%	80.0%	80.0%	80.0%	80.0%

invested in stocks earning an 8.5 percent return. The balance is in bonds earning 4.5 percent. I can justify the high allocation to stocks because the time horizon is long and the couple must earn competitive returns to fund the high cost of tuition. By the end of year five, Henry and Lisa have accumulated more than $134,517 in savings! This does not include their illiquid assets (house, cars, and furniture).

After the first five years, I've gradually reduced the stock allocation so that at retirement, they will have 50 percent of the retirement account in stocks and 60 percent of the surplus account in stocks. The education fund will have been used to fund college expenses for their boys. I assume that Henry and Lisa buy the Florida condo in twenty-one years, the year after their younger child graduates from college. The cost of the condo is $328,000 (adjusted for inflation), and the couple will use part of their surplus account for a 20 percent down payment. The balance of the cost will be funded through another mortgage. Note that at this point (year twenty-one), the couple have only four years remaining on their primary residence mortgage. I've also assumed that Lisa's father passed away in year fifteen, leaving them $50,000.

Figure 7.1

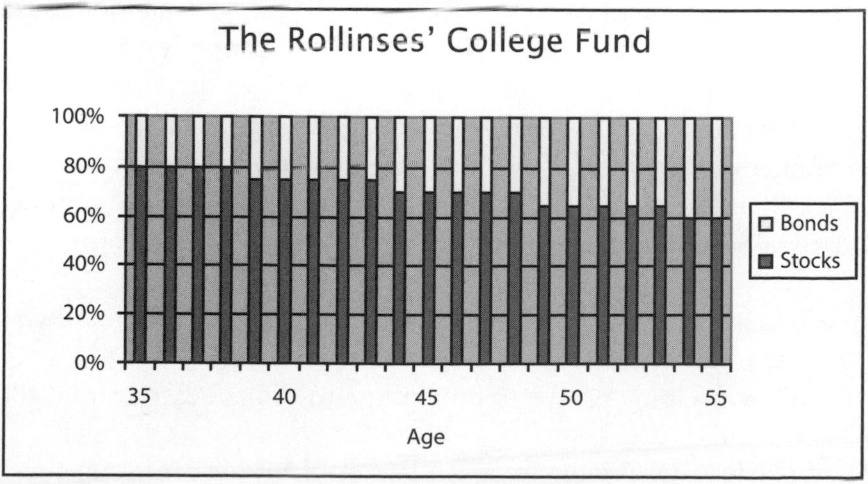

The Rollinses' College Fund

Figure 7.2

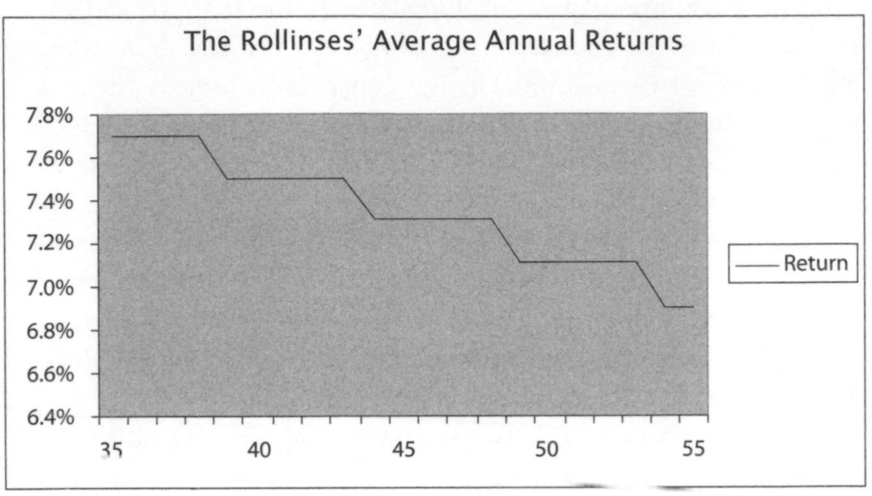

If we take this model out thirty years to the time of retirement, we can see that the Rollinses will be able to successfully fund 100 percent of their children's education at a four-year public university (assuming 6 percent growth in average costs, as reported in "Trends in College Pricing 2005" by the College Board, a nonprofit association of forty-five hundred schools, colleges, and universities). The cost of attending a four-year public university increases from $12,127 per year today to $27,418 in year fifteen and $36,691 in year twenty. Figure 7.1 shows the asset allocation, figure 7.2 the average annual return for each year given the selected mix of stocks and bonds, and table 7.3 the cash flows for their children's education fund.

The last five years of the couple's budget are detailed in table 7.4. This time period represents the years immediately prior to retirement when Henry and Lisa are ages sixty to sixty-five. As you will notice, by the time of retirement the Rollinses are running nearly a $54,000-per-year surplus, thanks to the following:

- Their income grew faster than their expenses, which grew at the inflation rate.
- They no longer have to contribute to the education fund for the kids.
- The kids are no longer dependent on them for living expenses.

Table 7.3
THE ROLLINSES' EDUCATION FUND CASH FLOW

Year	Amount Invested (end of each year)	Returns	Alex's Tuition	Jeff's Tuition	Balance
1	-	-			-
2	500	-			500
3	1,500	39			2,039
4	2,500	157			4,695
5	3,500	362			8,557
6	4,500	642			13,699
7	5,500	1,027			20,226
8	6,500	1,517			28,243
9	7,500	2,118			37,861
10	8,500	2,840			49,201
11	9,500	3,592			62,293
12	12,000	4,547			78,840
13	14,000	5,755			98,595
14	15,000	7,197			120,793
15	40,000	8,818	(27,418)		142,193
16	11,000	10,380	(29,063)		134,510
17	11,000	9,550	(30,807)	(30,807)	93,446
18	11,000	6,635	(32,655)	(32,655)	45,770
19	11,000	3,250		(34,615)	25,406
20	9,482	1,804		(36,691)	(0)

- Because the couple used fixed-rate loans, their mortgage and auto payments did not increase over time.

These benefits are partially offset by a higher mortgage payment on their condo, which replaced the mortgage on their primary residence (now paid off in full).

Table 7.4
THE ROLLINSES' BUDGET—FINAL FIVE YEARS

	Year 26	Year 27	Year 28	Year 29	Year 30
INCOME					
Salary					
Husband (net)	142,078	147,051	152,198	157,525	163,038
Wife (net)	-	-	-	-	-
Interest/ dividends	150	150	150	150	150
Total Income	***142,228***	***147,201***	***152,348***	***157,675***	***163,188***
EXPENSES					
Mortgage	28,278	28,278	28,278	28,278	28,278
Utilities	14,739	15,107	15,485	15,872	16,269
Real estate taxes	7,045	7,221	7,402	7,587	7,776
Homeowner's insurance	2,225	2,280	2,337	2,396	2,456
Home maintenance & repairs	3,708	3,801	3,896	3,993	4,093
Automobile loan	4,400	4,400	4,400	4,400	4,400
Auto insurance	5,006	5,131	5,259	5,391	5,525
Gas, maintenance, & repairs	4,820	4,941	5,064	5,191	5,321
Medical/dental	890	912	935	958	982
Food	8,676	8,893	9,116	9,344	9,577
Clothing	2,670	2,736	2,805	2,875	2,947
Entertainment	2,670	2,736	2,805	2,875	2,947
Activities	3,337	3,421	3,506	3,594	3,684

Vacations	5,562	5,701	5,843	5,989	6,139
Health insurance	2,670	2,736	2,805	2,875	2,947
Life insurance	534	547	561	575	589
Miscellaneous	4,820	4,941	5,064	5,191	5,321
Child care					
Total Expenses	***102,049***	***103,784***	***105,561***	***107,383***	***109,251***
SURPLUS/ (DEFICIT)	**40,179**	**43,417**	**46,787**	**50,291**	**53,937**
Education funding					
Vacation home					
Inheritance					
ADJUSTED SURPLUS/ (DEFICIT)	**40,179**	**43,417**	**46,787**	**50,291**	**53,937**
Retirement funding (netted out of income)	14,179	14,676	15,189	15,721	16,271
CUMULATIVE VALUES					
Education fund					
Retirement fund	959,519	1,038,482	1,123,250	1,214,229	1,311,853
Surplus	144,787	174,597	204,975	236,003	267,761
STOCK ALLOCATION					
College fund					
Retirement fund	55.0%	55.0%	55.0%	55.0%	50.0%
Surplus	60.0%	60.0%	60.0%	60.0%	60.0%

Building an Investment Portfolio

The budget here projects that at the time of retirement, the Rollinses will have $1.3 million in their 401(k) account and $268,000 in their taxable securities account. Figure 7.3 displays the asset allocation used for the 401(k) account. (Note that I recommend the typical thirty-five-year-old allocate at least 90 percent, if not 100 percent, to stocks given the thirty-year time horizon. Given the Rollinses' desire to limit risk to some degree, I started with an 80:20 stock-to-bond allocation and gradually brought this to 50:50 just before retirement.)

In addition, the Rollinses will own their primary residence outright and will have funded their children's education. Lisa did not go back to work, and they were able to purchase a condominium in Florida. Seems like utopia, right? Not so fast.

Our model tells us that Henry and Lisa still owe $130,000 on the condo mortgage, requiring them to make annual payments of more than $28,000. If they were to pay off the mortgage on their second home, they would be left with just $1.45 million in liquid investments. If they invest 50 percent of this in stock and 50 per-

Figure 7.3

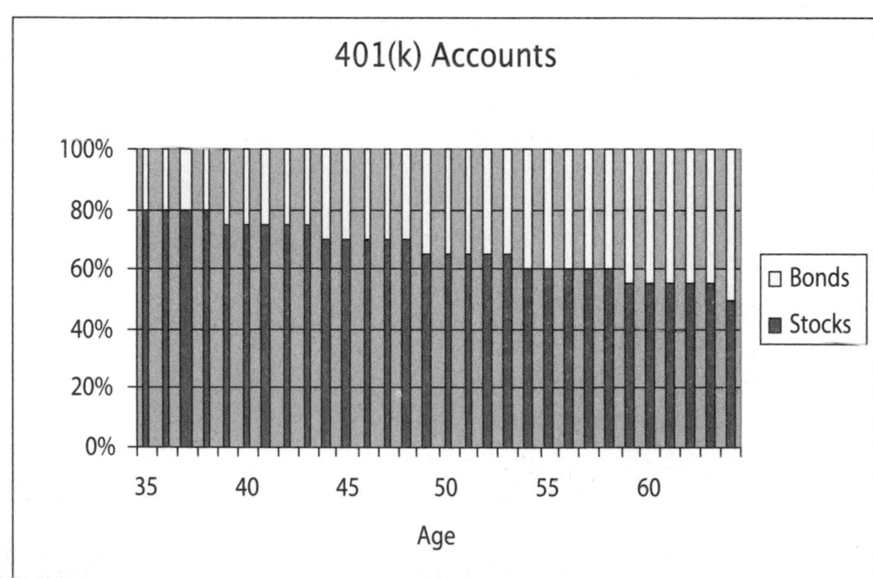

cent in cash (a conservative mix given their now advanced age), they can produce an estimated annual income of about $94,000 before taxes—significantly less than half of their gross income in the year immediately preceding retirement. According to the 2006 *Fortune* magazine retirement guide, "The conventional wisdom is that you'll typically need 70% to 80% of your working income" for retirement. *Fortune* also notes that "According to Fidelity's 2006 Retirement Index, the typical American worker retiring today without employer health coverage will probably need $200,000 for expenses not covered by Medicare throughout retirement." Therefore, the "medical/dental" expense line item in the budget may be understated.

Given these considerations, it looks like the Rollinses will need to make some choices. I recommend that Lisa consider going back to work, at least part time. Alternatively, they could postpone their condo purchase, pick something a little more modest (less expensive), or rent out the condo for half the year. Any of these options could increase their chances for financial security at retirement. In addition, they may find they have enough money to budget in the kitchen addition and new deck they have always wanted. What is clear is that given their goals, retirement security is no slam dunk.

You may have noticed that I did not give the family credit for Social Security benefits. I recommend you take this conservative approach as well. The current state of the Social Security program suggests that either younger workers will never receive benefits, or income tax rates will rise significantly to fund any benefits they do get. This model leaves the tax rates relatively stable and assumes no Social Security benefits. Also, the couple will own their primary residence outright, which is a significant positive. Under dire circumstances, the Rollinses could always downsize, sell their house and rent an apartment, or acquire a reverse mortgage. These options would be last resorts. I do not recommend that you consider your primary residence as an income-producing asset for retirement.

Table 7.5 shows the Rollinses' balance sheet at the time of retirement, assuming none of my recommendations are implemented. Assets have swelled to over $2.5 million while liabilities have

Table 7.5
THE ROLLINSES' PROJECTED NET WORTH AT RETIREMENT

ASSETS	
Liquid Assets	
Cash & money markets	
Checking accounts	5,000
Savings accounts	5,000
Certificates of deposit	
Savings and Investments	
Stocks	133,880
Bonds	133,880
Mutual funds	
Options	
Annuities	
Other brokerage assets	
Cash value of life insurance	
401(k)/IRAs	1,311,853
Fixed Assets	
Primary residence	524,392
Other real estate	409,627
Automobiles	23,000
Jewelry	
Furniture	20,000
Other assets	
TOTAL ASSETS	**2,566,633**
LIABILITIES	
Short-Term Debt	
Charge cards	
Bank loans	

Other debt due in less than one year	
Long-Term Debt	
Mortgage	130,000
Home equity loan	
Automobile loans	20,000
Other loans	
TOTAL LIABILITIES	**150,000**
TOTAL NET WORTH (ASSETS LESS LIABILITIES)	**2,416,633**

declined to just $150,000, producing a net worth of more than $2.4 million. Seems like a lot, doesn't it? Remember, however, that in today's dollars (adjusting for the 2.5 percent rate of inflation), that net worth amounts to just $1.15 million—only slightly more than $1 million! Without the mortgage on the Florida condo (costing them more than $28,000 per year), the couple may be able to get by on their savings. As it stands now, though, they will be deficit-spending the very first year after Henry's retirement. After several years their savings will dwindle, and they will find themselves in trouble.

$$\frac{\text{net worth}}{(1 + \text{inflation rate})^{\text{\# of years until retirement}}} = \frac{\$2,416,633}{(1 + 2.5\%)^{30}} = \$1,151,504$$

I caution you not to get overly confident when projecting your retirement savings. A net worth of more than $2.4 million does indeed seem like a lot, but it isn't nearly as much when you adjust for thirty years' worth of inflation. Again, time is on your side if you are young, but time also erodes purchasing power. Make the difficult choices and stick to your plan.

Freewheeling Ellen: A Single Neo-Boomer

Ellen Frasier is what I'd call an "Easy Rider." At the age of thirty-five, she is already thinking about her retirement. She's been in the workforce for seven years after receiving an MBA from Georgetown University. She worked for two years hawking residential real estate in New York City after getting her undergraduate degree. She made enough to get by—rent, cab fares, clothes, and nightlife—but nothing else.

Fortunately for Ellen, her parents paid for her undergraduate and graduate education. Having no student loans enabled her to buy a two-bedroom town house in Vienna, Virginia, three years ago for $237,500. She put 20 percent down on a thirty-year fixed mortgage at 6 percent. Based on principal and interest only, she would be paying $1,139.15 a month, but taxes in Vienna added approximately another $200.00, bringing her total to $1,380.65. That town house is now worth close to $325,000, but the bubble may be about to burst.

She lives well for a woman who started at $60,000 and now earns $75,000 at her midsize engineering firm.

Ellen's been a smart but not-so-smart financial planner for herself. From day one of her employment, she contributed 10 percent to her 401(k) plan, and her firm matched the first 7 percent of that. She now has $35,000 in her account, a tidy $1,000 for every year of her life.

Ellen has a friend in real estate who gave her a fair and reasonable assessment of the amount of equity she has built up in her town house, as well as its present market value. Ellen's like a lot of Americans. She's comfortable enough with her income, her 401(k), and her real estate holdings to feel that she can take on additional debt.

Ellen fancies herself a bit of an iconoclast, so instead of the usual car purchase, she went for Swedish and sunshine, buying a Saab 9-3 Aero Convertible. After tax, title, license, and options, the car cost was a little more than $45,000. She put down 20 percent and financed the balance for forty-eight months at 7.19 percent, giving her a monthly payment of $895.

She also had to furnish her town house, and the Dumpster diving in Vienna offers slim pickings, so she ordered the Pottery Barn catalog—not the glossy booklet, but the entire contents. Over the course of the last three years, she racked up $25,000 in credit card debt at a hefty 14 percent rate. She's been vigilant about paying down that debt, and at present stands at $15,000 owed to the Vizier of Visa.

Ellen came to see me because her father has just recently retired, sold her childhood home, and taken her mother to live in North Carolina. Suddenly, the reality of her situation and prospects for the future have hit home. She's single, she's thirty-five, and while she's been in a steady relationship for the last nine months, she fears he may be a commitment-phobe…and she's glad, even though the prospect of getting out there again doesn't thrill.

Ellen filled out the Simple Budget Worksheet I gave her (see page 72) and filled out her Retirement Wish List (see page 46). Knowing what she has, what she needs, and how much time she has left to her ideal retirement age (thirty years), I was able to devise a plan for her.

Table 7.6
ELLEN FRASIER'S SIMPLE BUDGET WORKSHEET

	Actual	Budget	First Review
INCOME:			
Take-home salary/ wages/commissions/ bonus	$4,187.50		
Interest/dividends			
Other income			
Total Income:	***$4,187.50***		
EXPENSES:			
Savings			
Rent/mortgage	$1,380.65		
Utilities (gas, electric, phone, water, cable, garbage)	$300.00		

Maintenance (dry cleaning, etc.)	$60.00		
Automobile (gas, etc.)	$90.00		
Clothing	$200.00		
Medical/dental	$45.00		
Entertainment	$350.00		
Food	$225.00		
Child-related			
Vacations			
Gifts/charity			
Insurance	$120.00		
Loan payments	$895.00		
Credit card payments	$200.00		
Miscellaneous	$150.00		
Other: List			
Total Expenses	***$4,015.65***		
CASH SURPLUS (DEFICIT)	**$171.85**		

Besides the equity in her home and the 401(k) account, Ellen has no real retirement savings. Like many her age, Ellen amassed considerable credit card debt in the early part of her career when her income was relatively low. Now making $75,000 per year, she is able to live within her means and even pay down some of the credit card debt each month.

Where She Wants to Go

Ellen hopes to be able to pay off her credit card debt and begin making regular contributions to a Roth IRA and after-tax savings account to reach a net worth of $1 million by the time she retires at age sixty-five.

How She Gets There

Priority one should be for Ellen to eliminate her credit card balances as soon as possible. She would effectively be earning 14 percent per year on every dollar of credit card debt she pays off. Next, she should maximize her 401(k) contribution at work ($15,000 a year in 2006). Then she should make regular contributions to a Roth IRA (up to $4,000 a year), as well as an after-tax savings account.

After her initial consultation with me, Ellen realized that her car payments were too high and were causing her monthly cash flow to fall short of her goals. Although she was living within her means, she was not able to start saving other than through her 401(k). After some soul searching, Ellen decided to bite the bullet: She sold her convertible and bought a used 2003 Honda Accord. This allowed her to cut her monthly car payment by more than half, to $405 a month.

Next, after comparing interest rates, she took out a home equity loan (at 7 percent) and used it to pay off all her outstanding credit card debt. This reduced her monthly interest by 50 percent and also allowed the interest to be tax deductible. She was able to keep her monthly payments below the $200 she'd been spending on credit cards as well as realizing the tax advantage.

Once the home equity loan is paid off, Ellen can continue to pay that same monthly amount into her taxable investment portfolio account. Later, as this investment account grows, I recommend that she invest the cash using the following asset allocation—which is suitable for many single thirty-five-year-olds.

Asset Allocation

Following Farr's Rules on asset allocation, Ellen should have zero invested in bonds until at least she reaches age fifty. This allocation allows for greater risk, but also greater returns, and utilizes Ellen's thirty-year investment time horizon (actually much longer, because she plans to continue investing well into retirement).

There are literally thousands of suitable equity investments available, and I could spend days analyzing which stocks and/or mutual funds Ellen should purchase with the money she has freed up to invest. As I stated previously—and I'll explain this further—Ellen might be best suited, at least at the start of her investment process, to contribute monthly to a low-cost index stock fund.

In Summary

- Ellen needed to reduce her monthly car payment.
- Ellen needed to eliminate her credit card debt.
- Ellen needed to begin contributing the maximum to her 401(k) plan.
- Ellen needed to begin contributing to a Roth IRA plan.*
- Ellen needed to invest the money she saved from her reduced car payment and the larger tax refund she realized from her home equity loan into a low-cost, no-load index fund.

The Forty-Five-Year-Old Tail End Boomers

Rick and Sally Taylor—whom we met in chapter 4—are both forty-five years old. They have been married for twenty years. Rick makes $44,000 per year as an administrator in the parks and recreation department, while Sally earns $42,000 per year as a branch manager for a small, locally owned bank. They have three children, ages sixteen, fifteen, and eleven. Two of the kids have braces; the third does not appear to need them. They have lived in the same house for the past seventeen years in Sarasota, Florida. A low interest-rate environment allowed them to refinance their previous mortgage loan in 2003 using a fifteen-year fixed-rate loan. They also pulled some cash out during refinancing, using some $28,000 to pay off their auto loans and $17,000 to add hurricane shutters to the house. Both Rick and Sally currently contribute 5 percent of their gross pay to their respective 401(k) plans.

*As noted earlier, the Roth IRA plan already has the income tax deducted from it. When you retire, you will not have to pay any tax on the money you withdraw from the account. Farr's Rule: Pay tax while you're still earning income, not after you've stopped working.

Establishing Net Worth

The Taylors' assets consist of the house (now worth $240,000); combined 401(k) holdings of $154,000 (50 percent in bond mutual funds, 50 percent in stock mutual funds); their two cars, worth an estimated $25,000; furniture worth an estimated $12,000; a separate taxable account with $15,000 in mutual funds (50 percent bonds, 50 percent stocks); and $15,000 in savings ($3,000 in checking and $12,000 in savings). Their only liability is their mortgage loan. They have paid off their auto loans, and they pay off their credit card bills each month. The remaining balance on the mortgage loan is $126,000.

The Taylors' main goal is to retire at age sixty. They would like to help with their kids' college as well, but Rick feels strongly that their children will be much better served if they pay their own tuition and "learn the value of a buck." As a compromise, Rick and Sally have decided to contribute their $15,000 in mutual funds to three Section 529 accounts—$5,000 for each child. Any college expenses beyond that will have to be borne by their kids. For our purposes, I've omitted the $15,000 in mutual funds from table 7.7, the beginning balance sheet.

After subtracting out the 529 contributions for the kids, the Taylors have a net worth of $320,000. However, their 529 contributions have left them a little light in liquidity. Their only liquid emergency resource, the $15,000 in bank deposits, represents just 15 percent of their combined income. I'd like to see that build to three to six months' worth.

Table 7.7
THE TAYLORS' BEGINNING NET WORTH

ASSETS	
Liquid Assets	
Cash & money markets	
Checking accounts	3,000
Savings accounts	12,000
Certificates of deposit	

Savings and Investments	
Stocks	
Bonds	
Mutual funds	
Options	
Annuities	
Other brokerage assets	
Cash value of life insurance	
401(k)/IRAs	154,000
Fixed Assets	
Primary residence	240,000
Other real estate	
Automobiles	25,000
Jewelry	
Furniture	12,000
Other assets	
TOTAL ASSETS	**446,000**
LIABILITIES	
Short-Term Debt	
Charge cards	
Bank loans	
Other debt due in less than one year	
Long-Term Debt	
Mortgage	126,000
Home equity loan	
Automobile loans	
Other loans	
TOTAL LIABILITIES	**126,000**
TOTAL NET WORTH (ASSETS LESS LIABILITIES)	**320,000**

Setting Returns Expectations

As a bank branch manager, Sally has a solid understanding of the capital markets. She also knows that real estate values are currently too high to achieve competitive risk-adjusted returns without speculating on further price appreciation. She is more optimistic with regard to stocks, especially given the low rates currently offered on savings and money market accounts. Rick, on the other hand, is still reeling over the losses sustained in his 401(k) account during the stock market correction. He continues to argue that "stocks are too risky," and that the couple should continue to limit their stock allocation to 50 percent in their retirement accounts. The balance, he argues, should be put in low-risk bonds or money market funds.

Both Taylors believe that their current annual 401(k) contributions are reasonable given their current expenses. Although far from the maximum, their modest 5 percent contributions do allow them to have a little savings left over after all their expenses are paid each year. In the past, they deposited these into a savings account at Sally's bank.

Determining Risk Tolerance

Rick and Sally have above-average *ability* to take risk. Their time horizon is long (fifteen years minimum to retirement), their goals are critical (funding retirement), and their current savings are not insignificant. They have sufficient income to cover their expenses, but they should ideally build their liquid rainy-day fund to a more acceptable level. Also, their medical/dental expenses are expected to remain a bit high given that two of their children need braces.

Rick and Sally seem to be divided on their *willingness* to take risk. Rick is still shell-shocked by the stock market correction, and he is distrustful of corporate management teams in the wake of the Enron and WorldCom scandals. Sally, on the other hand, recognizes through her experience in advising bank customers that stocks are the best-performing major asset class over long periods of time. She also believes that crackdowns and regulation changes are transforming the landscape of corporate governance for the better. She has firsthand experience in working with small-business owners and recognizes that the overwhelming majority of corporate executives are honest and scrupulous.

Both Rick and Sally had modest upbringings. Rick's parents were both high school teachers earning modest incomes throughout their lives. Sally's parents were immigrants from Ireland, and they built their own landscaping business from the ground up. Although Sally's parents are now considered financially secure, neither Sally nor Rick expects to receive any windfall inheritance.

I'm convinced that Rick should defer to Sally when determining their willingness to take risk. Sally has firsthand knowledge of the investment process, has experienced entrepreneurial risk taking through her parents, and has a justified faith in the corporate governance process. Therefore, I believe the Taylors' ability and willingness to take risk are both above average. Figure 7.4 shows the allocation I recommend for their retirement assets. The couple's tolerance for risk allows for a fairly aggressive allocation—80 percent stocks until age fifty-five. Entering retirement, I think a 60:40 ratio of stocks to bonds is both appropriate and necessary to accomplish their goals.

We can immediately identify two issues that may lead to trouble for the Taylors down the road. First, they are not taking full ad-

Figure 7.4

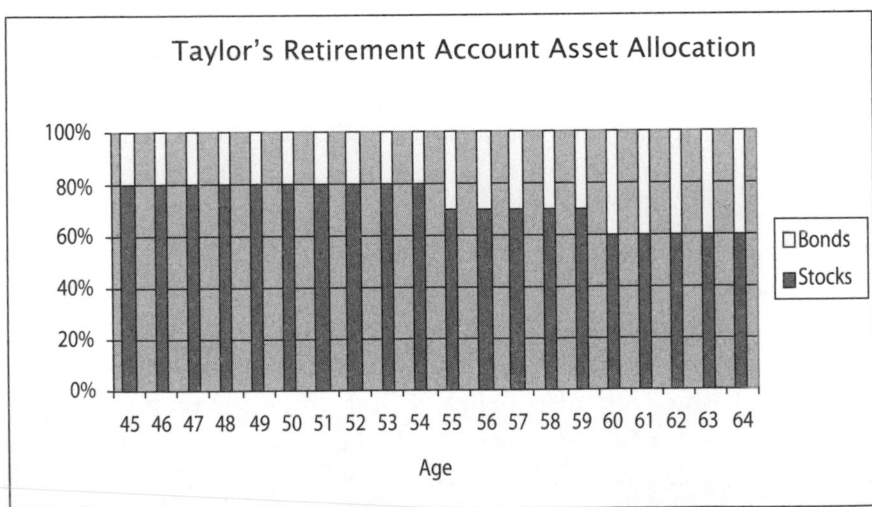

vantage of the tax benefits available to them. They contribute only 5 percent of their gross pay to their 401(k) plans, totaling less than $5,000 per year combined. Each of them is allowed to contribute pretax income up to $15,000. This money goes into the accounts on a pretax basis. Furthermore, the capital gains, dividend, and interest income earned on these accounts is deferred until you begin drawing on the account at retirement, allowing your account to compound at a much faster rate than it otherwise would.

The second problem is the Taylors' asset allocation in their 401(k) accounts. Given that Rick and Sally still have a minimum of fifteen years until retirement, they can afford to put a higher percentage into stocks than 50 percent. In chapter 6, I covered the historical returns on stocks relative to bonds. The Taylors will want to take advantage of these higher returns if they hope to hit their investment goals. Given that they cannot draw on their 401(k)s for another fifteen years without a 10 percent tax penalty anyway, why not earn higher returns?

Tables 7.8 and 7.9 demonstrate the difference that increasing 401(k) contributions and stock allocations can do for the Taylors. Table 7.8 shows the 401(k) account performance assuming 5 percent annual contributions and a 50 percent stock allocation; table 7.9 assumes 10 percent annual contributions and an 80 percent stock allocation (declining to 60 percent in year fifteen). Assume that stocks earn an annual return of 8.5 percent and bonds earn 4.5 percent. The latter approach results in almost $350,000 in additional account value by the age of sixty-five.

In creating a budget model, I assumed that the Taylors would take my advice and increase their 401(k) contributions to 10 percent of gross pay while simultaneously increasing their stock allocation to 80 percent. Table 7.10 shows the final five years of the model. It illustrates that working until age sixty (year fifteen) will result in less than $1 million in liquid assets. If, however, Rick and Sally continue to work to sixty-five and let their 401(k)s continue to accumulate, they will have $1.65 million at retirement. The value of $1.65 million in today's dollars is slightly over $1 million. The income they can produce from their $1.65 million will be slightly less than 70 percent of the income they were earning in the year prior to retirement. They should be in good shape.

Table 7.8
THE TAYLORS' 401(K)S WITH 5 PERCENT ANNUAL CONTRIBUTION AND 50 PERCENT STOCK ALLOCATION

Age	Balance	Return Percent	Return Amount	5% Contribution	New Balance	Today's Dollars
46	154,000	6.5%	10,010	4,300	168,310	168,310
47	168,310	6.5%	10,940	4,429	183,679	179,199
48	183,679	6.5%	11,939	4,562	200,180	190,535
49	200,180	6.5%	13,012	4,699	217,891	202,333
50	217,891	6.5%	14,163	4,840	236,894	214,614
51	236,894	6.5%	15,398	4,985	257,277	227,395
52	257,277	6.5%	16,723	5,134	279,134	240,696
53	279,134	6.5%	18,144	5,288	302,566	254,538
54	302,566	6.5%	19,667	5,447	327,680	268,942
55	327,680	6.5%	21,299	5,611	354,590	283,930
56	354,590	6.5%	23,048	5,779	383,417	299,525
57	383,417	6.5%	24,922	5,952	414,292	315,750
58	414,292	6.5%	26,929	6,131	447,352	332,631
59	447,352	6.5%	29,078	6,315	482,744	350,192
60	482,744	6.5%	31,378	6,504	**520,627**	368,462
61	520,627	6.5%	33,841	6,699	561,167	387,466
62	561,167	6.5%	36,476	6,900	604,543	407,235
63	604,543	6.5%	39,295	7,107	650,946	427,798
64	650,946	6.5%	42,311	7,320	700,577	449,186
65	700,577	6.5%	45,538	7,540	**753,655**	471,432

Table 7.9

THE TAYLORS' 401(K)S WITH 10 PERCENT ANNUAL CONTRIBUTION AND 80 PERCENT STOCK ALLOCATION

Age	Balance	Return Percent	Return Amount	10% Contribution	New Balance	Today's Dollars
46	154,000	7.7%	11,858	8,600	174,458	174,458
47	174,458	7.7%	13,433	8,858	196,749	191,951
48	196,749	7.7%	15,150	9,124	221,023	210,373
49	221,023	7.7%	17,019	9,397	247,439	229,772
50	247,439	7.7%	19,053	9,679	276,172	250,198
51	276,172	7.7%	21,265	9,970	307,407	271,703
52	307,407	7.7%	23,670	10,269	341,346	294,341
53	341,346	7.7%	26,284	10,577	378,206	318,172
54	378,206	7.7%	29,122	10,894	418,223	343,255
55	418,223	7.7%	32,203	11,221	461,647	369,654
56	461,647	7.7%	35,547	11,558	508,751	397,436
57	508,751	7.3%	37,139	11,904	557,795	425,120
58	557,795	7.3%	40,719	12,262	610,775	454,146
59	610,775	7.3%	44,587	12,629	667,991	484,575
60	667,991	7.3%	48,763	13,008	**729,763**	516,473
61	729,763	7.3%	53,273	13,399	796,435	549,911
62	796,435	6.9%	54,954	13,800	865,189	582,813
63	865,189	6.9%	59,698	14,214	939,102	617,173
64	939,102	6.9%	64,798	14,641	1,018,541	653,054
65	1,018,541	6.9%	70,279	15,080	**1,103,900**	690,520

Table 7.10
THE TAYLORS' BUDGET—FINAL FIVE YEARS

	Year 16	Year 17	Year 18	Year 19	Year 20
INCOME					
Salary					
Husband (net)	57,343	59,063	60,835	62,660	64,540
Wife (net)	60,073	61,876	63,732	65,644	67,613
Less 401(k) Contribution	(13,399)	(13,800)	(14,214)	(14,641)	(15,080)
Interest/ dividends	800	800	800	800	800
Total Income	***104,818***	***107,938***	***111,152***	***114,463***	***117,873***
EXPENSES					
Mortgage					
Utilities	7,560	7,749	7,943	8,141	8,345
Real estate taxes	7,821	8,016	8,217	8,422	8,633
Homeowner's insurance	6,517	6,680	6,847	7,018	7,194
Home maintenance & repairs	2,897	2,969	3,043	3,119	3,197
Automobile loan	3,600	3,600	3,600	3,600	3,600
Auto insurance	4,779	4,899	5,021	5,147	5,276
Gas, maintenance, & repairs	2,897	2,969	3,043	3,119	3,197
Medical/dental	3,476	3,563	3,652	3,743	3,837
Food	7,531	7,719	7,912	8,110	8,313
Clothing	1,738	1,781	1,826	1,872	1,918

Entertainment	2,086	2,138	2,191	2,246	2,302
Activities	2,607	2,672	2,739	2,807	2,878
Vacations	5,793	5,938	6,086	6,239	6,395
Health insurance	3,476	3,563	3,652	3,743	3,837
Life insurance	2,259	2,316	2,374	2,433	2,494
Miscellaneous	3,766	3,860	3,956	4,055	4,156
Child care					
Total Expenses	***68,802***	***70,432***	***72,103***	***73,816***	***75,571***
SURPLUS/ (DEFICIT)	**36,015**	**37,506**	**39,049**	**40,647**	**42,302**
Education funding					
Vacation home					
Inheritance					
ADJUSTED SURPLUS/ (DEFICIT)	**36,015**	**37,506**	**39,049**	**40,647**	**42,302**
Retirement funding (netted out of income)	13,399	13,800	14,214	14,641	15,080
CUMULATIVE VALUES					
Education fund					
Retirement fund	796,432	865,187	939,099	1,018,538	1,103,897
Surplus	295,084	350,281	410,300	475,482	546,190
STOCK ALLOCATION					
College fund					
Retirement fund	60.0%	60.0%	60.0%	60.0%	60.0%
Surplus	50.0%	50.0%	50.0%	50.0%	50.0%

If the Taylors Work Five More Years

The couple's balance sheet at age sixty-five (year twenty) will also look much better if they decide to work an additional five years. They will have no debt, and their assets will have increased to $2.1 million. The value of their net worth in today's dollars will be nearly $1.3 million.

Table 7.11
THE TAYLORS' PROJECTED NET WORTH AT RETIREMENT (AGE SIXTY-FIVE)

ASSETS	
Liquid Assets	
Cash & money markets	
Checking accounts	3,000
Savings accounts	21,673
Certificates of deposit	
Savings and Investments	
Stocks	273,095
Bonds	273,095
Mutual funds	
Options	
Annuities	
Other brokerage assets	
Cash value of life insurance	
401(k)/IRAs	1,103,897
Fixed Assets	
Primary residence	393,268
Other real estate	
Automobiles	25,000
Jewelry	

Furniture	12,000
Other assets	
TOTAL ASSETS	**2,105,028**
LIABILITIES	
Short-Term Debt	
Charge cards	
Bank loans	
Other debt due in less than one year	
Long-Term Debt	
Mortgage	
Home equity loan	
Automobile loans	
Other loans	
TOTAL LIABILITIES	
TOTAL NET WORTH (ASSETS LESS LIABILITIES)	**2,105,028**

The Fifty-Five-Year-Old Core Boomers

Jim and Nancy Anderson are both fifty-five-year-old lawyers. Jim makes $210,000 per year as a partner at a large and reputable corporate law firm. Nancy works for a nonprofit organization and makes $85,000 per year. The couple has four children, ages thirty-two, thirty, twenty-nine, and twenty-one. With the help of scholarships, Jim and Nancy paid for all of them to attend private universities. They are all out of school now and completely self-sufficient.

Establishing Net Worth

Jim and Nancy purchased their primary residence in Atlanta, Georgia, ten years ago for $750,000. It is now worth $1.1

million. They refinanced the house earlier this year with a fifteen-year fixed-rate loan for $529,000 at 6.25 percent. They also bought a house on the beach near Savannah fifteen years ago for $300,000. That house is now worth $500,000 and has been paid off in full. They do not plan on selling either house before or during retirement.

The couple's beginning balance sheet is presented in table 7.12. Calculating their assets minus their liabilities yields a current net worth of nearly $2.1 million. This seems like a lot, but as we shall discover, the Andersons have a very expensive lifestyle. Their goals are simply to be able to maintain this same extravagant lifestyle throughout retirement, which they plan for at age sixty-five. They would also like to leave some money to their children and the local church, if possible.

Setting Returns Expectations

The Andersons have been trying to "keep up with the Joneses" for several years now. They've never worried much about money, because they've always earned good livings. They buy what they need and want, and they assume that their current savings are enough to fund their retirement. However, they have never really sat down and forecast their retirement needs in any detail.

Jim has been managing their nontaxable stock account on his own for the past several years. He frequently trades in and out of stocks, often relying on tips from friends rather than his own research. He usually gets involved with whatever is hot at the time, and he places little if any emphasis on valuation when making investment decisions. He was heavily invested in technology stocks when the NASDAQ bubble popped, and now he favors commodity stocks. He has been completely convinced by recent articles discussing the insatiable demand for basic materials by huge emerging economies such as China and India. Roughly half of his portfolio is currently invested in oil stocks.

Jim has no idea how the portfolio has performed over time either on an absolute basis or relative to the market. He does know, however, that they "took a bath" as a result of the NASDAQ market correction a few years ago. He believes their account is still

Table 7.12
THE ANDERSONS' BEGINNING NET WORTH

ASSETS	
Liquid Assets	
Cash & money markets	
Checking accounts	15,000
Savings accounts	10,000
Certificates of deposit	
Savings and Investments	
Stocks	75,000
Bonds	75,000
Mutual Funds	
Options	
Annuities	
Other brokerage assets	
Cash valued life insurance	
401(k)/IRAs	643,748
Fixed Assets	
Primary residence	1,100,000
Other real estate	500,000
Automobiles	80,000
Jewelry	60,000
Furniture	72,000
Other assets	
TOTAL ASSETS	**2,630,748**
LIABILITIES	
Short-Term Debt	
Charge cards	7,600
Bank loans	

Other debt due in less than one year	
Long-Term Debt	
Mortgage	529,000
Home equity loan	
Automobile loans	
Other loans	
TOTAL LIABILITIES	**536,000**
TOTAL NET WORTH (ASSETS LESS LIABILITIES)	**2,094,148**

down 50 percent from its highs in 1999. Nancy has chosen to "let Jim have his fun" and not get involved in investment decisions.

Setting Risk Tolerance

It is pretty clear that the Andersons have an above-average willingness to assume risk. Jim has managed the account for years and seems unfazed by the sharp losses sustained when the NASDAQ crashed. Although the Andersons' personal knowledge about investing is probably low, they do not perceive it that way. They are very well educated but a little naive when it comes to investing and financial matters. They appear to be members of the herd—always chasing the hottest investment ideas in search of outsize gains. At the same time, however, their past successes and cursory knowledge of the financial markets have made them overconfident in their investment decisions.

Their ability to take risk, on the other hand, is a bit lower. Most important, they have only a short time horizon until retirement—ten years. While their goal is to maintain their current extravagant lifestyle, I don't view this as critical. They could certainly run a tighter ship if they made the effort. And finally, their portfolio of liquid assets isn't overly large given their short time to retirement and high spending needs. All of this suggests they should opt for a lower level of risk than the maximum they are willing to assume.

Running the Numbers

My budgeting model for Jim and Nancy is displayed in table 7.13. As you will notice, the couple contribute heavily to their 401(k) plans each year, beginning with $25,000 (combined) in year one. Because they spend so much, however, this leaves them with no savings after accounting for all their expenses. By age sixty-five, the year of expected retirement, the couple will have accumulated $1.64 million in their retirement accounts and $442,254 in their surplus accounts. Assuming a fifty-fifty mix of stocks and bonds, their accounts will only generate slightly more than $135,000 in income each year—well short of their combined income in the years preceding retirement. The Andersons will clearly have to make some concessions if they want to be financially secure.

I could make a number of suggestions to the Andersons to improve their outlook. The first would be to reign in their spending habits. However, this probably wouldn't make enough of an impact. The most significant impact would be made if the couple were to move into a smaller and more modest house. I've estimated that their primary residence will be worth more than $1.4 million at the time of retirement, and the remaining balance on their mortgage loan will be just $268,000. Even though they have only five years remaining on their mortgage, the $54,429 in payments they are making each year are crippling. If the couple were to downsize to a smaller house costing, say, $800,000, they would have no more mortgage payments—and they'd free up $340,000 to contribute to their surplus account. Their total expenses would go down dramatically, while the income from their investment accounts would rise meaningfully. I estimate that their accounts would generate close to $157,000 per year (50 percent stock, 50 percent bonds), while their annual expenses would decrease to about $162,164. The lower expense estimate assumes that utilities, real estate taxes, homeowner's insurance, and home repairs and maintenance costs all go down as well as a result of downsizing to a smaller (and newer) house. Chances are that the couple have less need for a big house now that their children have moved away from home.

Table 7.13
THE ANDERSONS' TEN-YEAR BUDGET

	Year 1	Year 2	Year 3	Year 4	Year 5	Year 6	Year 7	Year 8	Year 9	Year 10
INCOME										
Salary										
Husband (net)	161,919	167,586	173,452	179,523	185,806	192,309	199,040	206,007	213,217	220,679
Wife (net)	62,430	64,615	66,877	69,217	71,640	74,147	76,743	79,429	82,209	85,086
Less 401(k) contribution	(25,000)	(25,875)	(26,781)	(27,718)	(28,688)	(29,692)	(30,731)	(31,807)	(32,920)	(34,072)
Interest/dividends	800	800	800	800	800	800	800	800	800	800
Total Income	***200,150***	***207,127***	***214,348***	***221,822***	***229,558***	***237,565***	***245,851***	***254,428***	***263,305***	***272,493***
EXPENSES										
Mortgage	54,429	54,429	54,429	54,429	54,429	54,429	54,429	54,429	54,429	54,429
Utilities	16,900	17,323	17,756	18,199	18,654	19,121	19,599	20,089	20,591	21,106
Real estate taxes	16,000	16,400	16,810	17,230	17,661	18,103	18,555	19,019	19,494	19,982

Homeowner's insurance	8,000	8,200	8,405	8,615	8,831	9,051	9,278	9,509	9,747	9,991
Home maintenance & repairs	10,000	10,250	10,506	10,769	11,038	11,314	11,597	11,887	12,184	12,489
Automobile loan										
Auto insurance	6,000	6,150	6,304	6,461	6,623	6,788	6,958	7,132	7,310	7,493
Gas, maintenance, & repairs	4,000	4,100	4,203	4,308	4,415	4,526	4,639	4,755	4,874	4,995
Medical/dental	3,000	3,075	3,152	3,231	3,311	3,394	3,479	3,566	3,655	3,747
Food	14,300	14,658	15,024	15,400	15,785	16,179	16,584	16,998	17,423	17,859
Clothing	5,000	5,125	5,253	5,384	5,519	5,657	5,798	5,943	6,092	6,244
Entertainment	6,000	6,150	6,304	6,461	6,623	6,788	6,958	7,132	7,310	7,493
Activities	3,000	3,075	3,152	3,231	3,311	3,394	3,479	3,566	3,655	3,747

(continued)

Table 7.13
THE ANDERSONS' TEN-YEAR BUDGET
(continued)

	Year 1	Year 2	Year 3	Year 4	Year 5	Year 6	Year 7	Year 8	Year 9	Year 10
Vacations	10,000	10,250	10,506	10,769	11,038	11,314	11,597	11,887	12,184	12,489
Health insurance	2,400	2,460	2,522	2,585	2,649	2,715	2,783	2,853	2,924	2,997
Life insurance	12,000	12,300	12,608	12,923	13,246	13,577	13,916	14,264	14,621	14,986
Clubs & dues	12,500	12,813	13,133	13,461	13,798	14,143	14,496	14,859	15,230	15,611
Housekeeping	5,000	5,125	5,253	5,384	5,519	5,657	5,798	5,943	6,092	6,244
Miscellaneous	12,000	12,300	12,608	12,923	13,246	13,577	13,916	14,264	14,621	14,986
Total Expenses	***200,529***	***204,182***	***207,926***	***211,763***	***215,696***	***219,728***	***223,860***	***228,096***	***232,438***	***236,888***
SURPLUS/ (DEFICIT)	**(380)**	**2,945**	**6,423**	**10,059**	**13,862**	**17,837**	**21,991**	**26,332**	**30,867**	**35,605**
Education funding										
Vacation home										
Inheritance										

ADJUSTED SURPLUS/ (DEFICIT)	**(380)**	**2,945**	**6,423**	**10,059**	**13,862**	**17,837**	**21,991**	**26,332**	**30,867**	**35,605**
Retirement funding	25,000	25,875	26,781	27,718	28,688	29,692	30,731	31,807	32,920	34,072
CUMULATIVE VALUES										
Education fund										
Retirement fund	713,166	788,250	869,420	957,128	1,051,358	1,152,024	1,259,941	1,376,164	1,501,288	1,635,946
Surplus	156,370	169,555	186,416	207,321	232,669	262,887	298,437	339,817	387,564	442,254
STOCK ALLOCATION										
College fund										
Retirement fund	60.0%	60.0%	60.0%	60.0%	55.0%	55.0%	55.0%	55.0%	55.0%	50.0%
Surplus	50.0%	50.0%	50.0%	50.0%	50.0%	50.0%	50.0%	50.0%	50.0%	50.0%

Table 7.14 shows the difference that downsizing to a newer, smaller $800,000 house would make in the Andersons' budget. Downsizing gets them very close to breaking even in the first year. They may need to cut some additional expenses, however, because their expenses are increasing at the rate of inflation. Over a period of several years, they will eat into their savings, resulting in less inheritance for their children.

Building an Investment Portfolio

Figure 7.5 illustrates my suggested asset allocation for the Andersons.

If the Andersons do as I've suggested and cut back on their expenses, then this more conservative asset allocation plan will work for them.

Our case studies should have provided you with a good understanding of the process involved in creating your own financial plan. The next step is to walk you through the process of managing your investments through retirement.

One item I haven't yet addressed regarding asset allocation is *rebalancing*—the process of moving investments from one asset

Figure 7.5

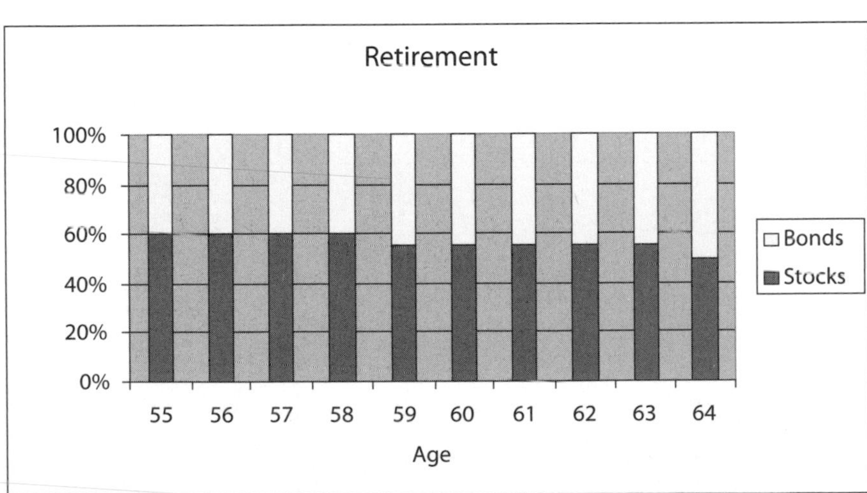

Table 7.14
THE ANDERSONS' BUDGET—DOWNSIZED

	Downsize Amount	Current Amount
INCOME		
Investments	157,000	135,000
Total Income	***157,000***	***135,000***
EXPENSES		
Mortgage	-	54,429
Utilities	14,433	21,633
Real Estate Taxes	14,986	20,481
Homeowners Insurance	7,681	10,241
Home Maintenance & Repairs	6,400	12,801
Auto Insurance	7,681	7,681
Gas, Maintenance, & Repairs	5,120	5,120
Medical/Dental	3,840	3,840
Food	18,305	18,305
Clothing	6,400	6,400
Entertainment	7,681	7,681
Activities	3,840	3,840
Vacations	12,801	12,801
Health Insurance	3,072	3,072
Life Insurance	15,361	15,361
Clubs & Dues	16,001	16,001
Housekeeping	3,200	6,400
Miscellaneous	15,361	15,361
Total Expenses	***162,164***	***241,450***
SURPLUS/(DEFICIT)	**(5,164)**	**(106,450)**

class to another to get back to the desired asset allocation. I believe you should undertake this process every twelve to eighteen months. Set up a time every year to a year and a half to review your portfolio and see how much each asset class has appreciated or depreciated. Based on your review, make the appropriate adjustments. Table 7.15 shows a sample rebalancing calculation.

Table 7.15
SAMPLE REBALANCING—DECEMBER 31, 2004

	Balance	Desired Allocation	Target Balances	Adjustment Needed
Bonds	184,500	70%	172,410	(12,090)
Stocks	61,800	30%	73,890	12,090
	246,300	100%	246,300	

The key is periodic reviews and rebalancing, not trying to time the market. Staying disciplined, dispassionate, and dedicated will lead you to the promised retirement Valhalla you seek. Protecting your investments is where we will turn our attention next.

CHAPTER EIGHT

Manage It

Monitor and Protect Your Investments Using Farr's Rules

I know the temptation must be setting in to breathe a hefty sigh of relief at the conclusion of a job well done. Just like the dieter who's shed thirty pounds and is flush with the excitement of the accomplishment—but knows that the maintenance phase is still ahead—as an investor you can't merely sit back. You've done the hard work, but not all of it. You still have to remain vigilant and maintain your control over your financial future. Simply put, now that you've implemented a plan, you have to monitor and manage it. More important, you have to monitor and manage another key contributor to the success of your Million-Dollar Mission—yourself. The next step in this plan calls for you to maintain your sell discipline. More on that important concept later in the chapter.

Don't Defeat Yourself

Have you ever heard the expression, *I've seen the enemy and it is me*? Unfortunately, inflation, downturns in the market, political and social crises, and the like often take a backseat to our own individual quirks when it comes to investment-management problems. In this chapter, we take a look at both internal and external factors you need to consider as you make your march toward the successful conclusion of your Million-Dollar Mission. I'll also discuss in some detail many of the other temptations that will test your investment discipline.

Behavioral factors such as emotion play an important part in the investment process. As noted earlier, investment decisions should be governed by not only your ability to accept risk, but also your willingness. However, not everyone is able to sit back and idly watch account values decline in a weak market. Instead, skittish investors sell their holdings at exactly the time when valuations are most compelling—after a market correction. Conversely, many people blindly buy stocks after huge rallies in an effort to get in on the action. Collectively, these foolish investors cause overreactions on both the upside and the downside—they artificially push up the price and then suffer when that overvalued stock returns to its "real" price. I call this the greater-fool theory: Some investments require a fool greater than you were who will pay more than you did, without regard to real value. Smart investors recognize these overreactions and use them as opportunities.

In 1999, some clients asked me to invest 100 percent of their assets in NASDAQ dot-coms. Those stocks were red hot at the time; share prices were rising through the roof. The clients, most of whom were seeing annual returns of more than 30 percent from a more conservative portfolio, felt that they were missing out and needed the almost 70 percent returns that stocks on the NASDAQ index were earning. Subsequently, the NASDAQ index was hurt the most and has not yet recovered to even 50 percent of its all-time highs. Before the United States invaded Iraq in early 2003, when the Dow was at 7,700, clients called me asking to get completely out of stocks and into bonds. At both times I heard clients say, "My dad wouldn't believe how much money I've made [or lost] in the stock market. He would think that I'm crazy." Emotion drives the wrong decisions time after time. And when we feel ourselves buffeted by the emotional gales, we often forget that the pressures on us are not singular and may even be coming from our parents' or grandparents' expectations or lessons.

Don't be that person! Don't be among those investors who watch the market rise and rise and buy near the top. These folks then enjoy a couple of months of increased asset satisfaction...only to watch the extended, elevated valuations decline. Of course, near the bottom the same investors are beating themselves up and feel ashamed. They know they should never have invested in the "damn market" and sell everything just as prices are beginning to move higher. The Million-Dollar Lesson: Have a plan and stick with it!

The efficient market hypothesis—a theory to which I *do not* recommend those of you on the Million-Dollar Mission subscribe—says that market prices already reflect the knowledge and expectations of all investors, making it futile to identify and profit from mispriced stocks. The theory also says that any new developments are quickly incorporated in the stock price, making it impossible to outperform the market. Only those investors possessing nonpublic information can possibly have an edge in this fantasy world. This theory is bunk because it fails to account for the behavioral effects that undoubtedly lead to overreactions in the market. Again, these overreactions create opportunity for those of us who do our homework, and they do indeed create opportunity to beat the market. So turn up your stereo and drown out all the noise! Ignore the talking heads on TV, including me, who may scare you into making foolish decisions. If you stick to your conviction and don't get greedy, you will be more likely to achieve your investment goals.

What follows are the common mistakes I see investors make. I've listed them here along with a few suggestions for how to avoid them or correct them.

Farr's Financial Rules

Make Decisions with Your Head, Not Your Gut or Heart

I've said this time and again, but you can't let emotion get the best of you. You need to use your head to make rational investment decisions. We all have a lot of emotional baggage tied up with money and how it was viewed and utilized in our families. It's helpful to talk with a spouse, partner, or trusted friend about those money experiences and attitudes and values that shaped your financial life. Getting them out in the open and examining them will help you realize why you make the decisions you do and respond the way that you do to various circumstances.

Keep Your Eyes on Your Own Paper

Everybody's financial situation, risk tolerance, goals, and so forth are unique; as a result, don't compare your situation with other people's. A number of my clients refer to their fathers, but they could have just as easily judged themselves against a sibling, friend, Warren Buffett, or anyone else. What your father might or might not have done has little relevance for you. The investing environment is constantly changing, as are your needs and desires. As you were told in school during a test, keep your eyes on your paper.

Don't Try to Find Fresh Grass Where the Herd Has Already Trampled

If everyone is buying a stock because earnings growth is accelerating, then the market is probably overestimating that growth. This may be a good time to trim back on your position in the stock. Conversely, when the masses become overly pessimistic about a particular stock or industry, it is very often the best time to buy. I love it when a great growth stock is beaten down for missing earnings in a quarter. It doesn't feel like the right thing to do at the time, but the sell-off gives me an opportunity to get involved on the cheap. You should look for similar opportunities.

I am not alone in my approach. In a market commentary report, the legendary Bill Miller, manager of the Legg Mason Value Trust, wrote the following: "Investing is all about probabilities, and just because there appears to be a strong consensus prices are going to keep going up, doesn't mean that is wrong, or right. The consensus does tend to be wrong at the turning points, being invariably bullish at the top and bearish at the bottom." These sentiments can be boiled down to simply this: Buy low and sell high. Nothing earth-shatteringly new there, but you'd be surprised how often this basic dictum gets trampled by the herd in their rush to cash in.

Incidentally, the same rationale can be applied to mutual funds as well as stocks. I wasn't surprised to read the following in an edition of *BusinessWeek* (June 26, 2006): "Typical stock fund investors gained an annualized 5.8% in the past decade, vs. 9.1% for the S&P 500, according to Dalbar, a Boston financial-services consultant. That's because they often do not buy a fund until it has already done very well." While I don't suggest going out and buying the worst-performing stock funds, it clearly doesn't work to simply pick the best performers, either. This goes against our natural inclinations—we all would clearly feel more comfortable buying the mutual fund with the best historical performance. It might feel bad to do otherwise, but research tells us that could be the best approach.

Avoid Living in a State of Denial

After reading Dr. Elisabeth Kübler-Ross's outstanding book on the five stages of dealing with death, I realized that novice investors usually go through three similar stages in responding to any bull or bear market: denial, acceptance, and capitulation. Think about it. How did you feel when the NASDAQ bull market began and stocks were doubling overnight simply for adding *.com* to the end of their name? You thought it was ridiculous, and you *denied* that it could last, right? But then it did last, for quite some time, and you began to accept the new paradigm. You reasoned, like everyone else, that the Internet had spawned a new world order, and that the money you could make was limited only by how much you had to invest. You *accepted* all the hype. Once convinced, maybe you felt you could no longer sit idly by while all your friends were making so much money. Did you open an account and start trading Internet stocks? Did you sell some of your General Electric to buy Yahoo!? If so, you *capitulated,* and probably just at the wrong time.

How did you feel about investing immediately after the events of September 11, 2001? Were you immediately apocalyptic about your investments, or did you take it in stride and realize the market would rebound eventually? My guess is that although you may have initially been somewhat fearful, you also reasoned that things would stabilize in fairly short order. You denied that the events of 9/11 could have such a drastic effect on the economy and keep the stock market in the doldrums for very long. But then the economy sank into recession, and we went to war in Iraq, and stocks dropped even further. You finally became exasperated and *accepted* the fact that the bubble had burst and that stocks would perform poorly for the indefinite future. Did you *capitulate* and sell some of your stock holdings when they were at the bottom?

Trends Always Last Longer than Anyone Expects

It takes time for the slowest bull in the herd to make it up a mountain. And it also takes time for investors to become comfortable and regain confidence in a market that has been unrewarding for a long time. Because nobody knows how to predict when sentiment will change, don't get started in this game. Your challenge is to overcome the feelings of denial, acceptance, and capitulation.

Do What Feels Bad

I know we're the generation that came up with the slogan, *If it feels good, do it.* That may work in some areas of your life, but not all of them—including investing. When I speak with my clients, I often tell them that the best course of action is to do what feels *bad.* If you accept the premise that the markets are inefficient and that investors exhibit irrational behavior, this doesn't seem like such a crazy idea. Doing what feels bad simply means going against the conventional wisdom. I know it felt bad to sell Internet stocks when they were reaching new highs every day. I know it is extremely difficult to buy stocks after a large market correction. I also know this is the way successful investors beat the market. I call it sticking to your discipline. I use the Farr Investment Technique to buy solid companies with above-average growth expectations and reasonable valuations, and I don't let my emotions shake my conviction. You can do it, too.

Enforce Your Sell Discipline

Despite the buy-and-hold philosophy that underpins the FIT, you should sell or reduce stock positions under certain conditions. This is known as sell discipline. Stocks are easy to buy but hard to sell. If they go up, our emotions tell us they may go higher. If they go down, we tell ourselves they will turn around because we just don't want to admit we were wrong. As discussed earlier, these are tendencies driven by emotions—in this case, fear and greed. The challenge in selling stocks is to recognize fear and greed. If your actions are based solely on either, you are probably making poor decisions. You need to get beyond the emotions and determine whether or not your fundamental reasons for owning the stock have changed.

So when *should* you sell?

- **Sell if valuation becomes excessive.** I generally trim positions to start, then continue selling if the market insists on giving the company credit for earnings growth that cannot possibly be achieved. This determination can't be made without doing some valuation work. At the very least, you need to compare a company's price-to-earnings ratio with that of its closest competitors and identify the reasons for any significant discrepancies. It is also helpful to compare a company's P/E ratio with its earnings growth rate. If the P/E multiple far exceeds the earnings growth rate and cannot be explained, the stock could be overvalued. At my company, we employ many different valuation techniques, including the discounted cash flow (DCF) analysis.
- **Sell out of a position completely if you believe the management team has become disingenuous.** If you sense any fraud or dishonesty, act first and ask questions later. We have all seen the effects of fraud on the likes of companies such as Enron and WorldCom. While fraud can be difficult to detect, it usually begins with dishonesty. Management teams should be given a little discretion, but you have to draw the line at some point.
- **If your original reason for owning the stock changes materially, sell.** The best example of this is if a company whose

stock you own makes a large acquisition in a completely unrelated industry in which it has no experience or expertise. If you cannot get comfortable with management's rationale for making the acquisition, it's likely time to hit the exit.

- **Any deterioration in fundamentals that threaten to materially affect the balance sheet.**
- **If circumstances affect a company's growth expectations, sell.** This is most likely to happen when a company starts to mature and cannot continue to grow at its historical above-average pace. I'm a growth investor because earnings growth is the single biggest determinant of stock prices over time.
- **If any single stock appreciates to more than 5 percent of your total portfolio value, trim.** Reduce the risk of overconcentration; simply put, keep your eggs in different baskets.

Don't Become a Trend Investor

As human beings, we have a natural desire to be part of the crowd. We change our hairstyles, listen to different music, and even eat different foods based on the latest fads. Investing is no different. Investors' emotions undoubtedly drive a large percentage of investment decisions, and psychological factors can play a huge role in the investment process. We have all seen what can happen as money moves in and out of the latest hot investments. Prices are bid up to unsustainable levels—until sentiment abruptly changes, leaving investors running for the hills. The most extreme instances of this phenomenon are called asset bubbles. More on these in a few pages.

Let me begin by stating what should be obvious by now: I am not a proponent of trend investing. I invest in bonds for stability, and I invest in stocks because over a long-term horizon, stocks have historically produced consistently higher returns than the other major asset classes. In other words, the *long-term* trend in stocks is up, and all the evidence suggests that this will continue. We live in a free, capitalistic society where innovation and new technologies are rewarded, productivity is increasing, trade barriers are breaking down, inflation is under control, and the government is stable. All these factors should help companies increase their earnings, and increasing earnings are the best predictor of stock prices over time. Companies with solid management teams operating in attractive industries have the wind at their backs. So if you are investing over a long-term horizon, "the trend is your friend." But you must understand the difference between the long-term trend for stocks and trend investing.

Trend investors generally seek quick profits by trading in and out of securities over a short period of time. They don't base their decisions on the long-term trend for stocks; rather, they use the near-term catalysts that can help them make a quick buck. I like to separate the trend investors into two distinct groups. The first group can be referred to as technicians or chartists. These investors chart trading patterns in an effort to identify current trends and forecast future price movements. They base their trading choices largely on the study of short-term supply and demand for a security, with little if any emphasis placed on company fundamentals. Technicians tend to be active traders—the supply-demand profile can change rather quickly.

The second group of trend investors can be referred to collectively as the herd because they make their investment decisions based on a herd mentality. The herd comprises uninformed, novice investors who simply want in on the action. These investors are more like gamblers, often relying on the greater-fool theory—as noted previously, the expectation that there are enough speculators in the market to keep pushing the price upward—rather than any sound investment rationale for owning a security. Those investing on this basis may have full knowledge that a stock is overvalued based on fundamentals, but they still believe that all the fools will continue to drive the price higher. If this sounds like a Ponzi scheme to you, then you have the right idea. These investors make us wonder who the real fools really are. Day traders, who often employ the greater-fool theory, would be considered part of the herd.

Both the chartists and the herd have an extremely short-term focus. Neither seeks to understand a company's financial standing or long-term growth drivers. Instead, both try to time their trades to take advantage of inefficient markets. They strongly disagree with the efficient market hypothesis and believe they can profit from the irrational behavior exhibited by market participants.

AN EXCEPTION TO THE RULE

In the late 1990s, we saw the genesis of the day trader. Ordinary people who had never been involved with the market or investing before began buying and selling stocks for profits ranging from $75 to several thousands of dollars.

I had a client named Stewart who was a successful software programmer in Florida. These were the days of the large floppy disk. His company went public, and this father of two retired at age thirty-five. Stewart used his computer skills to develop algorithms smoothing trading volatility, allowing him to be deliberate about buying and selling points for his technical trading scheme. This is a sophisticated approach to short-term trading. To the best of my knowledge, he remains retired at age fifty, providing for income by adhering to his short-term trading discipline. I need to tell you he is remarkable. He is an exception, not a rule. He continues to scare me because I have never seen anyone else remain profitable at what he does over extended periods.

Technical trading strategies are seductive. They make it look easy. Investing is much art as it is science. Since the advent of the computer, people have been trying to develop perfect programs to make us all rich. It hasn't been done, and I don't believe it can be. This sort of seemingly sensible empirical solution woos many people who find success to be very challenging. Remember, Stewart was the exception.

I am a fundamental investor. While I may utilize charts to determine the best timing for a trade, my actual trading decisions are determined solely by the careful study of a company's fundamentals. I seek companies that are growing faster than the market, but I am also extremely sensitive to valuation. This focus keeps me from chasing stocks that have run up based on excessive speculation. In fact, some may say I have a contrarian bias. A *contrarian* is an investor who seeks investments that are completely out of favor. *Barron's Dictionary of Finance and Investment Terms* states, "According to contrarian opinion, if everyone is certain that something is about to happen, it won't. This is because most people who say the market is going up are fully invested and have no additional purchasing power, which means the market is at its peak. When people predict decline they have already sold out, so the market can only go up."

I very often find myself going against the herd. However, this is not because I sense any near-term supply-demand imbalances such as the contrarians might identify. Instead, my valuation emphasis steers me toward stocks or industry sectors that are out of favor due to near-term issues. While these companies or sectors may have excellent long-term growth prospects, the market is simply unwilling to reward these prospects due to its obsession with near-term performance. This obsession allows me to exploit the inefficiency of time. I look beyond the next couple of quarters and focus instead on the next three to five years. The fact that trend investors are unwilling to look this far in the future creates the opportunity for me to buy solid companies at cheap prices (and sell companies that are getting more credit than they deserve).

Be a Good Student and Do Your Homework

Somewhere on the spectrum that ranges from uninformed trend investors to fundamentalist investors lie the semi-informed investors. These investors are generally well educated and have good jobs. They can be lawyers, doctors, astronauts, or teachers. They often excel at whatever they do. However, a history of consistent successes can get you into trouble in the world of stock trading. As I noted earlier, investing is all about probabilities. Professional money managers systematically produce volumes of research and analysis on any given stock, and they are thrilled to be correct 60 percent of the time. I like to use the baseball analogy. In baseball, you are inducted into the Hall of Fame if you get a hit in 30 percent of your at-bats throughout your career. In investing, the figure is much higher—perhaps 60 percent—but the lesson is the same: You need to be able to accept failure and being wrong some of the time. If you are unable to accept mistakes and cut your losses, it can be a very long road to a million dollars.

Honestly Assess Yourself

Semi-informed investors commonly think they're much smarter than they really are. For example, I have a friend who is a very intelligent medical doctor. He received highest honors in medical school and landed a highly sought-after job in one of the finest hospitals in the region. He was always up to date on the latest medical research and was on the cutting edge of his specialty. He also made a lot of money. Despite his sterling résumé, however, this doctor simply could not pick good stocks. He repeatedly came to me confounded over how much money he had lost on stocks that he had personally researched. How could someone of his intellect possibly pick bad investments?

I finally came to the conclusion that despite his claims of having "researched" these stocks, my friend had only a cursory understanding of the companies and their industries. Because he was such a leader in medicine, he assumed that he could get by with much less work than the average investor. This simply will not work. You must remember that there are incredibly smart people working around the globe trying to identify mispriced stocks and bonds. You are effectively competing with all the traders and analysts at Goldman Sachs and Merrill Lynch. Once a mispriced stock is identified by one of these guys, the price quickly changes and the opportunity is gone.

Farr's Rules in a Nutshell

Wouldn't it be great to find that pot of gold at the end of the investment rainbow? Well, since rainbows are pretty rare—occurring only when the circumstances are exactly right—prepare yourself to do some digging and panning elsewhere. I recommend you keep this list in a prominent place—either on your desk or inside a folder where you keep your investment papers—as a reminder of what you need to do to complete your Million-Dollar Mission:

- Take a humble approach to investing.
- Be prepared to be wrong, and be prepared to do your homework.
- Being a brain surgeon does not qualify you for blindly investing in technology stocks.
- What you read in the paper can very well be true, but before you even read it, the article has already been factored into a stock's price.
- The markets move very quickly.
- Your odds of consistently beating the pros to the punch are extremely small. Seek out companies with solid track records and strong management teams, and buy them at reasonable valuations.
- Stocks have gone up consistently over the long term. Don't try to get cute.
- *Hold on to them for a long time!*

Don't Chase Bubbles

An asset bubble could best be described as a situation in which the price of any asset increases to a level that does not reflect the underlying fundamentals. This situation is usually the result of speculative fervor by uninformed investors. Rather than relying on traditional measures of value such as the present value of future cash flows generated by an investment, investors are simply operating under the "greater fool theory." This theory holds that even though an asset may be expensive relative to its fundamentals, the purchase of the asset is justified because someone else will come along and buy it for a higher price. And the higher the price of the investment goes, the more tempting it becomes to other investors. By nature, many people find it exceedingly difficult to avoid the temptation of "getting in on the action" while watching their friends and neighbors hit the jackpot.

Unfortunately, most if not all asset bubbles end badly. A bursting bubble is characterized by frantic investors all running for the exits at the same time. Investors throughout time have been experiencing this frightening outcome, but nobody ever seems to learn. Therefore, it seems likely that learning to identify and avoid asset bubbles is a very important part of the investment process.

In the following section, I show you how to identify asset bubbles by describing three asset classes that are currently exhibiting signs of a bubble. While these examples are timely as of the writing of this book, they may be outdated at the time of your reading. Nevertheless, they should serve as examples of the phenomenon.

Former Federal Reserve Chairman Alan Greenspan said in a 2002 speech that it's "very difficult to definitely identify a bubble until after the fact—that is, when its bursting confirmed its existence." I would take issue with this assessment. Bubbles throughout history have all shown some common characteristics that should at least give smart investors pause. I would argue that the most important signal of all is uniformity of opinion. When the masses all begin to agree about some "paradigm shift" or "new world order," there is probably good reason for caution.

Consider the most notorious bubble in recent years—the NASDAQ stock market. The NASDAQ lost two-thirds of its value from the beginning of 2000 to the end of 2002. At its peak, nearly everyone was talking about how the Internet had created a paradigm shift that would lead to increased productivity, higher corporate profits, and better standards of living for all. Indeed, the Internet was and still is a very important source of our recent productivity gains. However, investors collectively accepted all the hype and overestimated the benefits. Eventually, the herd got involved and took the market to astronomical levels. Many smart investors recognized the mania and reduced positions in high-flying technology stocks. I was one such investor. I remember taking a cab ride in 1999 and listening to the driver talk about all his hot technology stocks. This was just one indicator of the spell we were all under. While it felt bad at the time, I recognized that the market was way ahead of itself and trimmed back my positions in overvalued stocks. My client accounts beat the S&P 500 by nearly 9 percent from 2000 to

2002. That's the kind of disciplined management of your portfolio you're going to have to exhibit to successfully complete your Million-Dollar Mission—especially in light of some of the other temptations that are on the horizon.

Today's Bubbles

I am clearly seeing signs of other bubbles as I write. The most visible is the housing market in certain urban coastal areas. I have listened patiently for years now as investors have touted the positive attributes of real estate relative to stocks. I'm certain that you've also heard these same arguments. Resist the temptation—and here's why. These investors argue that real estate is a hard, tangible asset and stocks are not. They say there is only limited land available for development. Or they argue that immigration will always ensure strong future demand. I could never figure out why these issues just became important in the past five years. These new arguments seem to push over into the tipping point of popular acceptance. Yet hasn't there always been a finite supply of land? Haven't we always had immigration? What changed in the investor psychology to attract people to tangible assets?

I think that initially, investors sought the relative safety of real estate after the stock market correction. The Fed enhanced the attractiveness by reducing interest rates to multiyear lows. Housing affordability increased, and prices started to rise. As prices rose, more investors wanted to get involved. Ordinary moderate-income Americans began buying investment properties using new and exotic financing alternatives offered by the banks, which only increased affordability even more. A plethora of new finance companies emerged offering mortgage loans to lower-income Americans who could never have qualified for a loan in the past. These sub-prime loans increased the homeownership rates in the country to all-time highs. And then, of course, there were those investors seeking to flip properties in a short period of time.

All the above created the perception that real estate investing was the only game in town. To make matters worse, real estate agents and mortgage brokers beat it into our heads that we had better get involved in real estate now or risk being priced out of the market forever. The masses began to accept the notion that housing demand had suddenly increased permanently while the supply of land was simultaneously in rapid decline. Housing prices continued to soar as person after person capitulated to the hysteria. Why invest in stocks or bonds when you can make 50 percent with no risk in real estate?

Real Estate

Real estate has been a wonderful place for your money to be for the past five years. According to the Office of Federal Housing Enterprise Oversight, home prices increased 9.5 percent per year nationwide from the first quarter of 2001 to the first quarter of 2006. This compares with a 4.0 percent annual total return for the S&P 500 Index over the same time period (dividends reinvested). Inflation over this time, as measured by the Consumer Price Index, averaged 2.5 percent. Therefore, inflation-adjusted (or real) returns averaged 7.0 percent for real estate and 1.5 percent for the S&P 500 from early 2001 to early 2006.

In hindsight, it would have been great to know that real estate was going to appreciate so much! But what is the longer-term performance of real estate as an asset class? *From March 1975 through March 2006 housing prices increased 6.2 percent per year, surpassing inflation by just 1.8% per year.* If we look at the time frame from early 1975 to early 2001, housing prices increased just 5.5 percent per year compared with an average inflation rate of 4.8 percent—a real return of just 0.7 percent per year! The dramatic increases in real estate prices over the past five years are responsible for more than half of the meager inflation-adjusted returns since 1975. It is also worth noting that the housing price data do not adjust for money spent on renovations, maintenance, and transaction costs (closing costs, sales commissions), which we all know can be significant. So how does the performance of housing compare with stocks?

The S&P 500 produced a total annual return of 12.8 percent from March 1975 to March 2006. From March 1975 to March 2001, the total annual return was 14.6 percent. So even though we experienced a dramatic correction in the stock market and a huge

Table 8.1
AVERAGE ANNUAL RETURNS

	March 2001–March 2006	March 1975–March 2001	March 1975–March 2006
Housing	9.5%	5.5%	6.2%
S&P 500	4.0%	14.6%	12.8%
Inflation	2.5%	4.8%	4.4%

Source: OFHEO and Bloomberg Financial

increase in housing prices since 2000, stocks still *far outperformed* real estate over the thirty-one years through March 2006.

Some people may argue that returns on real estate are actually higher due to the amount of leverage investors generally employ. For instance, if you were to make a 10 percent down payment on a $200,000 condominium, your investment would only amount to $20,000. A 5 percent increase in the price of your condo would yield a 50 percent return on your money! However, I strongly urge you to remember that leverage is a double-edged sword. Had your condo fallen 5 percent in value, you would have lost 50 percent of your investment. Furthermore, stock investors also have the ability to leverage their investments through margin borrowing (although it is usually limited to about 50 percent of account value).

Investing in residential real estate is starkly different from *speculating* in residential real estate. Real estate investors buy properties with the goal of using rental income received from a tenant to cover their expenses. These expenses include the monthly mortgage payment, property taxes, utilities (in some cases), condo fees, insurance, and maintenance. In a perfect world, tenant rents would cover all these ongoing expenses while simultaneously paying down the principal balance of the investor's mortgage loan. Over the course of many years, the declining principal balance on the investor's mortgage loan should lead to a competitive return relative to the risk assumed and the time spent on the property. In a normal environment, housing price appreciation is considered icing on the cake for investors. Smart real estate investors generally do not expect or factor in big increases in housing prices when deciding whether or not to make an investment.

Real estate speculators, on the other hand, *do* factor in price appreciation when making their investment choices. These investors buy properties with the expectation of significant price appreciation bolstered by the leverage they employ in financing the property. They usually either expect to flip the property in a short period of time, or are willing to go out of pocket to cover the difference between the rent they receive from a tenant and their monthly ownership expenses. Both of these approaches entail a large amount of risk. Not surprisingly, the masses have underestimated the extent of this risk as housing prices have soared. We have all heard stories about how our friends have made thousands of dollars flipping condos before they are even completed. We have yet to see how the story will ultimately play out. I suspect that when the music stops, there will be many an investor left without a chair.

Over the long run, houses are only worth what someone will pay you for them, and the value of real estate as an investment is simply the amount of cash it will generate for the investor over time. Using the aforementioned example of a $200,000 condo, you would need monthly rental income of more than $1,500 to cover your mortgage payment, property taxes, condo fees, and insurance (assuming utilities are paid by the tenant). If you are unable to find a renter willing to pay this much, you must make up the difference out of your own pocket. Each time you reach into your pocket, you are placing more importance on price appreciation, increasing your risk, and lowering your potential return. Table 8.2 depicts the hypothetical ownership expenses in the first year for the $200,000 investment condo.

At today's housing prices in the DC metropolitan area, real estate investors cannot possibly cover all their ownership expenses through rental income received from a tenant. Lured by the promise of double-digit annual price increases, speculators have continued to buy nonetheless. The result has been a state of disequilibrium between the ownership and rental markets. When these two variables—rental rates and housing prices—get too far out of line, a

Table 8.2
OWNERSHIP EXPENSES—FIRST YEAR

Mortgage Payment	
Principal	$1,828
Interest	$12,542
Taxes	$2,000
Condo fees	$1,200
Insurance	$600
Maintenance	$300
Total ownership expenses	$18,171
Average monthly ownership expenses (First Year)	**$1,514**

problem usually results. As housing price increases slow, prospective buyers will begin to realize that renting makes a lot more sense. Homeowners with large unrealized gains will be more inclined to take their chips off the table by selling out and renting or accelerating retirement plans and moving to a more affordable locale. It is also likely that rental rates will increase to reflect the higher cost of ownership. What is completely clear is that in the long run, housing prices and rental rates must adjust such that we get to a more long-run equilibrium level. Double-digit annual increases in housing prices are simply not sustainable over time.

As you may have guessed, I am not a big proponent of investing in residential real estate for the average investor. While there is definitely money to be made by those with the time and expertise, most of us have other jobs and already have a significant amount of our net worth in real estate through the ownership of our homes. Furthermore, the high transaction costs associated with active real estate management (seller closing costs average 6 to 7 percent of the home value) make flipping properties a losing proposition in all but the most irrational markets.

In my view, the surge in real estate prices has mostly been the function of the lower-interest-rate environment; the surge of creative financing alternatives such as adjustable-rate mortgages (ARMs) and interest-only mortgages (IOs); and an easing in bank credit standards, making homeownership possible for lower-income people. It can be argued that the latter two factors represent a permanent structural change in the way we Americans finance our home loans. Some may even say that the changes are positive because they produce higher homeownership rates by increasing affordability for lower-income Americans. While I do not disagree, I also believe that the changes also increase the risks in the banking system. While banks are currently enjoying low mortgage foreclosure rates due to the positive economic environment (low unemployment), I find it unlikely that banks will be so willing to extend credit in the face of increasing loan losses. We are already beginning to see the effects of higher interest rates on those homeowners who decided to use ARMs to finance their home. As foreclosures increase, I believe many will reevaluate the wisdom of the recent structural changes in the home finance market.

In summary, don't fall victim to the real estate hysteria. Avoid emotional decisions and stick to your discipline. You likely have more than enough exposure to real estate if you already own your home. Real estate investing requires both expertise in a given local market and time to manage properties. I think you probably have better things to do. Historically, stocks have consistently produced higher returns over long periods of time, and I see no reason why this will change in the future. So drown out all the stories about your friends making fortunes overnight in real estate. It feels bad to be the guy who missed the big opportunity, but sticking with your plan is more important. You have a long-term time horizon that will enable you to reach your goals. Remember that the trend *really is* your friend when you invest in stocks for the long term.

Commodities

I have also seen signs of a commodities bubble in recent years. Everything from oil to copper to sugar has appreciated dramatically, rallying new entrants to the market in search of a piece of the action. Commodity investors have come up with a plethora of excuses why we have entered a new paradigm for commodities. Once again quoting from Bill Miller's quarterly report, recent commodity price increases have been driven by "insatiable demand from China, India and the developing world, 20 years of underinvestment in production capabilities, sources of supply are either depleted or in geographically unstable parts of the world, skepticism about the sustainability of the price move, greater capital discipline on the part of the companies who produce commodities, massive new investment demand which is permanent since it is driven by indexation and thus will not leave even if prices decline." Again I ask, were all these issues not relevant just three years ago? How did we get into such a supply-demand imbalance so quickly? Did nobody see this coming?

Not surprisingly, Miller goes on to refute the hysteria surrounding commodities: "The time to own commodities is (or at least has been) when they are down, when everybody has lost money in them, and when they trade below the cost of production. That time is not now." I agree.

To invest in commodities at these prices is to ignore some of the basic tenets of economics. Entrepreneurs are motivated by profits, and many of them undoubtedly see an opportunity to get involved in the production of commodities given today's prices. This would increase supply and ultimately lower prices. Second, we cannot ignore the impact that technological improvements will continue to improve the productivity of commodity producers. In fact, these technological improvements have led to a decline in inflation-adjusted commodity prices over time. Third, if prices remain high, enterprising entrepreneurs will undoubtedly introduce substitutes for many commodities. The most obvious example here is the hybrid automobile, which requires less gasoline. And finally, we have to assume that at some point, high commodity prices will lead to reduced demand. Ultimately, lower demand will lead to lower prices.

Despite these irrefutable arguments, however, more and more investors are accepting the new paradigm and capitulating. Even some top-tier investment firms are doubling their recommended portfolio weightings in commodities. If these professionals have bought into the hype, why shouldn't you? Because I cannot possibly answer that question any better than Bill Miller did in his quarterly report, I will borrow his thoughts one last time:

> The excitement and enthusiasm surrounding commodities, and the belief that they will continue to rise, is not surprising. People want to buy today what they should have bought 5 or 6 years ago; call it the 5-year psychological cycle. Today people want commodities, emerging market, non US assets, and small and mid-cap stocks. Those were all cheap 5 years ago and had you bought them then you would be sitting on enormous gains. But 5 or 6 years ago, everyone wanted tech and Internet and telecom stocks, and venture capital and US mega caps. The time to buy them was in 1994 or 1995, when they were cheap...In general, you can get a good sense of what to buy now by looking to see what the worst performing assets or groups were over the past five or six years. That is long term for most people, and long enough to convince them that the malaise is permanent and to have migrated their money elsewhere, such as to whatever has done best in the past 5 or 6 years.

I would like to point out that oil may indeed be a special case. I am sure that most of you have read articles talking about peak oil. According to the Web site Lifeaftertheoilcrash.net, *peak oil* refers to the point at which "the endowment of oil has been 50 percent depleted. Once the peak is passed, oil production begins to go down while cost begins to go up." While the site offers somewhat far-fetched doomsday consequences as a result of our reaching peak oil, there may certainly be negative implications for oil prices as a result of the finite supply of oil. Prices could very well remain elevated and even go higher as we seek viable alternative fuel sources in the future. However, to suggest that the human race is incapable of finding alternative fuels is a very pessimistic view. In my opinion, efforts to develop alternative fuel sources will accelerate as oil reserves decline. The price of oil will likely fluctuate based on the success rate of these endeavors. Given the importance of this issue to the global economy, though, I have no doubt that we will be successful over the long run.

The Dollar

I also believe that the US dollar may be exhibiting some signs of a bubble. The dollar's strength has contributed to our record trade deficit. Americans are effectively buying foreign products using money borrowed from foreign sources, and a strong dollar makes imports cheaper relative to domestically produced goods. According to *BusinessWeek* magazine (June 26, 2006), "A new study from a team of economists led by Richard H. Clarida of Columbia University calculates that the US current-account deficit, now almost 7% of GDP, is substantially above the 2 to 3% level that should have triggered a large-scale dollar depreciation." The US government also continues to deficit-spend by using money borrowed from foreign central banks. These twin deficits cannot continue indefinitely. A weaker dollar may be the only effective way to bring the deficits back into balance.

However, Bush administration members say its policy is to support a strong dollar. They want a strong dollar because if foreign central banks believe the dollar is going to fall, they may be less likely to invest in our Treasury bonds and fund our deficits. We are completely reliant on these sources to fund excessive spending by both the government and consumers. If the appetite for US debt by foreigners were to decrease, higher interest rates would be needed to attract the foreign capital to fund the deficits. Currency traders recognize this dilemma and invest accordingly.

The government knows that a strong dollar has its drawbacks. Most important, a strengthening dollar makes it more difficult for US companies to compete in the global marketplace. US exports become relatively more expensive for foreign consumers, and foreign imports become relatively less expensive for US consumers. This will only exacerbate our trade imbalance. The vicious cycle must be broken at some point.

My view is that the dollar will eventually resume the downward slide that began in 2005. While the US economy is growing faster than its major counterparts, the trade imbalance must eventually be addressed. We cannot continue to deficit-spend using money borrowed from foreigners. This is unsustainable. Eventually (perhaps as US economic growth slows and growth in the European

Union and Japan pick up), foreign central banks will want to diversify their reserve holdings away from the dollar.

Incidentally, Warren Buffett and Bill Gross (manager of Pacific Investment Management Company, PIMCO) both agree with me and are making large bets against the dollar. These investing legends know it feels bad to go against the herd, and they have both taken some heat for the losses sustained in doing so. However, history tells us that they will eventually be right. Do you recall when Warren Buffett was endlessly criticized for not investing in Internet stocks as the NASDAQ was peaking? Even Buffett himself finally accepted the new paradigm and apologized to his investors for not recognizing the new world order. Well, we all know how that story played out. Will it happen again with the dollar?

Doing What Feels Bad Redux

To summarize, doing what feels bad means going against the conventional wisdom. In other words, you need to buy low and sell high. It seems so easy, but so many of us do exactly the opposite. The temptation is extraordinary to jump on the bandwagon with all your friends when a stock is soaring. It may be just as hard to avoid the temptation of selling out after a stock has gone down. It is true that you may miss out on some quick money in the process, but you are likely to save a lot more by avoiding bubbles and buying quality investments when they are cheap.

When Your Assets Multiply

Mutual funds have been a godsend to the small individual investor. They have brought professional investment management to the masses at a reasonable cost and made it easier to invest.

As good as mutual funds are, in the later stages of your Million-Dollar Mission you will reach a point at which they lose some of their effectiveness. At a level of liquid investable assets of about $200,000, it makes sense to think about using an individual investment adviser. How does this fit in with my refrain of being in control? The simplest answer is that by choosing someone to assist you—someone who has the expertise and the experience you may lack—you *are* in control of the situation. You recognize that someone else can do a better job than you can, but you don't cede complete control. That's one of the problems I have with mutual funds—you don't have much say in who manages that sector of the fund and what they do. Ultimately, with a money manager the responsibility still lies with you. Think of this professional as another source of information and research.

One of the main financial benefits of money managers is the ability to tailor your portfolio to your own special needs. They will sit down with you, get a comprehensive picture of your situation and your goals, and create a portfolio that most closely executes your plan for you. Your particular growth and income needs, risk tolerance, and tax considerations are factored into the portfolio. A mutual fund is unable to do this because all money is pooled together, effectively resulting in one large account containing interests held by clients with vastly different investment horizons and objectives.

Part of the problem with the pooling of funds from a cross section of investors is the inability to optimize the tax consequences for each fund holder. Mutual fund managers may try to minimize taxes passed through the fund to you, but they cannot be sensitive to your particular situation. Did you know that you can inherit a substantial tax burden just from investing in a mutual fund? If you get in at a time when the fund is doing a lot of selling, the tax on gains falls to you as a current holder even if the initial investment by the fund occurred before you became an investor? A fund that has a lot of portfolio turnover runs the risk of passing higher tax consequences to its holders. Besides that, a personal money manager can determine your particular appetite and tolerance for current income and capital gains, and can invest in a manner that minimizes your tax burden.

Some of you might be prone to just hand your money over and let the professionals take care of it. Others might like to be very involved in the process. Either way, a money manager is very accessible. I don't know that any mutual fund managers take calls from individual investors to talk about issues. Portfolio decisions are made by the management firm without input from investors.

Mutual funds are only required to make public their holdings every six months. A money manager, on the other hand, can discuss every actual or prospective trade with you every day if you so desire.

Lastly, an individual money manager may actually be cheaper than a mutual fund. Even with no-load funds, you are paying fees every year to the mutual fund company. The investment adviser gets a fee; in addition, all the processing that is required to trade, keep track of fund holders, report to holders and regulators, and much more can add 1 percent or more of your account. Technology has allowed individual fund managers to offer individualized, reasonably priced service to clients at an ever-decreasing level of investable assets.

How Do You Pick a Money Manager?

Hiring a money manager based on recent track record or the advice of a co-worker or neighbor who claims to have made a killing is not a good way to get peace of mind or maximize your assets. You need to really know managers, and they really need to take the time to get to know you in order to be effective. A feeling of trust and comfort helps. Track record is important—you do want to do the best you can—but numbers can be deceiving. The important thing is that they take the time to know what your objectives are, and they do the best possible job to meet those objectives.

Do they take the time to fully grasp your situation and goals? A thorough interview should include an analysis of your entire financial picture as well as some of the nonfinancial issues that may impact your financial situation now or later on. Do they spend the time to get to know your risk tolerances and your personal situation? Someone who raises issues and provides good counsel is more valuable than someone who promises everything you want and doesn't discuss trade-offs, priorities, and alternatives.

Are they willing to tailor their approach to meet your needs? Cookie-cutter solutions are rarely ideal. Be careful if they promise too much, focusing only on positives and not explaining the risks. Ensure that they give you the information you need in order to feel comfortable. Sketchy information, an unwillingness to provide details, or explanations that seem purposely complicated are not good signs. Managers should also provide the level of accessibility you require in order to feel comfortable.

They should be able to provide general references as well as some examples of situations that are close to yours. In addition, all advisers who provide investment advice must register with the Securities and Exchange Commission and file Form ADV, a lengthy document that provides information that can help you know more about them. Ask for a copy from them or from the SEC to find:

- A breakdown of their income sources—sales of investment products, money management, and so on.
- Relationships and affiliations with other companies.
- Each adviser's educational and employment history.
- Types of securities they deal in.
- Their fee schedule.

The SEC can also tell you whether the adviser is registered and whether any complaints have been made. Your state also will have a department that tracks financial advisers.

Track record is important, but must be viewed in perspective. It would take an entire college course to explain the intricacies of performance and analysis, but here are a few tips. Of course, short-term performance is no indicator of an adviser's capability. Riding today's wave is no assurance that the adviser will be able to steer you all the way through to retirement or even a business cycle. Performance should be measured over at least a full business cycle. Ensure that managers earn their money by beating a benchmark that closely resembles their style. Of course, performance is affected by the extent that they personalize individual portfolios, so try to get an explanation for any discrepancies. Data about volatility and risk versus return, separate performance and risk measures during down and up markets, and the performance of each holding could help you decide whether their risk-return profile matches yours.

CHAPTER NINE

Pass It On
Creating a Financial Legacy for Your Family

Movies, television shows, and novels are filled with dramatic stories of families torn apart by the complexities, financial and emotional, of a loved one's death and the passing on of the estate he or she accumulated. After working hard all your life, you don't want to be King Lear extorting loyalty and love from your daughters—nor do you want to be a fool of any kind with an estate wiped out by taxes or caught in legal limbo. As I've said before, much of the Million-Dollar Mission is about assuming control—of your saving, your spending, and your investing. Though it's not pleasant to consider, at the end of our lives, we need to maintain that control as we consider what is going to happen to our money once we die.

From another perspective, estate planning is the best kind of financial problem you can have. What it means is that you accumulated more than you needed to fund retirement. You've succeeded in accomplishing the Million-Dollar Mission. I've had clients who have done everything to ensure that they spend every last dollar they've made, and I've had others with genuine concern that family members are well taken care of after they've passed on. Still others have a strong desire to see that their legacy is memorialized through charitable donations, whether that means contributing to their alma mater, funding the addition of a wing to a hospital, or bequeathing their money to their favorite charity to use as it sees fit. While I'm not one to be critical of anyone's philanthropic efforts, I am also a pragmatist. Sometimes those charitable donations are motivated as well by a desire not to see the government take what it considers its share of your hard-earned money. When you consider Warren Buffett's announcement in 2006 that he was donating his considerable fortune to the Bill and Melinda Gates Foundation, does it really matter what his motivations are? In this case, I'd prefer to focus on the good that can be done with that money and not what good might accrue to Mr. Buffett.

If you've been diligent in your Million-Dollar Mission, you'll be accumulating a substantial amount of money. That's a good thing. What if you are one of the fortunate who has more than they could possibly spend? Where would you want your money to go? What if you should die before you're able to enjoy your wealth—have you taken steps to ensure that your family will be taken care of and will get the full benefit of your hard work? The tax and legal systems will play a large role in who gets your money and how much they get. The so-called death tax is truly a grim reaper of your hard-earned and wisely invested money. Of course, without proper planning, the government will take a substantial cut off the top before anyone else sees a piece of your estate. Even if the tax man doesn't get you, you still have to be prudent. If you don't write instructions for how your estate is to be divided, the courts will, and results of those efforts might not be to anyone's liking. A little planning goes a long way toward saving money, hassles, and regrets for your heirs.

The nonfinancial issues are the ones that you will likely anguish over. Who are going to be your beneficiaries? How much will you leave to each of them? Do you divide it equally or base the amounts on need or loyalty? How do you satisfy their needs or wants versus your desires and abilities to deliver? Maybe they want items that provide memories rather than a fat bank account. How do you provide for your spouse or significant other and still maximize your ability to bequeath to your children? What if you have a family structure complicated by divorce and remarriage? What if you want to leave money to a charity or school? You can leave your estate to whomever you wish, but unless it is a blood relative you must have a will to do so. Whom will you choose as the executor of your estate? Before you even seek estate-planning help, you and your significant other need to discuss most of these issues. A qualified professional will be able to help you accomplish your goals and alert you to pitfalls.

Compared with the emotional issues, figuring out the amount of your estate is relatively simple. The net worth that you've calculated through the exercises in this book is nearly identical to the way your estate is calculated. Any asset held in your name is part of your estate. If it is solely in your name, it is 100 percent part of the estate. If you hold something jointly, only your portion of the asset is considered part of your estate. For instance, if you and your spouse share ownership of your home, only your ownership portion is part of your estate. If you own a portion of a business, only your percentage of the value is included in your estate. As we'll discuss later in the chapter, assets held in an irrevovable trust are not technically yours, so they are not included. If you've kept ownership of property you both use in your spouse's name, it is not part of your estate. Likewise, spouses can have separate assets for estate tax purposes.

Default Inheritance

Many people leave no will. Death comes sooner than they expected, or they just don't want to deal with the issue. Unfortunately, dying intestate (without a will) means that laws must be used to determine how the estate is handled. I use the word *unfortunately* because the law may not coincide with what you would have wanted or what would be most beneficial to your heirs. State law governs how an estate without a will gets distributed, and rules vary by state. For the most part, a current spouse gets at least a share of the estate. In some states, the spouse gets everything; in others the surviving children get portions. That may or may not fit your desires. After that, things get very convoluted. If there's no surviving spouse, any "legitimate" children from any partner can receive equal shares. If they pre-decease you, their children get their shares. If you had no children, your living parents are next in line. If no living parents, your siblings become your heirs. If they

A CASE IN POINT

Plan for the continuance of your financial affairs beyond your death, but don't go so far overboard that you will be disappointed not to die. This is exactly the conversation I had with a sixty-five-year-old retiring lawyer in Washington. Mel was facing forced retirement from his law firm. He was not shy at all about informing me that he was a very good lawyer and an excellent investor. With retirement looming, he was getting all his affairs in order. Though he was an investor with a multimillion-dollar portfolio, he knew that his wife and children did not have the aptitude to invest. This is why Mel decided to hire a money manager like me. Mel's plan for retirement was impressive and thorough. Indeed, Mel's two main interests were practicing law and managing his stock portfolio.

The idea that he would choose to quit both for a "World Without Mel Plan" struck me as premature. When I told him that the only thing I saw wrong with his plan was that he would likely live for another twenty years after retirement, he got upset. He had everything worked out. He had prepared for a seamless transition. And here I went and played the bad guy, disrupting his plans! Moreover, if Mel was as good as he said at managing his portfolio, he should continue to do so.

In the end, my firm took over monitoring Mel's accounts, and I meet with him annually. I have also prepared to take a more active role if and when he would like me to do so.

There is an old rule among TV talking heads: "If you tell people *where* the market is going to go, don't tell them *when*." The best-laid plans have a way of finding their own calendar and timing. So the lesson is: Preparation is good; turning into a control freak is not.

are deceased, their children—your nieces and nephews—share in your estate. The state will continue to look for a blood relative (in-laws at any level are not heirs) at your estate's expense, and if no one is found the estate goes to the state. The latter fact means that if you have a prospective beneficiary who is not a blood relative it is imperative that a will be drafted to specify that non-blood beneficiary.

Spouses

A nearly universal goal is to provide for the surviving spouse after your death. Unfortunately, two seemingly beneficial steps many of us take can actually backfire. Co-owned marital assets are a complicating issue. Earlier I stated that any assets in your name are part of your estate. That's true, but some assets are held in both you and your spouse's names. You might own property, particularly your home, in joint tenancy. Joint tenancy (some states add the phrase "with right of survivorship") means that you share equal ownership of the property and have equal right to its use. If one of you dies, the other automatically receives the deceased's share of the property. That sounds like a good idea; however, it may be bad if your estate is of sufficient size that a substantial estate tax credit will be wasted. By automatically passing to the surviving spouse it increases that spouse's estate and increases the tax burden to your eventual heirs.

You might be tempted to not leave a will because having your estate go to your spouse by default might be exactly what you planned to do anyway. Your spouse will need to live off the assets you've collectively accumulated for the remainder of her life, so let her decide what to do with what's left over after she dies. What's remaining can be passed by your spouse to your children or other beneficiaries. Even in the simple case in which the default state laws are acceptable to you, however, other factors may make it a bad choice. Many of us are under the mistaken notion that anything passed to the surviving spouse is tax-free. In theory, that is true, but in practice it is not. Yes, your spouse can inherit everything tax-free from you. Whatever is left over after both of you die, though, will be taxed. As of 2006, the government gives each person an exemption of $2 million for their estate. The first $2 million of your estate passes tax-free to heirs. In total, a married couple would have $4 million of exemption—$2 million each. If you pass your entire estate to your spouse, you increase the estate he will leave and waste your exemption. As a result, your overall estate will be reduced by the 45 percent estate tax rate on the portion you wasted. For example, when you pass your $2 million estate to your spouse, who also has a $2 million estate, no taxes are paid. When he dies, however, taxes will be due. Assuming the estate doesn't fall in value, the tax will be 45 percent of $2 million ($4 million minus the $2 million exclusion of your spouse), which is $900,000. If you had directly bequeathed your $2 million to your children, you could have passed the entire $4 million to them tax-free. By not doing so, they end up with $900,000 less.

Estate Taxes

Aside from methods to get your estate into the right hands, estate planning is about reducing your estate tax burden. Congress is looking to revamp the estate tax system, but taxes are still onerous. The exemption will increase and tax rates will gradually decline through 2009. In 2010, there will be no estate tax at all—just for that year. Lawmakers have not come to agreement about what to do after that. As the law stands today, in 2011 and beyond, the exclusion would revert back to $1 million, and the top tax rate would return to 55 percent.

Why avoid taxes? Even with higher exemptions and lower rates, the burden is high. You pay taxes on your gross estate minus charitable bequests and certain expenses related to managing the estate settlement process. All property left to a surviving spouse who is a US citizen is also removed in the tax calculation. Then refer to the estate tax schedule to determine the amount of tax due on the remaining net amount. Finally, subtract the unified credit to arrive at your net estate taxes.

As an example, let's assume your estate is worth $3,995,000 when you die in 2008. Your tax would be $555,800 on the first $1,500,000 of value plus $1,122,750 (45 percent of $2,495,000) on the amount

Table 9.1
ESTATE TAX RATES THROUGH 2009

IF TAXABLE AMOUNT IS:				
More Than:	*But Not Over:*	*The Tax Is:*	*Plus:*	*Of the Amount Over:*
$0	$10,000	$0	18%	$0
10,000	20,000	1,800	20%	10,000
20,000	40,000	3,800	22%	20,000
40,000	60,000	8,200	24%	40,000
60,000	80,000	13,000	26%	60,000
80,000	100,000	18,200	28%	80,000
100,000	150,000	23,800	30%	100,000
150,000	250,000	38,800	32%	150,000
250,000	500,000	70,800	34%	250,000
500,000	750,000	155,800	37%	500,000
750,000	1,000,000	248,300	39%	750,000
1,000,000	1,250,000	345,800	41%	1,000,000
1,250,000	1,500,000	448,300	43%	1,250,000
1,500,000	—	555,800	45%	1,500,000

Table 9.2
UNIFIED CREDIT AGAINST ESTATE TAXES

An Individual Dying In . . .	Receives a Unified Credit Of . . .	Which Eliminates the Tax for Estates Valued Up To:
2006–2008	$780,800	$2,000,000
2009	$1,455,800	$3,500,000

by which $3,995,000 exceeds the $1,500,000 category floor. From the tax, you can then subtract the unified credit of $780,800 (the tax on the first $2 million) to find that you owe $897,750. (Please note that this schedule applies to federal estate taxes only; state and local taxes are separate.) Quite a large chunk of your assets. No wonder a whole industry exists to lessen the burden.

Reducing the Tax Burden Through Gifts

One way to better control your estate is to give it away while you are alive. You have control over its distribution, and you get to enjoy the emotional reward of helping others. Of course, you must balance gifting with your own needs. It would be unfortunate to give away your estate and then require help living out your last years.

By bestowing gifts, you also enjoy the benefit of possibly eliminating the need for probate. Gifted assets stay out of probate, which isn't triggered until after death. You don't necessarily escape taxes on those gifts, though. Large gifts are added to your taxable estate to determine your "gift and estate tax" bill when you die, from which the unified credit is subtracted. The *unified* descriptor is used for the tax credit because it is to be applied to the combination of large lifetime gifts and your eventual estate. As of 2006, you and your spouse can each give up to $12,000 to an individual in one year without incurring any gift tax. Any gift exceeding $12,000 becomes a large gift, and as a result is subject to gift tax. However, you don't have to pay a gift tax unless the cumulative total of all large gifts you have ever made exceeds $1,000,000 (the maximum amount of the unified tax equivalent you can use toward gifts). Once you exceed that $1,000,000 amount individually (your spouse gets an equivalent amount), you will start paying gift taxes. Also, any unified tax credit you use up on gifts during your lifetime reduces dollar for dollar the credit you can apply toward your estate. So if you can keep your gifts below $12,000, you will be able to eventually save on your estate taxes.

Gifted property does not avoid taxes forever. When giving away appreciated property, the person you give it to will take over your cost basis. She eventually will have to pay income taxes on it when she sells it. The good news is that the gain is figured from what you *originally* paid for the asset, not the value at the time you gifted it.

On the other hand, if you pass it to people through inheritance, their cost basis is the value of the asset at your death. For example, let's say that you have a thousand shares of a $100 market-value stock that you bought for $25. If you give it to your daughter during your lifetime, eventually she will have to pay taxes on the $75-per-share appreciation in value. If you give it to her through your estate, her cost basis becomes $100, and she will only have to pay taxes on the appreciation above that level. Of course, your estate will pay taxes on the $75-per-share appreciation, so collectively, either way you do it you and your daughter are eventually paying taxes on the full appreciation. The difference is in the tax rates used and the exemptions available. If you are under the unified credit amount, you will pay no estate taxes on that stock. If not, then your estate will be paying at a 45 percent rate. Capital gains taxes for your daughter currently don't exceed 15 percent, so if you are going to be over the unified credit, a gift saves you 30 percent (the 45 percent estate tax rate minus the 15 percent capital gains rate) of the asset's value. Plus, it's deferred until she actually sells it.

It is important to remember that in order for your handing over of an asset to be a true gift, you must relinquish all rights to it. You can't give away shares of stock but continue to receive the dividends or remain custodian of the account. If you do, you legally still own it.

Tuition

Sometimes parents or grandparents are in a financial position that allows them to help their children or grandchildren. For instance, a grandchild might need help with college tuition. In the budget section of chapter 4, I explained several advantageous ways for you to save for college tuition. One of them, the ESA, is a program that grandparents, and even strangers, can fund for a future student. The account grows tax-free and remains so as long as proceeds are used at a qualifying institution and for qualifying expenses. By gifting a contribution of $12,000 or less, the contribution is exempted from the donor's estate. What do you do if the student is now in or entering school and is short of funds? A $12,000 ESA contribution at this point might not be enough. If the donor pays a qualifying (legitimate) school directly for specified learning-related expenses, there is no limit to the amount that is exempt from the gift tax. As an additional bonus for this kind of gift, the amount contributed isn't even included in the determination of lifetime total gifts or the eventual estate. If you or someone close to the student is willing to fund his or her education to some degree, this is a good way to do so when an ESA won't be sufficient. Since ESA proceeds are factored into the need/aid calculations most schools use (and may therefore reduce the amount of other financial aid—grants, loans, what have you—the student is eligible for), this may also make sense as an alternative to an ESA. This is an attractive choice provided the donor can afford the larger lump-sum payments while the student is in school rather than the annual ESA contributions leading up to school.

For the large-sum donations, don't make the mistake of giving an amount over $12,000 to the student directly to then be used to pay tuition. The payment must reach the school directly from you to qualify for the tax benefits of that large lump-sum payment. If you can't afford those large chunks, then setting aside whatever you can each year and contributing it to an ESA makes sense. The other option, obviously, is to create a separate account that you keep in your name, let the magic of compounding and rise in stock's value do their work, and then make the lump-sum payment to the school directly. Just as in planning for your own retirement, looking ahead, starting early, and making regular contributions to the account will pay dividends in the end.

Medical Expenses

Paying medical expenses for someone else is treated just like the direct education payments described in the previous section. You can pay expenses for diagnosis, cure, mitigation, treatment, or prevention of disease, or for the purpose of affecting any structure or function of the body. You can also pay for transportation and medical insurance for another individual.

Make the payment directly to the health-care provider and you avoid the $12,000 limit—*and* save your gift tax credit for something else.

Home Down Payment

Often, young homebuyers rely on help from parents or grandparents to afford a new home. Their ability to qualify for a mortgage might depend on the promise that the money the parents provide is guaranteed to be a gift. If $48,000 isn't enough ($12,000 each to husband and wife by each of the couple's parents), you, the donor, might run into gift tax penalties. You have two main alternatives to get more money into their hands. First, you could use the education and medical expense exclusions to increase your gift to them. Pay their medical expenses—remember, even insurance premiums can be paid by you—so that their money can be freed up to support the down payment. If that's not enough, you could loan them a larger amount with terms that require an annual payment that falls under the gift tax exclusion level of $12,000 per year per donor per beneficiary ($48,000 in our case). The homebuyers will get the money upfront when they need it, and you will get your full gift tax break.

Trusts

If your estate is large enough that you will be facing tax consequences, or if you want to put some controls on the distribution of your assets after you die, you could benefit from the use of trusts. Trusts seem very secretive and even devious, but they are fairly straightforward and legitimate ways to protect your assets. They are certainly not a do-it-yourself project or something a lawyer can do as a sideline. Mistakes can be costly tax-wise, so I recommend that you work with a well-established and reputable provider in order to get sound advice and bulletproof trusts. Stay away from providers who make wild claims or try to use a trust that hasn't been tested in tax court.

At their core, trusts are merely a legal entity set up to own property. Through their use, you can transfer possession of your property to the trust, which then holds the property for the benefit of another person. Because of the transfer, the assets are not in your possession or estate, and because the trust holds them, the beneficiary also does not have them in possession. The assets basically disappear for legal and tax purposes. Taxes will only be paid on distributions of earnings or principal to the beneficiary.

Credit-Shelter Trusts

We learned earlier that passing everything to the surviving spouse isn't a good idea for estates that exceed a couple's combined unified credit. The unified credit of the first spouse to die goes unused, so the overall tax bill on the assets by the time the surviving spouse passes away is more than it needs to be. In order to fully use the credit, then, credit-shelter trusts were created. The trust is set up so that when the first spouse dies, the amount that qualifies for the estate tax credit—$2,000,000 through 2009—goes into a trust instead of going directly to the surviving spouse. The trust owns the assets, but the surviving spouse receives income from the trust. For instance, if you have your dividend-paying stocks in the trust, your spouse will receive the quarterly dividend checks. When the surviving spouse dies, the assets in the trust go to the children or other heirs. Final distribution of the assets from the trust when the second spouse dies does not create a taxable event. The income your spouse receives from the trust while alive is taxed.

The credit-shelter trust has other benefits:

- The assets are professionally managed by the trustee—someone you appoint or someone the trust administrator supplies. Your spouse does not need to worry about managing the assets.
- The trust can name the eventual receivers of the assets when your spouse dies.
- The assets do not become part of your spouse's estate, so they avoid taxation as part of an estate.
- The appreciation on the assets held in trust isn't subject to estate taxes. The eventual receivers will pay taxes when and if they sell, but their capital gains tax rate is almost always lower than the estate tax rate.

You can only put your own assets into the trust—jointly owned assets are not allowed. You don't need to give up ownership of the assets the moment you sign the trust documents; transfer occurs at a later date or at your death. Many times it makes sense to use your will to direct the assets into the trust at the time you die.

Living Trust to Avoid Probate

A living trust is not necessarily a mechanism to reduce your estate taxes, but it is a useful way to control your estate. It allows you to accomplish the same tasks as a will while avoiding the probate process. The basics of a living trust are simple:

- While you're still alive, you place any or all of your assets in the trust. In your lifetime, you maintain complete control over the assets. The law and the IRS still view them as belonging to you, and you have the ability to remove them or change the assets in the trust at any time if you name yourself as the trustee and put in a clause stating that the trust is revocable.
- You can name a successor trustee—the person who will manage the trust when you die.
- You can name the trust beneficiaries—the people who will receive the assets in trust after you die.
- As long as the trust is revocable, the IRS views the assets in it as belonging to you. You pay taxes, and so forth, just as if you held them in your name.
- When you die, your successor trustee takes the property and transfers it to your beneficiaries with no need for probate or other court proceedings.

If you also want to avoid some taxes, you can set up the living trust as an irrevocable trust. If you hold the assets in an irrevocable trust, you have fully relinquished control over the assets and the trust arrangement. You can't even change beneficiaries. Because of this, an irrevocable trust is viewed as an entity separate from you, the grantor. It pays its own income taxes (unless the income doesn't remain in the trust but is distributed to beneficiaries). For estate tax purposes, however, the value of the assets is frozen at the date the assets are put in the trust. So, any appreciation will not increase the size of your estate. Thus, you might stay below the unified estate tax credit or at least maximize its effectiveness. One of the most effective strategies would be to put $2 million of assets in the irrevocable trust (the maximum amount of estate value sheltered by the unified estate tax credit). Afterward, you can add $11,000 per year per beneficiary per donor (maximum tax-free gift), and as the assets grow, your estate and its possible tax liability remain constant.

Testamentary Trust

Testamentary trusts allow you to be more specific about who should get your assets—and when. These trusts, established through instructions in your will, don't exist until you die. A QTIP trust (qualified terminable interest property trust) is a useful testamentary trust with particular interest if you have heirs from a prior marriage. A QTIP works well to satisfy, or at least control, the needs of your present spouse and children from a previous marriage. Your current spouse needs financial support, and your children need assurance that their stepparent isn't going to loot your estate or remarry and leave your estate to someone else. To satisfy your spouse's need for financial support after you die, this type of trust gives the surviving spouse or partner the income generated from the assets in the trust. To satisfy the children's concerns that their stepparent will spend your estate dry and leave nothing for them, the trust retains ownership of the assets; as long as your current partner is not the trustee, that partner has no control over the assets. Eventually they pass to your children—or whomever else you designate—upon your current partner's death.

In addition, the trust can have any number or type of clauses restricting access to the assets. You could specify that your spouse can live in the house but not own it, for instance; if he would like to move or sell it, the eventual beneficiaries, your children, would have to approve the sale.

Charitable Remainder Trusts

Ever wonder how a hospital wing, school library, or other institution ends up with the name of a huge donor across its face? Sometimes the donors are still alive, and it seems astounding that they could give away so much money and still maintain their standard of living. Yes, they do have a lot of money, but they get some help through the use of a charitable remainder trust. A CRT allows you to donate assets to a nonprofit organization, receive the tax breaks from the donation, and still receive the income from the assets while you are alive. For instance, a gift of highly appreciated stock allows you to collect the dividends even though you have donated the shares to your favorite charity.

Those of us who aren't in the upper echelons can benefit from CRTs, too. If you set up the trust as an irrevocable living trust, it gives you an immediate tax deduction for your charitable contribution and also allows you to receive the income from those assets while the assets are in the trust. In the trust agreement, you can arrange for the charity to get the trust's assets at some later date—after your death or even sometime later; maybe when your youngest child graduates from college. If you set it up as a testamentary trust (meaning that it's created upon your death), you can specify that the trust will provide income to your heirs for life and that the remainder of its assets go to a nonprofit organization upon their deaths. This strategy, in addition to providing current income tax benefits and ongoing income, also reduces the value of your taxable estate.

You can receive a great financial bonus from using CRTs, which are ideal for retired Americans who have assets that have greatly appreciated. These folks have reached the point at which they are more interested in current income from their investments than growth and appreciation, so they would like to sell the highly appreciated assets and replace them with bonds or dividend-paying stocks that will support their present cash needs. To sell the highly appreciated assets would incur a huge tax bill, however. But by putting them in a CRT, the tax bill is eliminated altogether. The CRT sells the assets, incurring no taxes because the beneficiary is a nonprofit. The full value of the property remains in the trust, and the trust then is able to buy more income-generating assets and provide you with more income than if you had sold the assets instead. With a larger asset base, the trust is able to have larger holdings and generate more current income for the holder.

As you can see, estate-planning issues are many, and the complications and choices are in abundance. I started off this book by talking about Abundance Guilt, and in planning for the final stage of your financial life, you really have the opportunity to rid yourself of that nasty emotional baggage. I don't know any of my clients who entered this phase of their planning regretting the wealth they'd accumulated over the years. Whether they are going to be able to fund charitable organizations, their grandchildren's education, or simply not leave their loved ones with money worries or debt, they've been able to sit back and smile at a job well done.

I've only briefly touched on the major issues here. I hope that this information has allowed you to become a more educated and better-prepared consumer as you seek out the expert advice of an estate planner or as you work with a money manager, accountant, tax attorney, or other adviser. You've reached your goal, and now is not the time to drop the ball. Sharing the responsibility while still maintaining control is the ultimate step in your Million-Dollar Mission. Congratulations on getting here, and for having the foresight and discipline to make it all happen for yourself and your family.

CHAPTER TEN

Review It

A Look Back and to the Future

I don't know how many of you remember the television show *Mission Impossible*. I loved that original program, and I especially loved the hissing self-destructing tape that the agent listened to with its ominous words, "Your mission, should you decide to accept it..." Of course he was going to accept it! No doubt in his mind, and we wouldn't have had a show if he'd elected to do anything but risk life and limb to battle the forces of evil.

Now that you've finished reading this book, I hope you realize that the stakes are not as high as they were in that fictional world. World domination is not the aim here. The Million-Dollar Mission is one that you should find far easier to accept and far easier to complete. That doesn't mean that it won't take some work and some sacrifice on your part. As I've reminded you throughout, managing risk and investing is all about control. As most psychologists will tell you, the only thing that you can ever control is your response to other people's behaviors and the events of the world. You can control the decisions you make, and I hope that armed with the knowledge you've acquired in reading this book, you will make solid decisions that lead to you making real the vision for your retirement.

I want to remind you of a few basic principles that should serve to guide you as you navigate your way through the process. First, resolving your internal conflict about money and its rewards is important. Abundance Guilt and egonomics are a part of your Boomer mentality. You can control each of them. Second, remember that small changes in lifestyle can make a big difference when you factor in the magic of compounding. Save a little and earn a lot when you take the Farr view. In addition, remember that investing in the stock market really is the only game in town. When you look at inflation-adjusted returns, you will see that no other investment vehicle outpaces inflation and the cost-of-living increases that result from it. Simply put: If you're not in the market, the chances are great that you will be losing ground. To select good-quality stocks at the right valuation, here again are the factors to look for:

- A history of superior performance and consistency.
- A company that is a leader in its market, with a competitive advantage its counterparts can't easily match.
- A healthy balance sheet and great income to generate strong cash flows.
- Sustainable growth markets that don't require mergers and acquisitions for growth.
- Strong, proven management.
- Not overpriced, with below-market P/Es.
- Not overly risky—a stock with financial leverage more conservative than its peers.
- Large enough for trading to be liquid and information to be available. Market capitalization of $20 billion is average; $1 billion is a minimum.

Remember that you can exploit the inefficiency of time in the market by using this method to select stocks and hang on to them for a long time—and use your sell discipline to know when to make the necessary moves out of them.

Remember that a lot of trend investors believe that they are trendsetters, but more of them are in fact part of the herd than out in front. I firmly believe that if you do what makes you feel bad, if you adopt a quasi-contrarian perspective, you will be well served. I'd rather see you reaping rewards than chasing the next big thing—chases are exhausting and often fruitless. Sprinters may excel at the chase, but in terms of funding your retirement, you're in a marathon, not a hundred-meter dash. Here's a reminder of how you can best get in financial shape for the Million-Dollar Mission:

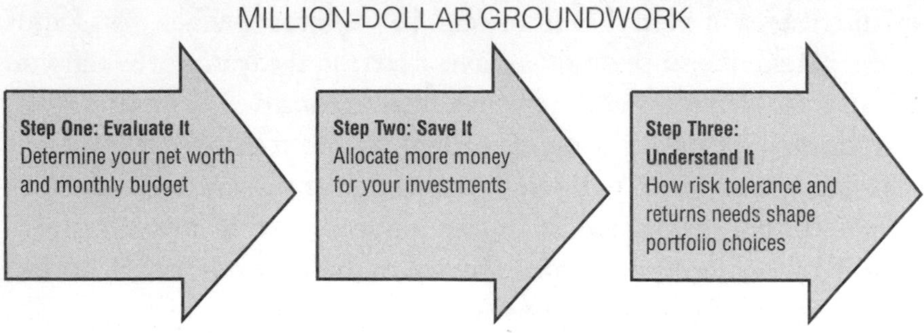

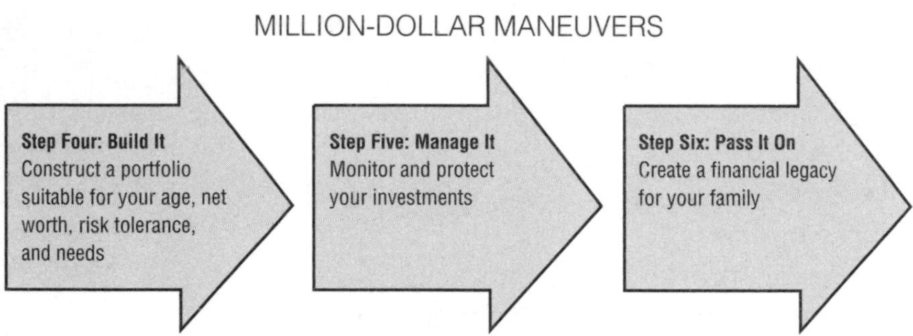

MILLION-DOLLAR MANEUVERS
Step Four: Build It
Construct a portfolio suitable for your age, net worth, risk tolerance, and needs
Step Five: Manage It
Monitor and protect your investments
Step Six: Pass It On
Create a financial legacy for your family

These are the same steps I employ in working with my clients. I hope that, like many of those clients, you will be able to rest easy knowing that you are in control of your financial future. You've succeeded in many other parts of your life, and I've no doubt that with the right mind-set, the proper information and research, and the kind of dedication and perseverance you've demonstrated in other areas of your life, your Million-Dollar Mission will be a success. I'll be at the finish line cheering you on, knowing that you'll be looking for more challenges.

Hitting the finish line and looking beyond it for more challenges is exactly what Jason Lee did. If you will recall, Jason was the son of a wealthy client of mine named Adam Lee. Jason didn't get started planning and saving for his retirement until he married and decided to begin a family at age forty. Jason had a cushion that most of us can't count on having—his father would match whatever amount Jason had accumulated in his retirement accounts. He first came to see me in 1990, and, using the methods I've outlined here, seventeen years later and seven years into receiving more than twenty thousand dollars a year from each of his parents, he has far exceeded the million-dollar goal he set for himself. In fact, the money that Jason receives each year, instead of going toward his two children's education—which he has funded completely—is going toward a future matching-fund program just like the one Adam set up for him. Jason hopes that the lessons in saving and investing he's passed on to his children will produce the same results for his future grandchildren.

That's the thing about a mission. Once you get started on it, it tends to take on a life of its own. I wish you the best of luck in starting the ball rolling for you, for your family, and for future generations.

Resources

Books

Your Renaissance Years: Making Retirement the Best Years of Your Life by Robert L. Veninga (Little, Brown, 1991).

Looking Forward: An Optimist's Guide to Retirement by Ellen Freudenheim (Stewart, Tabori, and Chang, 2004).

Too Young to Retire: 101 Ways to Start the Rest of Your Life by Marika Stone and Howard Stone (Plume, 2004).

My Time: Making the Most of the Rest of Your Life by Abigail Trafford (Basic Books, 2003).

The Third Age: Six Principles for Growth and Renewal After Forty by William A. Sadler, PhD (Perseus Books, 2000). Also see www.thirdage.com.

Prime Time: How Baby Boomers Will Revolutionalize Retirement and Transform America by Edgar Bronfman and Catherine Whitney (G. P. Putnam, 2003).

The New Retirement: The Ultimate Guide to the Rest of Your Life by Jan Cullinane and Cathy Fitzgerald (Rodale Press, 2004).

Retirement Places Rated by David Savageau (Wiley Publishing, 2004).

The Grown-Up's Guide to Retiring Abroad by Rosanne Knorr (Ten Speed Press, 2001).

What Should I Do with My Life? by Po Bronson (Random House, 2002).

What Do You Want to Do When You Grow Up? Starting the Next Chapter of Your Life by Dorothy Cantor and Andrea Thompson (Little, Brown, 2002).

Organizations and Web Sites

- AARP, www.aarp.org
- Experience Corps, www.experiencecorps.org
- www.bestplaces.net
- www.retirementliving.com
- www.escapeartist.com
- www.internationalliving.com
- www.eons.com
- www.mynextphase.com
- www.elderhostel.org
- www.volunteermatch.org
- ReServ, www.reserveinc.org

Index

About the Authors

MICHAEL K. FARR is president and majority owner of investment management firm Farr, Miller & Washington, LLC, in Washington, D.C. He has been in the investment business for over twenty years. Mr. Farr, a contributor for CNBC television, is quoted regularly in the *Wall Street Journal, BusinessWeek, USAToday,* and many other publications. He was a longtime recurring panelist on PBS's *Wall $treet Week* and does a great deal of public speaking. He is a member of the Economic Club of Washington and the Young President's Organization. He is the chairman of the Sibley Memorial Hospital Foundation and serves on the Board of Trustees at Sibley Hospital; he's the former vice chairman of the Board of the Salvation Army and a former member of the Board of Trustees of Ford's Theater. A graduate of the University of the South in Sewanee, Tennessee, Mr. Farr is married and has two children. To contact him, go to www.michaelkfarr.com.

GARY BROZEK is a freelance writer based in Evergreen, Colorado. He has coauthored or ghostwritten more than a dozen books on a variety of subjects ranging from personal finance and psychology to sports and memoirs.